Rust for Web and Networking Services

Maxwell Vector

Contents

3

4

7

11

Chapter 1

High-Performance Asynchronous Programming in Rust

Foundations of Asynchronous Execution

Asynchronous execution represents a paradigm in which computational tasks are structured to operate without imposing blocking behavior on system resources. The evolution of such techniques has been driven by the necessity to manage concurrent input/output operations and high-volume network traffic while preserving computational efficiency. Early event-driven models have matured into sophisticated frameworks that utilize cooperative multitasking and refined scheduler coordination. In such frameworks, system calls related to input/output are handled in a non-blocking fashion, thereby minimizing idle cycles and reducing the overhead introduced by traditional thread context switching. This approach permits efficient utilization of both processing units and underlying hardware, which is particularly critical in high-performance web and networking environments.

The Async/Await Paradigm in Rust

Rust incorporates asynchronous programming directly into its syntax through the introduction of the keywords *async* and *await*.

This paradigm is distinguished by its ability to transform functions that contain asynchronous operations into state machines during compile-time. In this design, execution suspension is denoted explicitly by the use of an *await* expression, which signals the precise location at which a function yields control to the scheduler. The resulting state machine encodes internal state transitions and variable context, ensuring that when an asynchronous operation resolves, control is resumed accurately at the predetermined suspension point. Such a design affords a clear, linear presentation of asynchronous logic while maintaining the non-blocking execution model required for high-performance network services.

1 Internal Mechanics of Asynchronous Functions

Within Rust, asynchronous functions undergo a compilation process that transforms them into resumable state machines. Each function systematically enumerates its progression through distinct states, with suspension points annotated implicitly by the *await* operator. At these junctures, the active computation is paused, and its state—comprising local variables, control flow markers, and execution context—is preserved. The state machine is designed to facilitate a seamless resumption once the asynchronous operation for which it waited has reached completion. This transformation mechanism not only provides a structured way to handle the intricacies of task pausing and continuation, but it also ensures that the overhead associated with context switching is kept to a minimum. The precise management of state enables optimization of task scheduling and resource allocation, which are crucial in the domain of high-throughput network services.

2 The Role of the *Future* Trait

Central to Rust's asynchronous infrastructure is the *Future* trait, which serves as an abstraction for computations whose outputs are not immediately available. The *Future* trait sets forth a protocol wherein asynchronous tasks are polled periodically to determine their resolution status. Such a design imbues asynchronous operations with a type-safe contract, ensuring that their eventual completion adheres to the stringent memory and concurrency guarantees provided by Rust's safety model. By integrating the *Future* trait into the type system, Rust enforces rigorous control over lifetimes and ownership in concurrent contexts. The interplay between the *Future* trait and the *await* operator underpins the model of asynchronous execution, facilitating a system in which concurrent operations are managed in a deterministic and resource-efficient manner.

Concurrency and Non-Blocking I/O Integration

The practical application of asynchronous programming in high-performance network services hinges on the integration with non-blocking input/output operations. Rust's async runtime is engineered to interface directly with low-level system calls and event notification mechanisms, thus enabling efficient I/O multiplexing. In this architecture, asynchronous tasks are scheduled in a manner that aligns computational processing with incoming I/O events. This orchestration is achieved through a robust polling mechanism in which the runtime continuously assesses the readiness of various asynchronous operations without incurring the penalties of thread-based blocking. The result is a system capable of managing numerous simultaneous I/O operations concurrently, while concurrently processing high volumes of computational tasks. This integration of non-blocking I/O with the asynchronous execution model capitalizes on modern hardware capabilities and allows for the scalable design of web and networking services that are both performance-oriented and resource-efficient.

Rust Code Snippet

```rust
use std::future::Future;
use std::pin::Pin;
use std::task::{Context, Poll};
use std::time::Duration;
use std::thread;
use std::sync::{Arc, Mutex};

//-----------------------------------------------------------------------
// TimerFuture:
// This custom future illustrates a basic asynchronous timer using a
//   state-machine pattern.
// It waits for a specified duration before completing, mirroring
//   the async/await transformation
// where the suspension of execution is captured as part of the
//   future's internal state.
```

18

```rust
struct TimerFuture {
    // Shared state between the TimerFuture and the spawned thread.
    shared_state: Arc<Mutex<SharedState>>,
}

// SharedState holds the completion status of the timer.
struct SharedState {
    completed: bool,
}

impl TimerFuture {
    // Constructs a new TimerFuture that completes after 'duration'.
    fn new(duration: Duration) -> Self {
        let shared_state = Arc::new(Mutex::new(SharedState {
        ↪    completed: false }));
        let thread_shared_state = Arc::clone(&shared_state);

        // Spawn a thread to simulate the non-blocking wait.
        thread::spawn(move || {
            thread::sleep(duration);
            let mut state = thread_shared_state.lock().unwrap();
            state.completed = true;
        });

        TimerFuture { shared_state }
    }
}

impl Future for TimerFuture {
    type Output = ();

    // The poll method acts as the state machine's engine, checking
    // ↪   if the timer has elapsed.
    // If not, it yields control, simulating a suspension point
    // ↪   corresponding with 'await'.
    fn poll(self: Pin<&mut Self>, cx: &mut Context<'_>) ->
    ↪   Poll<Self::Output> {
        let state = self.shared_state.lock().unwrap();
        if state.completed {
            Poll::Ready(())
        } else {
            // In practice, the executor would re-register the waker
            // ↪   to be notified upon state change.
            cx.waker().wake_by_ref();
            Poll::Pending
        }
    }
}

//------------------------------------------------------------------------
// CounterFuture:
// This future manually demonstrates a state machine by iteratively
// ↪   incrementing
```

19

```rust
// a counter until a maximum value is reached. It embodies the
//    algorithmic transition
// through different states that an async function undergoes before
//    reaching completion.
struct CounterFuture {
    current: usize,
    max: usize,
}

impl CounterFuture {
    // Creates a new CounterFuture with an upper bound defined by
    //    'max'.
    fn new(max: usize) -> Self {
        CounterFuture { current: 0, max }
    }
}

impl Future for CounterFuture {
    type Output = usize;

    // The poll method simulates state transitions:
    // It advances the counter and yields control (simulating
    //    'await') until the final state is reached.
    fn poll(mut self: Pin<&mut Self>, cx: &mut Context<'_>) ->
    //    Poll<Self::Output> {
        if self.current < self.max {
            println!("State Machine: current count = {}",
            //    self.current);
            self.current += 1;
            // Mimic suspension by re-waking the task for subsequent
            //    polling.
            cx.waker().wake_by_ref();
            Poll::Pending
        } else {
            // Once the counter reaches the max state, the future is
            //    ready.
            Poll::Ready(self.current)
        }
    }
}

//-----------------------------------------------------------------------
// Asynchronous workflow demonstrating the integration of custom
//    futures using async/await.
// This function ties together the TimerFuture and CounterFuture,
//    showcasing how asynchronous
// computations can be elegantly composed in Rust.
async fn asynchronous_workflow() {
    println!("Starting the TimerFuture...");
    // Await the timer future which completes after a 2-second
    //    delay.
    TimerFuture::new(Duration::from_secs(2)).await;
    println!("TimerFuture completed after 2 seconds.");
```

```rust
    println!("\nStarting the CounterFuture state machine...");
    let final_count = CounterFuture::new(5).await;
    println!("CounterFuture completed with final count: {}",
    ↪  final_count);
}

#[tokio::main]
async fn main() {
    // Execute the asynchronous workflow.
    asynchronous_workflow().await;
}
```

Chapter 2

Tokio Runtime Fundamentals for Network Services

Tokio's Reactor Pattern in Asynchronous Contexts

Tokio employs a refined reactor pattern that forms the foundational backbone for asynchronous I/O management in network services. At its core, the reactor pattern is responsible for the efficient demultiplexing of I/O events and the subsequent mapping of these events to suspended tasks. This design leverages low-level operating system primitives, such as *epoll* on Linux, *kqueue* on BSD-derived systems, and IOCP on Windows, to monitor multiple file descriptors simultaneously in a non-blocking manner. The reactor continuously polls for readiness events, ensuring that tasks suspended awaiting I/O can be promptly resumed once the underlying event occurs. By isolating I/O event detection from task execution, this architecture minimizes kernel-user space transitions and reduces context switching overhead, thereby optimizing resource utilization in high-throughput network environments.

The reactor's operation is intrinsically tied to the concept of event-driven programming. It registers interest in specific events and subsequently notifies the runtime when these events transpire. Each notification is paired with a corresponding wake-up mechanism that triggers the re-scheduling of suspended tasks. This systematic approach to event handling allows for a clear separation of concerns between the detection of I/O readiness and the execution of computational logic, a separation which is paramount in achieving scalable and resilient network services.

Task Scheduling Mechanisms within the Tokio Runtime

The scheduling infrastructure in Tokio is designed to manage asynchronous tasks with remarkable efficiency. The runtime adopts a cooperative multitasking model, wherein tasks voluntarily yield execution upon encountering operations that would otherwise block if executed synchronously. This yielding is facilitated by intrinsic mechanisms that re-enqueue tasks based on the availability of requisite resources. The scheduling system is not only engineered to honor fairness but also to maximize throughput by minimizing idle cycles.

A sophisticated work-stealing algorithm underpins Tokio's scheduler, enabling an equitable distribution of tasks across available processing units. This dynamic redistribution ensures that computational resources are utilized optimally, even under conditions of uneven task loads. The scheduler judiciously tracks task states, promptly responding to wake-up signals issued by the reactor. Such signals are propagated via waker abstractions, which encapsulate the logic required to reinsert suspended tasks into the execution queue. In environments where high concurrency is commonplace, the scheduler's ability to manage tasks in a non-blocking and efficient manner is essential to maintain responsiveness and to accommodate the volatile demands of network traffic.

Core Abstractions in Tokio's Asynchronous Infrastructure

The architecture of Tokio is sustained by a collection of core abstractions that encapsulate the complexities inherent in asynchronous programming. A central element is the abstraction of the task. In the Tokio runtime, a task represents an encapsulated unit of asynchronous computation, typified by its state and control flow. Each task is constructed in such a manner that it embodies a finite state machine, transitioning between states as it awaits the completion of I/O operations or internal computations. This state machine is orchestrated via the *Future* trait, thereby imposing a type-safe contract on tasks and guaranteeing that their completions are predictable and deterministic.

Another fundamental abstraction is the waker mechanism. Wakers are responsible for reactivating tasks that have been suspended on the occurrence of specific events. This mechanism ensures that once a task's awaited operation becomes available, the corresponding task is promptly rescheduled without incurring superfluous delays. The integration of wakers with the reactor and scheduler results in a highly efficient asynchronous execution loop, wherein tasks can be paused and resumed with minimal overhead.

Additionally, Tokio encapsulates inter-task communication and resource management within its core abstractions. These constructs facilitate the synchronization of state among concurrently running tasks while preserving the principles of memory safety inherent in the language. By abstracting these elements, Tokio provides a unified framework that mitigates the complexities of non-blocking I/O and concurrent execution. Collectively, the interplay between these core abstractions—the task, the waker, and the scheduler—enables the runtime to harness the full capabilities of modern hardware, supporting network services that are both scalable and performant.

Rust Code Snippet

```rust
use std::future::Future;
use std::pin::Pin;
use std::sync::{Arc, Mutex};
use std::task::{Context, Poll, Waker};
use std::time::Duration;
use std::sync::mpsc::{self, Receiver, SyncSender};
use std::thread;
use futures::task::{waker_ref, ArcWake};

/// A simple Future that completes after a specified Duration.
/// This simulates an asynchronous I/O event (e.g., waiting for
↪ readiness)
/// in a reactor-like pattern.
struct TimerFuture {
    shared_state: Arc<Mutex<SharedState>>,
}
```

```rust
/// Shared state between the TimerFuture and the waiting task.
struct SharedState {
    /// Whether the timer has completed.
    completed: bool,
    /// The waker for the task that is waiting for this future.
    waker: Option<Waker>,
}

impl TimerFuture {
    /// Constructs a new TimerFuture that will be completed after
    /// `duration`.
    fn new(duration: Duration) -> Self {
        let shared_state = Arc::new(Mutex::new(SharedState {
            completed: false,
            waker: None,
        }));

        // Spawn a thread to simulate an asynchronous I/O event.
        let thread_shared_state = Arc::clone(&shared_state);
        thread::spawn(move || {
            // Simulate waiting for an I/O readiness event.
            thread::sleep(duration);
            let mut shared_state =
                thread_shared_state.lock().unwrap();
            shared_state.completed = true;
            // If a waker is registered, wake the task.
            if let Some(waker) = shared_state.waker.take() {
                waker.wake();
            }
        });

        TimerFuture { shared_state }
    }
}

impl Future for TimerFuture {
    type Output = ();

    fn poll(self: Pin<&mut Self>, cx: &mut Context<'_>) ->
        Poll<Self::Output> {
        let mut shared_state = self.shared_state.lock().unwrap();
        // If the timer has completed, signal readiness.
        if shared_state.completed {
            Poll::Ready(())
        } else {
            // Register the task's waker so that it can be notified
            // when the event occurs.
            shared_state.waker = Some(cx.waker().clone());
            Poll::Pending
        }
    }
}
```

25

```rust
/// The Task struct encapsulates an asynchronous computation (a
↪  Future)
/// along with a means of rescheduling itself via a channel. This
↪  simulates
/// the cooperative multitasking and scheduling aspects of Tokio.
struct Task {
    /// The asynchronous computation wrapped in a Mutex for safe
    ↪  concurrent access.
    future: Mutex<Pin<Box<dyn Future<Output = ()> + Send>>>,
    /// Channel handle to reschedule the task once it is woken.
    task_sender: SyncSender<Arc<Task>>,
}

impl Task {
    /// Polls the task's future once. If the task is not complete,
    /// it will be rescheduled via its waker.
    fn poll(self: Arc<Self>) {
        // Create a waker from the task itself.
        let waker = waker_ref(&self);
        let mut context = Context::from_waker(&*waker);
        // Lock the future and attempt to poll it.
        let mut future_slot = self.future.lock().unwrap();
        match future_slot.as_mut().poll(&mut context) {
            Poll::Pending => {
                // The task is not complete. It will be woken and
                ↪  rescheduled later.
            }
            Poll::Ready(()) => {
                // The task has completed.
            }
        }
    }
}

// Implementing ArcWake allows the Task to wake itself
// and get re-scheduled in the executor's task queue.
impl ArcWake for Task {
    fn wake_by_ref(arc_self: &Arc<Self>) {
        arc_self.task_sender.send(arc_self.clone())
            .expect("Task queue closed");
    }
}

/// A simple executor that drives asynchronous tasks to completion.
/// This executor mimics the scheduling mechanism and work-stealing
/// ideas by re-inserting tasks into a channel when they need to be
↪  resumed.
struct Executor {
    task_sender: SyncSender<Arc<Task>>,
    task_receiver: Receiver<Arc<Task>>,
}

impl Executor {
```

```rust
/// Creates a new Executor with a bounded task queue.
fn new() -> Self {
    let (task_sender, task_receiver) = mpsc::sync_channel(128);
    Executor { task_sender, task_receiver }
}

/// Spawns a new asynchronous task onto the executor.
fn spawn(&self, future: impl Future<Output = ()> + Send +
↪ 'static) {
    let task = Arc::new(Task {
        future: Mutex::new(Box::pin(future)),
        task_sender: self.task_sender.clone(),
    });
    self.task_sender.send(task).expect("Task queue full");
}

/// Runs the executor until all tasks have been processed.
/// This mimics the event-loop scheduling, where tasks are
↪ polled
/// and re-scheduled as necessary.
fn run(&self) {
    while let Ok(task) = self.task_receiver.recv() {
        task.poll();
    }
}
}

fn main() {
    // Create the executor instance.
    let executor = Executor::new();

    // Spawn a task simulating waiting for an asynchronous I/O
    ↪ event.
    executor.spawn(async {
        println!("Task: Waiting for simulated I/O event...");
        TimerFuture::new(Duration::from_secs(2)).await;
        println!("Task: I/O event occurred, resuming execution.");
    });

    // Spawn another task to simulate concurrent processing.
    executor.spawn(async {
        println!("Task2: Starting computation...");
        TimerFuture::new(Duration::from_secs(1)).await;
        println!("Task2: Computation complete after delay.");
    });

    // Run the executor. The loop will continue until all tasks have
    ↪ completed.
    executor.run();

    println!("All tasks completed.");
}
```

Chapter 3

Customizing Asynchronous Tasks with Tokio

Tokio Task Model and Customization Fundamentals

Tokio's approach to asynchronous execution is centered around a task model that encapsulates units of computation as state machines implementing the *Future* trait. In this model, each task represents a self-contained asynchronous operation whose progression is governed by successive invocations of its *poll* method. The intrinsic design leverages a cooperative multitasking paradigm wherein tasks are expected to yield control willingly upon encountering operations that potentially block synchronous execution. This paradigm is made robust by the integration of the *Waker* abstraction, which provides an efficient mechanism to signal tasks when the underlying events that they depend on have occurred.

A detailed examination of the task lifecycle reveals that tasks are dynamically scheduled, suspended, and eventually resumed based on event notifications. The customization of such tasks demands a deep understanding of the interplay between the task's internal state and the scheduling framework employed by Tokio. Alterations to the conventional state transitions or the conditions under which a task yields or is reactivated can introduce refined control over the rate and order of task execution. This level of customizability is particularly pertinent in network services, where the fine-tuning of concurrency parameters directly influences throughput and latency.

Techniques for Optimizing Task Scheduling and Resource Management

The inherent design of the Tokio runtime supports an adaptable scheduling infrastructure that can be customized to meet the demanding requirements of high-concurrency network environments. Optimizing task scheduling in such contexts often involves the judicious manipulation of the work-stealing algorithm that underpins Tokio's scheduler. This algorithm is engineered to distribute outstanding tasks across available computational resources in a manner that minimizes idle cycles and reduces context switching overhead.

Customization techniques in this area include the modulation of task resumption protocols and the refinement of the wake-up mechanism. By altering the way in which tasks are rescheduled upon the occurrence of relevant events, it is possible to fine-tune the balance between throughput and responsiveness. For example, a nuanced adjustment of the criteria for task re-enqueueing can mitigate the overhead associated with overly frequent context switches, which is a critical consideration in handling bursty network traffic. Furthermore, modifications to the internal bookkeeping of task states and priorities can lead to enhanced resource utilization, ensuring that the system remains robust under variable load conditions.

Customizing Task Execution for Concurrent Network Operations

Network service implementations frequently necessitate a level of concurrency control and task orchestration that exceeds the capabilities provided by generic asynchronous frameworks. Within Tokio, the execution of asynchronous tasks can be customized to articulate fine-grained concurrency strategies that are expressly tailored to the operational characteristics of network workloads. Such techniques often involve the integration of task-specific execution policies that take into account the predictability and variability of network traffic patterns.

One approach is the deliberate structuring of tasks to encapsulate both computational and I/O-bound operations in a manner that minimizes interference between concurrent executions. This technique leverages the isolation of I/O event monitoring—facilitated by operating system primitives such as *epoll*, *kqueue*, and IOCP—from the execution of the computational logic inherent in each task. By customizing the interaction between these two domains, it becomes possible to achieve a form of concurrency control that is both efficient and deterministic. In addition, tailoring the execution pipeline can involve the explicit adjustment of task priorities and the dynamic modulation of task scheduling intervals. Such mechanisms allow for the construction of bespoke task dispatch pipelines that are engineered to respond deterministically under conditions of high load, thereby ensuring that system resources are apportioned optimally across all active tasks.

The detailed exploration of these customization techniques highlights the potential for achieving significant performance improvements in network services. By leveraging the intrinsic flexibility of Tokio's task model and scheduling infrastructure, it is feasible to design asynchronous operations with an unprecedented level of control over concurrency dynamics.

Rust Code Snippet

```
use std::future::Future;
use std::pin::Pin;
use std::sync::{Arc, Mutex};
use std::task::{Context, Poll, RawWaker, RawWakerVTable, Waker};
use tokio::time::{sleep, Duration};

/// A custom asynchronous task simulating a network operation.
/// It demonstrates the internal state transitions and the use of
↪   the wake mechanism.
struct CustomTask {
    state: Arc<Mutex<TaskState>>,
}

/// Internal state for our CustomTask tracking a simple counter.
#[derive(Debug)]
struct TaskState {
    count: usize,
    limit: usize,
}
```

30

```rust
impl Future for CustomTask {
    type Output = String;

    /// The poll method mimics the task's progression as a state
    /// ↪ machine.
    /// Each poll increments a counter until a limit is reached,
    /// ↪ then returns Ready.
    fn poll(self: Pin<&mut Self>, cx: &mut Context<'_>) ->
    ↪ Poll<Self::Output> {
        let mut state = self.state.lock().unwrap();
        if state.count < state.limit {
            println!("[CustomTask] Poll count: {}", state.count);
            state.count += 1;
            // In a real-world scenario, this is where one might
            // ↪ adjust the scheduling criteria.
            // Here we invoke wake_by_ref to simulate the task being
            // ↪ re-enqueued.
            cx.waker().wake_by_ref();
            Poll::Pending
        } else {
            println!(
                "[CustomTask] Completed after {} polls",
                state.count
            );
            Poll::Ready(format!("Completed after {} polls",
            ↪ state.count))
        }
    }
}

/// Custom waker implementation using the RawWaker API.
/// This waker logs events to simulate custom wake-up and scheduling
/// ↪ behavior.
fn custom_raw_waker() -> RawWaker {
    // Allocate a dummy data pointer.
    let data = Box::into_raw(Box::new(())) as *const ();
    RawWaker::new(data, &VTABLE)
}

unsafe fn waker_clone(data: *const ()) -> RawWaker {
    println!("[CustomWaker] clone invoked");
    custom_raw_waker()
}

unsafe fn waker_wake(data: *const ()) {
    println!("[CustomWaker] wake invoked");
    // As wake consumes the waker, free up the allocated memory.
    Box::from_raw(data as *mut ());
}

unsafe fn waker_wake_by_ref(data: *const ()) {
    println!("[CustomWaker] wake_by_ref invoked");
```

31

```rust
    // When waking by reference, we do not free the data.
}

unsafe fn waker_drop(data: *const ()) {
    println!("[CustomWaker] drop invoked");
    Box::from_raw(data as *mut ());
}

// Define the vtable for our custom waker.
static VTABLE: RawWakerVTable =
    RawWakerVTable::new(waker_clone, waker_wake, waker_wake_by_ref,
    ↪ waker_drop);

/// Helper function to create a Waker from our custom raw waker.
fn create_custom_waker() -> Waker {
    unsafe { Waker::from_raw(custom_raw_waker()) }
}

#[tokio::main]
async fn main() {
    // --- Part 1: Manually Polling a Custom Future with a Custom
    ↪ Waker ---
    println!("--- Manual Polling of CustomTask ---");
    let custom_task = CustomTask {
        state: Arc::new(Mutex::new(TaskState { count: 0, limit: 5
        ↪ })),
    };

    // Create a custom waker and context for manual polling.
    let custom_waker = create_custom_waker();
    let mut context = Context::from_waker(&custom_waker);
    // Pin the custom task on the heap.
    let mut pinned_task = Box::pin(custom_task);

    // Manually poll the task to simulate customized scheduling.
    loop {
        match pinned_task.as_mut().poll(&mut context) {
            Poll::Ready(result) => {
                println!("[Main] CustomTask result: {}", result);
                break;
            }
            Poll::Pending => {
                // Simulate a delay between polls to allow state
                ↪ changes.
                sleep(Duration::from_millis(100)).await;
            }
        }
    }

    // --- Part 2: Spawning Concurrent Tasks to Simulate Optimized
    ↪ Scheduling ---
    println!("\n--- Spawning Simulated Network Tasks ---");
    let mut handles = Vec::new();
```

32

```
    for id in 0..3 {
        // Each spawned task simulates a concurrent network
        ↪   operation.
        handles.push(tokio::spawn(network_simulation_task(id)));
    }

    // Await completion of all spawned tasks.
    for handle in handles {
        match handle.await {
            Ok(result) => println!("[Main] Network task completed:
            ↪   {}", result),
            Err(e) => println!("[Main] Task failed: {:?}", e),
        }
    }
}

/// An asynchronous function simulating a network operation with
↪   mixed computation and I/O.
/// It mimics realistic scheduling by inserting delays that vary
↪   with task identity.
async fn network_simulation_task(id: usize) -> String {
    println!("[NetworkTask {}] Starting", id);
    // Simulate a series of steps in the network task.
    for step in 0..3 {
        println!("[NetworkTask {}] Executing step {}", id, step);
        // Delay to emulate non-blocking I/O and computation.
        sleep(Duration::from_millis(50 * (id as u64 + 1))).await;
    }
    println!("[NetworkTask {}] Completed", id);
    format!("Result from network task {}", id)
}
```

Chapter 4

Implementing Custom Futures and Streams

Foundations and Theoretical Underpinnings

Within the domain of asynchronous computation, the Future and Stream traits serve as the principal abstractions for encapsulating deferred and potentially non-deterministic computations. The Future trait is conceived as a state machine, where a computation evolves over discrete steps and is driven by successive invocations of its polling function. Formally, a future is characterized by a function

$$poll\colon Pin < mut\ Self > \times Context \to Poll < T >,$$

where the output type $Poll < T >$ signifies whether the computation is complete with an output of type T or requires further progress. The design adheres to principles of lazy evaluation, wherein the computational steps are advanced only when explicitly polled. In contrast, the Stream trait extends this paradigm by modeling sequences of asynchronous outputs. Conceptually, a stream represents an asynchronous iterator, yielding multiple items over an arbitrary time span, thus broadening the asynchronous workflow paradigm beyond the single-result computation that characterizes futures.

The abstraction offered by these traits encapsulates not only the discrete computation of a final value but also the intricate orchestration of intermediate state transitions. The state transitions are governed by well-defined invariants that ensure memory safety and concurrency correctness. These invariants become particularly critical when dealing with low-level operating system primitives for event notification and task scheduling. The integration of the waker mechanism, which signals the runtime for the availability of new data or readiness for further processing, further enriches the theoretical model underlying custom future and stream implementations.

Implementing Custom Futures

The implementation of custom futures begins with the careful definition of the state machine that encapsulates the underlying asynchronous operation. A custom future is designed such that it meticulously tracks its progress through a series of intermediate states. The challenge is to design these states in a manner that preserves the contract of the Future trait, thereby ensuring that each call to the poll function meaningfully processes the current state and, when appropriate, yields a final result. The poll method is defined with the signature

$$poll\colon Pin < mut\ Self > \times Context \to Poll < Self\colon\colon Output >,$$

and must treat the provided context, and in particular its embedded waker, as the critical mechanism for resuming execution once the necessary conditions are met.

In the rigorous design of a custom future, one must carefully consider the semantics of state progression. The internal representation often involves one or more counters, flags, or even a composite structure that determines which branch of the computation is to be executed. For instance, a common pattern involves incrementally processing data or performing computations until a threshold condition is satisfied. In each invocation of the poll function, the future may opt to re-register its interest in further computation by invoking the waker mechanism, ensuring that the future is revisited by the scheduler. This design must also handle the transition from a pending state to a completed state with precision, releasing any resources that were allocated and yielding a result that is both coherent and free of race conditions. The interplay between the custom state machine and the underlying runtime scheduler is managed through careful state bookkeeping, which is imperative to avoid spurious wake-ups or inadvertent deadlocks.

Designing Custom Streams

While the Future trait concerns itself with the eventual production of a single value, the Stream trait extends this model to a series of asynchronous outputs. The design of a custom stream necessitates an implementation of a poll-based mechanism that repeatedly yields items until the end of the stream is reached. Each poll operation returns a value encapsulated within a result type, typically

$$Poll < Option < T >>,$$

where the use of the Option type reflects the possibility of an early termination of the stream. The stream, as a higher-level abstraction, requires a meticulous design strategy to handle backpressure, resource allocation, and synchronization of state across multiple poll invocations.

In crafting a custom stream, the primary focus is on managing the internal buffering of values and ensuring that each produced element is coherent with respect to the overall asynchronous workflow. The stream's implementation must define a clear protocol for transitioning between states: from yielding a new element, signaling the absence of an element, to handling any errors that arise during the generation of items. Furthermore, the interplay between the stream and consumer code is critical in maintaining a high degree of responsiveness, achieved through the careful coordination of wake-up signals and efficient context switching. This architecture often employs a loop that polls for new data and conditions that allow the emission of successive items, all the while guarded by invariants ensuring that state transitions adhere to the requisite safety properties.

Synchronization and Memory Safety Considerations

Both custom futures and streams necessitate a robust approach to synchronization and memory management, especially in the presence of concurrent operations and asynchronous execution. The enforcement of memory safety in these implementations leverages

Rust's borrowing rules and its type system. The explicit use of pinning via *Pin* ensures that computed memory addresses remain invariant throughout the duration of the asynchronous operation. This is essential in contexts where the internal state of a future or stream is accessed repeatedly through mutable references across multiple scheduler invocations.

The careful design of state transitions, combined with explicit management of the waker mechanism, fosters a deterministic behavior in the face of concurrency. It is vital to ensure that any resources allocated during the asynchronous computation are eventually released when the future or stream transitions to its final state. In particular, the deallocation of resources should be synchronously aligned with the termination of the asynchronous process. This synchronization is achieved through rigorous state invariants that mandate the orderly progression and eventual finality of the computation.

Moreover, the encapsulation of internal state within custom futures or streams must account for possible contention points when integrated into larger asynchronous workflows. The potential for concurrent access underscores the necessity for atomic operations or mutex-based synchronization, which, when used judiciously, prevent data races while still affording high-performance throughput. The intricate balance between coarser-grained locking strategies and fine-grained synchronization primitives is central to achieving both safety and efficiency in custom asynchronous implementations.

Rust Code Snippet

```
//! This example demonstrates the implementation of a custom Future
↪    and a custom Stream
//! as discussed in this chapter. Both abstractions rely on the poll
↪    mechanism:
//!
//! For the Future trait:
//!    poll: Pin<&mut Self> × Context -> Poll<Self::Output>
//!
//! For the Stream trait:
//!    poll_next: Pin<&mut Self> × Context ->
↪    Poll<Option<Self::Item>>
//!
//! The custom future is implemented as a state machine with
↪    discrete states,
```

```rust
//! transitioning based on a counter. The stream repeatedly yields
//    values until a maximum is reached.
//!
//! These examples also illustrate the use of the waker mechanism by
//    invoking `cx.waker().wake_by_ref()`
//! to re-register interest in subsequent execution.

use std::pin::Pin;
use std::task::{Context, Poll};
use std::future::Future;
use futures::stream::Stream;
use futures::executor::{block_on, LocalPool};
use futures::task::LocalSpawnExt;

//
// ------------------------------------------------------------------------
// Custom Future Implementation
//
// ------------------------------------------------------------------------

#[derive(Debug)]
enum CustomFutureState {
    Start,
    Waiting,
    Done,
}

struct CustomFuture {
    state: CustomFutureState,
    counter: u32,
}

impl CustomFuture {
    fn new() -> Self {
        Self {
            state: CustomFutureState::Start,
            counter: 0,
        }
    }
}

impl Future for CustomFuture {
    type Output = u32;

    // The poll method follows the signature:
    // fn poll(self: Pin<&mut Self>, cx: &mut Context<'_>) ->
    //    Poll<Self::Output>
    //
    // It simulates a computation progressing through discrete
    //    states.
    fn poll(mut self: Pin<&mut Self>, cx: &mut Context<'_>) ->
        Poll<Self::Output> {
        match self.state {
```

```rust
            CustomFutureState::Start => {
                // Initial state: transition to Waiting after
                // ↪  performing first step.
                self.counter += 1;
                println!("CustomFuture: transitioning from Start to
                // ↪  Waiting (counter = {})", self.counter);
                self.state = CustomFutureState::Waiting;
                // Register interest to be woken up when conditions
                // ↪  change.
                cx.waker().wake_by_ref();
                Poll::Pending
            },
            CustomFutureState::Waiting => {
                // In the waiting state, perform additional work.
                self.counter += 1;
                println!("CustomFuture: in Waiting state (counter =
                // ↪  {})", self.counter);
                if self.counter < 3 {
                    // If not complete, signal for further polling.
                    cx.waker().wake_by_ref();
                    Poll::Pending
                } else {
                    // Once the counter reaches the threshold,
                    // ↪  complete the computation.
                    println!("CustomFuture: computation complete
                    // ↪  with counter = {}", self.counter);
                    self.state = CustomFutureState::Done;
                    Poll::Ready(self.counter)
                }
            },
            CustomFutureState::Done => {
                // Polling after the future is complete is a logic
                // ↪  error.
                panic!("CustomFuture polled after completion");
            },
        }
    }
}

//
// ↪  ----------------------------------------------------------------
// Custom Stream Implementation
//
// ↪  ----------------------------------------------------------------

struct CustomStream {
    counter: u32,
    max: u32,
}

impl CustomStream {
    fn new(max: u32) -> Self {
        Self { counter: 0, max }
```

```
        }
    }

    impl Stream for CustomStream {
        type Item = u32;

        // The poll_next method follows the signature:
        // fn poll_next(self: Pin<&mut Self>, cx: &mut Context<'_>) ->
        ↪    Poll<Option<Self::Item>>
        //
        // It simulates an asynchronous sequence, yielding items until a
        ↪    maximum count is reached.
        fn poll_next(mut self: Pin<&mut Self>, cx: &mut Context<'_>) ->
        ↪    Poll<Option<Self::Item>> {
            if self.counter < self.max {
                self.counter += 1;
                println!("CustomStream: yielding value {}",
                ↪    self.counter);
                // Wake up the executor for the possibility of further
                ↪    items.
                cx.waker().wake_by_ref();
                Poll::Ready(Some(self.counter))
            } else {
                println!("CustomStream: reached maximum value {}",
                ↪    self.max);
                Poll::Ready(None)
            }
        }
    }

    //
    ↪    -----------------------------------------------------------------------
    // Main Execution
    //
    ↪    -----------------------------------------------------------------------

    fn main() {
        // Demonstrate the custom future.
        println!("Starting CustomFuture execution:");
        let future_result = block_on(CustomFuture::new());
        println!("CustomFuture completed with result: {}\n",
        ↪    future_result);

        // Set up a local executor to run the custom stream.
        let mut pool = LocalPool::new();
        let spawner = pool.spawner();

        // Spawn an async task to process the stream.
        spawner.spawn_local(async {
            use futures::stream::StreamExt;
            let mut stream = CustomStream::new(5);
            println!("Starting CustomStream execution:");
            // Process each item yielded by the stream.
```

40

```
        while let Some(item) = stream.next().await {
            println!("Received from CustomStream: {}", item);
        }
        println!("CustomStream execution completed.");
    }).expect("Failed to spawn stream task");

    // Run the executor until the stream task completes.
    pool.run();
}
```

Chapter 5

Synchronization and Shared State Management

Atomic Reference Counting and Arc

The use of atomic reference counting, as embodied in Arc, provides a mechanism for safe, shared ownership of immutable data among concurrently executing tasks. Arc employs hardware-level atomic operations to increment and decrement its reference counter, ensuring that the underlying data is deallocated precisely when no references remain. In this context, the semantics of Arc guarantee that every additional clone performs a well-synchronized update to the reference count, following the established memory ordering constraints such as acquire and release semantics. This guarantees that changes made to data prior to the increment of the counter become visible to subsequent accesses. Furthermore, in an asynchronous environment where multiple tasks may acquire references almost simultaneously, the lock-free properties of Arc prove indispensable in avoiding race conditions and ensuring deterministic memory management under heavy load.

Mutual Exclusion via Mutex

The Mutex construct enforces exclusive access to mutable data, thereby preventing concurrent modifications that could lead to inconsistent or erroneous state. In its core design, a Mutex wraps a data value and ensures that at most one asynchronous task or thread holds the lock at any given time. The act of acquiring the lock is typically realized via an atomic state transition that, if unsuccessful, requires the caller to yield or suspend its operation, thereby integrating naturally with asynchronous scheduling interfaces. The enforceable critical section provided by a Mutex ensures that complex state modifications occur in a controlled fashion. Under high contention, the proper integration of the Mutex with the asynchronous runtime means that tasks can be efficiently descheduled and reactivated via wake-up signals, maintaining both safety and performance without resorting to busy-wait loops or other blocking strategies.

Concurrent Access through RwLock

RwLock extends the paradigm of mutual exclusion by differentiating between read and write access. Whereas a Mutex permits only a single concurrent user, RwLock allows multiple readers to access the shared data simultaneously, while still ensuring that write operations obtain exclusive access. This dual mode of access is particularly advantageous when read operations significantly outnumber writes, as it minimizes contention and reduces latency. In the rigorous framework of asynchronous execution, RwLock must carefully mediate access among tasks that may be suspended and later resumed, ensuring that ongoing read operations do not preclude the eventual acquisition of the lock for writing. The underlying algorithms are designed to prevent writer starvation by guaranteeing that a pending write request eventually receives exclusive access after all active readers complete, a balance that is critical under heavy and dynamically varying load conditions.

Shared State Management in Asynchronous Environments

Within asynchronous systems, the combined use of Arc, Mutex, and RwLock forms the foundation for managing shared state while mitigating the challenges imposed by concurrent accesses. The design principles underpinning these abstractions emphasize non-blocking synchronization, wherein tasks release control rather than repeatedly polling for lock availability. This ensures that the scheduler can efficiently redistribute computational effort among tasks, even when contention for shared data peaks. Concretely, the archetypal pattern involves wrapping a shared resource within an Arc to facilitate shared ownership, and then encapsulating the mutable state within either a Mutex or an RwLock depending on the access patterns. The interactions among these components are subject to strict invariants regarding memory visibility and ordering; for instance, every release of a Mutex or RwLock is associated with a corresponding memory fence that guarantees the propagation of state modifications. Furthermore, these constructs are designed to operate under the assumption of asynchronous yield points, wherein the invocation of a wake-up mechanism informs the runtime when a lock may have become available. In environments characterized by sustained high load, the judicious application of these synchronization primitives is paramount to achieving both correctness and scalability without compromising on performance or safety.

Rust Code Snippet

```rust
use std::sync::{Arc, Mutex, RwLock};
use std::sync::atomic::{AtomicUsize, Ordering, fence};
use tokio::time::{sleep, Duration};
use tokio::task;

/// This example demonstrates the use of Arc, Mutex, RwLock, and
↪    AtomicUsize in an asynchronous context.
/// Each asynchronous task updates a shared counter (protected by
↪    Mutex), increments a lock-free atomic counter,
/// and reads shared data protected by a RwLock. Memory ordering is
↪    explicitly handled using atomic operations,
/// illustrating the acquire and release semantics discussed in the
↪    chapter.

#[tokio::main]
```

```rust
async fn main() {
    // Shared mutable counter protected by a Mutex.
    let counter = Arc::new(Mutex::new(0));

    // Shared data vector protected by a RwLock to allow concurrent
    //   read access.
    let shared_data = Arc::new(RwLock::new(vec![10, 20, 30, 40,
    //   50]));

    // An atomic counter that uses lock-free operations for fast,
    //   concurrent updates.
    let atomic_counter = Arc::new(AtomicUsize::new(0));

    // Vector to collect task handles.
    let mut handles = Vec::new();

    // Spawn 10 asynchronous tasks to simulate concurrent
    //   operations.
    for i in 0..10 {
        let counter_clone = Arc::clone(&counter);
        let data_clone = Arc::clone(&shared_data);
        let atomic_counter_clone = Arc::clone(&atomic_counter);

        let handle = task::spawn(async move {
            // Simulate work by delaying the task execution.
            sleep(Duration::from_millis(100 * (i as u64))).await;

            // Increment the atomic counter.
            // Using Ordering::Release to ensure that prior writes
            //   are visible to other threads that use acquire.
            atomic_counter_clone.fetch_add(1, Ordering::Release);
            // Fence with Ordering::Acquire ensures that this task
            //   sees all memory effects up to this point.
            fence(Ordering::Acquire);

            // Update the counter inside the Mutex critical section.
            {
                let mut num = counter_clone.lock().unwrap();
                *num += 1;
                println!("Task {}: Mutex counter updated to {}", i,
                //   *num);
            }

            // Read shared data concurrently using a RwLock.
            {
                let data = data_clone.read().unwrap();
                let sum: i32 = data.iter().sum();
                println!("Task {}: Sum of RwLock data is {}", i,
                //   sum);
            }
        });
        handles.push(handle);
    }
```

```rust
    // Wait for all tasks to complete.
    for handle in handles {
        let _ = handle.await;
    }

    // Print the final values after all asynchronous tasks are
    ↪  complete.
    println!("Final Mutex counter value: {}",
    ↪   *counter.lock().unwrap());
    println!("Final AtomicUsize counter value: {}",
    ↪   atomic_counter.load(Ordering::Acquire));

    // Modify the shared data by acquiring a write lock via RwLock.
    {
        let mut data = shared_data.write().unwrap();
        data.push(100);
        println!("After write, RwLock data: {:?}", *data);
    }
}
```

Chapter 6

Non-blocking TCP Server Design

Foundations of Asynchronous I/O for TCP Servers

Non-blocking I/O constitutes the cornerstone of scalable network server architectures designed for high concurrency. The model operates on the principle of event-driven execution, wherein tasks relinquish control during idle periods and subsequently resume operation upon the occurrence of pertinent events. This paradigm exploits operating system facilities such as *epoll*, *kqueue*, and *IOCP* to monitor file descriptors for readiness, thereby eliminating the inefficiencies associated with traditional blocking system calls. The architectural approach enables a minimal set of threads to manage an extensive number of simultaneous connections, reducing overhead and facilitating operation under sharply varying loads. In this context, the asynchronous framework orchestrates I/O operations by leveraging futures and task schedulers, ensuring that system resources are judiciously allocated and that latency remains low even in high-throughput scenarios.

Architectural Strategies in Non-blocking TCP Server Design

The design of a non-blocking TCP server necessitates a clear separation of concerns between connection acceptance, I/O processing, and protocol-specific logic. Central to the architecture is an event loop that functions as a reactor, continuously monitoring for input/output events and dispatching work to appropriate handlers. This reactor pattern not only minimizes system call overhead but also enhances data locality and cache utilization, which are critical for maintaining high performance. The architecture typically features a layered approach in which low-level socket operations are abstracted from higher-level connection management, thereby isolating hardware-dependent behaviors from application logic. Such a modular design ensures that each component—even under heavy load—adheres to strict performance and scalability requirements by confining blocking operations exclusively to the boundaries of the asynchronous interface.

Integration with Rust Networking Libraries

Rust's ecosystem provides a comprehensive suite of libraries that seamlessly integrate asynchronous I/O techniques with its robust type system and memory safety guarantees. These libraries encapsulate operating system networking APIs within a framework that leverages the language's native constructs for concurrency. Through a design centered on futures and task scheduling, the libraries expose high-level abstractions for socket operations, connection management, and event notification. The integration respects Rust's ownership and borrowing disciplines, ensuring that the concurrent handling of network events does not compromise memory integrity or induce data races. This architectural coupling permits the server to adopt a fully asynchronous operational model, where non-blocking calls are represented as composable tasks and scheduling decisions are made in accordance with explicit resource management strategies.

Advanced Connection Handling and Concurrency Management

In the realm of high-performance TCP server design, the management of a multitude of concurrent connections is achieved through meticulous control over asynchronous events and resource allocation. The event loop continually receives and aggregates notifications from numerous sources, scheduling tasks in a manner that precludes blocking while permitting fine-grained concurrency. Each established connection is monitored for state changes—readability, writability, and error conditions—with the inherent design ensuring that even transient spikes in activity are accommodated without inducing systemic delays. Concurrency control is further enhanced by the adoption of lock-free data structures and minimal locking strategies, which are employed to safeguard state transitions and ensure atomicity across asynchronous contexts. This approach provides a framework wherein scheduling, load distribution, and resource reclamation are tightly interwoven to achieve efficient, deterministic performance under variable network conditions.

Robust Error Handling and Resource Management

Error detection and resource reclamation are intrinsic to the non-blocking design of a TCP server, particularly when operating in a highly concurrent environment. The asynchronous model mandates that all I/O events be scrutinized rigorously for potential error conditions, with mechanisms in place to propagate failures through well-defined channels without stalling the event loop. In this design, error handling routines are executed within the same non-blocking paradigm, permitting the graceful degradation of service in the face of transient network anomalies and systemic resource constraints. Resource cleanup, including the deallocation of sockets and associated buffers, is performed deterministically under the auspices of Rust's ownership model, ensuring that no residual state persists once a connection has been terminated. The consistent application of atomic operations and explicit memory ordering constraints guarantees that resource deallocation and error propagation occur in a predictable and controlled manner, thereby preserving the overall integrity and resilience of the server under sustained load.

Rust Code Snippet

```rust
use tokio::net::{TcpListener, TcpStream};
use tokio::io::{AsyncReadExt, AsyncWriteExt};
use std::time::{Instant, Duration};
use std::sync::atomic::{AtomicUsize, Ordering};
use std::error::Error;

/// Global atomic counter tracking the number of active connections.
static ACTIVE_CONNECTIONS: AtomicUsize = AtomicUsize::new(0);

/// Entry point launching the asynchronous non-blocking TCP server.
#[tokio::main]
async fn main() -> Result<(), Box<dyn Error>> {
    // Bind the TCP listener to a local address.
    let listener = TcpListener::bind("127.0.0.1:8080").await?;
    println!("Server listening on 127.0.0.1:8080");

    loop {
        // Accept an incoming connection.
        let (socket, addr) = listener.accept().await?;
        ACTIVE_CONNECTIONS.fetch_add(1, Ordering::SeqCst);
        println!("New connection from {} | Active connections: {}",
                addr, ACTIVE_CONNECTIONS.load(Ordering::SeqCst));

        // Spawn a new task to process the connection without
        // ↪ blocking the event loop.
        tokio::spawn(async move {
            if let Err(e) = handle_connection(socket).await {
                eprintln!("Error handling connection from {}: {:?}",
                    ↪ addr, e);
            }
            ACTIVE_CONNECTIONS.fetch_sub(1, Ordering::SeqCst);
            println!("Connection from {} closed | Active
            ↪ connections: {}",
                    addr,
                    ↪ ACTIVE_CONNECTIONS.load(Ordering::SeqCst));
        });
    }
}

/// Handles an individual TCP connection using non-blocking I/O.
///
/// This function demonstrates important aspects:
///    - Asynchronous reading and writing with futures.
///    - Throughput calculation using the equation:
///        throughput (bits/sec) = (total_bytes * 8) /
↪  elapsed_time_in_seconds
```

```
///    - A simple token bucket rate-limiting algorithm to simulate
↪  flow control:
///        tokens = (elapsed_time * refill_rate) -
↪  total_bytes_transferred
///    If tokens fall below zero, the task waits for a calculated
↪  duration before resuming.
async fn handle_connection(mut socket: TcpStream) -> Result<(),
↪  Box<dyn Error>> {
    let mut buf = [0u8; 1024];

    // Record the initial time to measure throughput and to drive
    ↪   the token bucket.
    let start_time = Instant::now();
    let mut total_bytes = 0;

    loop {
        // Read data from the socket into the buffer (non-blocking).
        let n = match socket.read(&mut buf).await {
            Ok(0) => break, // Zero bytes read implies the
            ↪   connection was closed.
            Ok(n) => n,
            Err(e) => {
                eprintln!("Read error: {:?}", e);
                return Err(e.into());
            }
        };

        total_bytes += n;

        // Echo back the received data.
        if let Err(e) = socket.write_all(&buf[..n]).await {
            eprintln!("Write error: {:?}", e);
            return Err(e.into());
        }

        // --- Rate Limiting via a Simple Token Bucket Algorithm ---
        // Equation:
        //    tokens = (elapsed_time_in_seconds * refill_rate) -
        ↪   total_bytes_transferred
        // Where:
        //    refill_rate is the rate of token replenishment (in
        ↪   bytes per second).
        //    total_bytes_transferred is the cumulative number of
        ↪   bytes processed.
        // If the token count falls below zero, the connection is
        ↪   momentarily throttled.
        let elapsed = start_time.elapsed().as_secs_f64();
        let refill_rate = 1000.0; // tokens (i.e., bytes)
        ↪   replenished per second (example value)
        let tokens = (elapsed * refill_rate) - total_bytes as f64;
        if tokens < 0.0 {
            let wait_duration = Duration::from_secs_f64((-tokens) /
            ↪   refill_rate);
```

51

```rust
        // Suspends the task for the calculated time without
        ↪   blocking the event loop.
        tokio::time::sleep(wait_duration).await;
    }
}

// Calculate and print the throughput using the formula:
//    throughput (bits/sec) = (total_bytes * 8) /
↪   elapsed_time_in_seconds
let elapsed = start_time.elapsed().as_secs_f64();
if elapsed > 0.0 {
    let throughput = (total_bytes as f64 * 8.0) / elapsed;
    println!("Connection throughput: {:.2} bits/sec",
    ↪   throughput);
}

Ok(())
}
```

Chapter 7

Non-blocking TCP Client Development

Foundations of Asynchronous I/O for TCP Clients

The development of non-blocking TCP clients is founded upon a radical departure from traditional synchronous communication paradigms. In this approach, connection initiation, data transmission, and reception are all executed via asynchronous calls that preclude the use of blocking system calls. The operational model relies on low-level operating system mechanisms such as *epoll*, *kqueue*, and *IOCP* which monitor socket file descriptors for state changes, thereby enabling a single thread or a limited pool of threads to manage multiple concurrent connections. By representing I/O operations as futures or promises, the client defers execution until a corresponding event is signaled, thus realizing a high degree of concurrency without compromising resource efficiency.

Architectural Patterns and Modular Design

The architectural design of non-blocking TCP clients adheres to the principles of modularity and separation of concerns. At the lowest level, raw socket operations are encapsulated within an abstraction layer that handles asynchronous event notification, while higher-level modules are responsible for connection management and protocol-specific logic. This layered architecture follows the reactor design pattern, wherein a central event loop orchestrates the dispatching of connection events and data transfer operations. Such a configuration permits the decoupling of the syntactic intricacies associated with low-level non-blocking I/O from the substantive business logic, rendering the overall system more adaptable and maintainable. In addition, the division of responsibilities facilitates rigorous formal verification of each module's behavior under concurrent conditions.

Concurrency Mechanisms and Connection Lifecycle Management

The efficient management of concurrent connections is an essential requirement in the non-blocking paradigm. Each TCP client instance is treated as an independent entity that undergoes a lifecycle comprising connection establishment, data exchange, and eventual disconnection. Handling these state transitions requires the employment of advanced concurrency mechanisms that minimize synchronization overhead and prevent race conditions. State transitions are managed via finely tuned state machines that track the progress of asynchronous operations. Lock-free data structures and atomic variables are often integrated into these mechanisms to ensure that connection state updates occur in a deterministic fashion. This model not only optimizes resource allocation but also simplifies error recovery during transient network disruptions, thereby sustaining high degrees of parallelism in connection management.

Performance Optimization and I/O Efficiency

The performance of a non-blocking TCP client is intrinsically linked to the efficiency of its I/O operations and the underlying scheduling policies. Asynchronous non-blocking calls allow the client to process multiple events concurrently, dramatically reducing the latency inherent in waiting for synchronous operations to complete. Performance metrics such as throughput and round-trip time (RTT) are essential indicators of system efficiency and are used to fine-tune both resource allocation and task scheduling. The client's architecture is designed to minimize the number of context switches and optimize system resource usage by consolidating multiple I/O events into singular operation batches. In addition, adaptive scheduling techniques, which may incorporate dynamic rate limiting and predictive buffering strategies, are employed to mitigate the effects of network contention and to sustain a continuous flow of data even under high-load conditions.

Robust Asynchronous Error Handling and Resource Clean-Up

Integral to the reliability of non-blocking TCP clients is a robust framework for error handling and deterministic resource management. Asynchronous operations are inherently more susceptible to transient errors, including socket timeouts, abrupt connection terminations, and other network anomalies. In this context, error propagation is managed through a well-defined series of handshaking protocols and asynchronous signaling channels that ensure errors are detected and handled with minimal impact on ongoing operations. Resource deallocation routines are tightly coupled with the ownership and borrowing semantics inherent to the language, providing deterministic cleanup of network buffers and socket descriptors upon the termination of a connection. This mechanism prevents the accumulation of residual state, ensuring that the client maintains operational integrity even in scenarios of sustained network instability.

Rust Code Snippet

```rust
use tokio::io::{self, AsyncReadExt, AsyncWriteExt};
use tokio::net::TcpStream;
use tokio::time::{sleep, Duration};

#[derive(Debug)]
enum ConnectionState {
    Connecting,
    Connected,
    Disconnected,
    Error(String),
}

struct TcpClient {
```

```rust
    address: String,
    connection_state: ConnectionState,
}

impl TcpClient {
    // Initiates an asynchronous connection to the server.
    async fn connect(&mut self) -> io::Result<()> {
        self.connection_state = ConnectionState::Connecting;
        match TcpStream::connect(&self.address).await {
            Ok(stream) => {
                println!("Connected to server at {}", self.address);
                self.connection_state = ConnectionState::Connected;
                self.handle_connection(stream).await;
                Ok(())
            }
            Err(e) => {
                self.connection_state =
                ↪   ConnectionState::Error(e.to_string());
                Err(e)
            }
        }
    }

    // Manages the connection lifecycle: send handshake, process
    ↪   responses, and echo acknowledgments.
    async fn handle_connection(&self, mut stream: TcpStream) {
        // Example of initiating a handshake.
        let handshake = b"HELLO from client\n";
        if let Err(e) = stream.write_all(handshake).await {
            eprintln!("Failed sending handshake: {:?}", e);
            return;
        }
        // Buffer to store incoming data.
        let mut buffer = vec![0u8; 1024];
        loop {
            match stream.read(&mut buffer).await {
                Ok(0) => {
                    // Connection gracefully closed by server.
                    println!("Server closed connection");
                    break;
                }
                Ok(n) => {
                    let response = &buffer[..n];
                    println!("Received data: {}",
                    ↪   String::from_utf8_lossy(response));

                    // Simulate computational processing delay (e.g.
                    ↪   RTT calculation).
                    // RTT estimation could be modeled as:
                    //   RTT = t_end - t_start
                    // For demonstration, we use sleep to mimic
                    ↪   processing delay.
                    sleep(Duration::from_millis(100)).await;
```

```rust
            // Echo a PONG message as an acknowledgement.
            if let Err(e) =
            ↪   stream.write_all(b"PONG\n").await {
                    eprintln!("Error sending PONG: {:?}", e);
                    break;
                }
            }
            Err(e) => {
                eprintln!("Failed reading from stream: {:?}",
                ↪   e);
                break;
            }
        }
    }
}

// TokenBucket implements a dynamic rate limiting algorithm using
↪   the token bucket model.
// The refill formula is: tokens = min(capacity, tokens +
↪   refill_rate)
struct TokenBucket {
    capacity: usize,
    tokens: usize,
    refill_rate: usize, // tokens added per interval
}

impl TokenBucket {
    fn new(capacity: usize, refill_rate: usize) -> Self {
        Self {
            capacity,
            tokens: capacity,
            refill_rate,
        }
    }

    // Attempts to consume a token. Returns true if successful.
    fn try_consume(&mut self) -> bool {
        if self.tokens > 0 {
            self.tokens -= 1;
            true
        } else {
            false
        }
    }

    // Refill the token bucket based on the refill_rate.
    fn refill(&mut self) {
        self.tokens = std::cmp::min(self.capacity, self.tokens +
        ↪   self.refill_rate);
    }
}
```

```
#[tokio::main]
async fn main() -> io::Result<()> {
    println!("Starting Non-blocking TCP Client Development Sample");

    // Initialize the TCP client with the target server address.
    let mut client = TcpClient {
        address: "127.0.0.1:8080".to_string(),
        connection_state: ConnectionState::Disconnected,
    };

    // Spawn an asynchronous task to demonstrate dynamic rate
    ↪ limiting using a token bucket.
    let rate_limit_task = tokio::spawn(async {
        let mut token_bucket = TokenBucket::new(10, 1); // capacity
        ↪ of 10 tokens, 1 token per interval
        loop {
            if token_bucket.try_consume() {
                println!("Token consumed. Remaining tokens: {}",
                ↪ token_bucket.tokens);
            } else {
                println!("No tokens available. Refilling
                ↪ bucket...");
                token_bucket.refill();
            }
            sleep(Duration::from_millis(200)).await;
        }
    });

    // Attempt to connect to the server asynchronously.
    if let Err(e) = client.connect().await {
        eprintln!("Error connecting to server: {:?}", e);
    }

    // In a real application, the rate limit task may run
    ↪ indefinitely.
    // Here, we abort it for demonstration purposes once the client
    ↪ connection ends.
    rate_limit_task.abort();
    println!("Client connection ended.");
    Ok(())
}
```

Chapter 8

Efficient UDP Communication Patterns

Asynchronous Foundations in UDP Communications

The design of asynchronous UDP services is predicated on the intrinsic characteristics of the User Datagram Protocol (UDP), wherein the absence of connection management enables a naturally non-blocking mode of operation. In this model, input/output events are managed via event-driven paradigms that leverage system-level mechanisms such as *epoll*, *kqueue*, and *IOCP*. UDP datagrams are encapsulated as independent packets, and asynchronous processing ensures that the reception and transmission of these datagrams are handled without incurring the delays usually associated with blocking system calls. The absence of connection state inherently simplifies the scheduling of operations, as each packet is processed independently; however, it simultaneously imposes the requirement for robust error detection and handling strategies at the application layer. This paradigm necessitates a fine-grained orchestration of asynchronous events and the adoption of non-blocking state machines that monitor socket descriptors for readiness events, thereby permitting rapid response times and enhanced throughput when managing multiple simultaneous datagram streams.

Broadcasting Mechanisms

Broadcasting in the context of UDP services involves the transmission of datagrams to all network nodes within a specified subnet, effectively enabling a wide dissemination of information without the overhead of managing multiple individual connections. Implementation of broadcasting necessitates the careful configuration of socket options to allow the dispatch of packets to the universal broadcast address, commonly represented in IPv4 as 255.255.255.255. In an asynchronous setting, the utilization of non-blocking socket APIs allows for simultaneous dispatch of broadcast packets while concurrently processing incoming responses. This pattern is particularly advantageous in scenarios where rapid dissemination of control messages, discovery protocols, or state updates is required. The architecture supporting broadcasting must therefore manage issues such as packet collision, variable network latency, and potential packet loss; hence, detailed mechanisms for error handling, confirmation of packet reception, and, where applicable, gradual retransmission strategies are incorporated to maintain a consistent level of service reliability.

Multicasting Paradigms

Multicasting extends the principles of broadcasting by targeting only a subset of hosts that subscribe to a specific multicast group. The mechanism requires the configuration of specialized socket options to join multicast groups, thereby allowing datagrams to be delivered exclusively to members of the group. Within asynchronous UDP services, multicasting is orchestrated by embedding group management within the event loop infrastructure. Management protocols, such as the Internet Group Management Protocol (IGMP) for IPv4 or Multicast Listener Discovery (MLD) for IPv6, are employed to regulate group membership, ensuring that multicast datagrams are efficiently delivered to all subscribed endpoints. The asynchronous design enables concurrent handling of multiple multicast groups, each with heterogeneous data exchange requirements. This paradigm facilitates rapid data exchange by minimizing the overhead associated with unicast communications and leveraging the multicast distribution capabilities inherent in modern network infrastructures. Detailed attention is given to mechanisms ensuring that datagram delivery is handled effectively despite the inherent unreliability of UDP, including techniques for sequence numbering, redundancy, and adaptive retransmission policies.

Architectural Considerations in Asynchronous UDP Services

The construction of UDP services within an asynchronous framework relies on a carefully layered architectural design, wherein the separation of concerns is paramount. At the lowest level, raw UDP socket operations are abstracted into a non-blocking event dispatch mechanism. This abstraction ensures that all incoming datagrams are efficiently queued and routed to higher-level processing units without inducing undue latency. The middleware layer is responsible for the implementation of protocol-specific logic, which includes addressing the stateless nature of UDP by incorporating custom mechanisms to delineate session context on a per-datagram basis. Modular design patterns are employed to encapsulate broadcasting and multicasting functionalities into distinct components that interface seamlessly with the central event loop. Furthermore, the implementation of error detection and state synchronization routines is intertwined with the architecture to mitigate packet loss and to enforce the deterministic handling of datagram sequences. The resultant system is inherently scalable, allowing for rapid adjustments in operational load by dynamically modulating the event scheduling policies and prioritizing latency-critical operations.

Performance Optimization and I/O Efficiency

In the realm of rapid data exchange, performance optimization of asynchronous UDP services is critically underscored by the minimization of processing overhead and the efficient management of I/O operations. The removal of connection establishment procedures, inherent in the UDP protocol, serves as a fundamental advantage; yet, the design must account for the possibility of out-of-order delivery and the absence of acknowledgment mechanisms. Advanced scheduling techniques within the asynchronous runtime environment facilitate the consolidation of multiple I/O events into cohesive operation batches, thereby reducing the frequency of context switches and the overall computational load. Techniques such as adaptive rate control, predictive buffering strategies, and fine-tuning of event loop frequency are systematically integrated to enhance throughput and reduce latency. The deployment of these methods contributes to a marked improvement in performance metrics, such as datagram round-trip time and overall exchange rate, all while maintaining high levels of system stability and resource efficiency. The architectural blueprint is thus characterized by an intricate balance between the speed of data propagation and the robustness of error recovery protocols, ensuring that rapid data exchange is achieved without compromising the integrity of the service.

Rust Code Snippet

```
//! Comprehensive Example: Asynchronous UDP Service with Adaptive
↪   Rate Control
//! This example demonstrates:
//!   - Asynchronous UDP reception and transmission using Tokio.
//!   - Implementation of broadcasting and multicasting paradigms.
//!   - A token bucket algorithm for adaptive rate control.
//!
//! Cargo.toml dependencies:
//! [dependencies]
//! tokio = { version = "1", features = ["full"] }

use tokio::net::UdpSocket;
use tokio::time::{self, Duration, Instant};
use tokio::sync::Mutex;
use std::error::Error;
use std::sync::Arc;
use std::net::{UdpSocket as StdUdpSocket, SocketAddr, Ipv4Addr};

/// TokenBucket implements a simple adaptive rate control algorithm.
/// It follows the token bucket model where tokens accumulate at a
↪   steady rate.
struct TokenBucket {
    capacity: usize,
    tokens: usize,
    refill_rate: usize, // tokens per second
    last_refill: Instant,
}

impl TokenBucket {
```

```rust
    /// Creates a new TokenBucket with a specified capacity and
    /// refill rate.
    fn new(capacity: usize, refill_rate: usize) -> Self {
        Self {
            capacity,
            tokens: capacity,
            refill_rate,
            last_refill: Instant::now(),
        }
    }

    /// Attempts to consume a given number of tokens.
    /// Returns true if sufficient tokens exist, else false.
    fn try_consume(&mut self, amount: usize) -> bool {
        self.refill();
        if self.tokens >= amount {
            self.tokens -= amount;
            true
        } else {
            false
        }
    }

    /// Refills tokens based on the elapsed time since the last
    /// refill.
    /// The formula applied: tokens_to_add = elapsed (in seconds) *
    /// refill_rate.
    fn refill(&mut self) {
        let now = Instant::now();
        let elapsed = now.duration_since(self.last_refill);
        let tokens_to_add = (elapsed.as_secs_f64() *
            self.refill_rate as f64) as usize;
        if tokens_to_add > 0 {
            self.tokens = std::cmp::min(self.capacity, self.tokens +
                tokens_to_add);
            self.last_refill = now;
        }
    }
}

#[tokio::main]
async fn main() -> Result<(), Box<dyn Error>> {
    // Bind a standard UDP socket on a local address for
    // asynchronous operations.
    let local_addr: SocketAddr = "0.0.0.0:8080".parse()?;
    let std_socket = StdUdpSocket::bind(local_addr)?;
    std_socket.set_nonblocking(true)?;

    // Multicasting Paradigms:
    // Join a multicast group (here using the IPv4 multicast address
    // 224.0.0.1).
    let multicast_v4: Ipv4Addr = "224.0.0.1".parse()?;
```

63

```rust
std_socket.join_multicast_v4(&multicast_v4,
    &Ipv4Addr::UNSPECIFIED)?;

// Convert the standard socket into a Tokio UdpSocket for async
    management.
let socket = UdpSocket::from_std(std_socket)?;

println!("UDP service listening on {}", local_addr);

// Broadcasting Mechanisms:
// Enable the broadcast option on the socket.
socket.set_broadcast(true)?;

// Create a shared TokenBucket instance for adaptive rate
    control.
let rate_limiter = Arc::new(Mutex::new(TokenBucket::new(10,
    5)));

// Clone the UDP socket for the asynchronous reception task.
let recv_socket = socket.try_clone().expect("Failed to clone
    socket for receiving");

// Asynchronous Foundations in UDP Communications:
// Spawn a task to continuously receive UDP datagrams.
tokio::spawn(async move {
    let mut buf = [0u8; 1500]; // Buffer size approximates the
        typical MTU.
    loop {
        match recv_socket.recv_from(&mut buf).await {
            Ok((n, src)) => {
                println!("Received {} bytes from {}: {:?}", n,
                    src, &buf[..n]);
                // Insert advanced error detection, sequence
                    numbering, or redundancy logic here.
            },
            Err(e) => {
                eprintln!("Error receiving datagram: {}", e);
            },
        }
    }
});

// Task for sending UDP datagrams with broadcasting and
    multicasting.
let send_task = {
    let rate_limiter = Arc::clone(&rate_limiter);
    async move {
        // Define target addresses.
        let broadcast_addr: SocketAddr =
            "255.255.255.255:8080".parse()?;
        let multicast_addr: SocketAddr = format!("{}:{}",
            multicast_v4, 8080).parse()?;
```

```rust
        // Set up an interval timer to trigger send operations
        // ↪ periodically.
        let mut interval =
        ↪   time::interval(Duration::from_millis(200));
        loop {
            interval.tick().await;
            let mut limiter = rate_limiter.lock().await;
            if limiter.try_consume(1) {
                // Broadcasting Mechanisms:
                let broadcast_msg = b"Async UDP Broadcast
                ↪   Message";
                match socket.send_to(broadcast_msg,
                ↪   broadcast_addr).await {
                    Ok(n) => println!("Broadcasted {} bytes to
                    ↪   {}", n, broadcast_addr),
                    Err(e) => eprintln!("Error sending
                    ↪   broadcast: {}", e),
                }

                // Multicasting Paradigms:
                let multicast_msg = b"Async UDP Multicast
                ↪   Message";
                match socket.send_to(multicast_msg,
                ↪   multicast_addr).await {
                    Ok(n) => println!("Multicasted {} bytes to
                    ↪   {}", n, multicast_addr),
                    Err(e) => eprintln!("Error sending
                    ↪   multicast: {}", e),
                }
            } else {
                println!("Rate limiter: Insufficient tokens;
                ↪   delaying send.");
            }
        }
        // This return is unreachable but necessary for type
        // ↪ inference.
        #[allow(unreachable_code)]
        Ok::<(), Box<dyn Error>>(())
    }
    };

    // Execute the sending task indefinitely.
    send_task.await?;

    Ok(())
}
```

Chapter 9

Scalable Socket Programming with Mio

Foundations of Mio in the Context of Low-Level I/O

Mio is conceived as a lightweight, cross-platform abstraction layer for non-blocking input/output that exposes a uniform interface to underlying operating system primitives such as *epoll*, *kqueue*, and *IOCP*. The design of Mio is predicated on providing fine-grained control over socket state and event notification, allowing the explicit management of I/O events. The emphasis on low-level operations is evident in the manner in which Mio forgoes complex abstractions in favor of direct access to the native event mechanisms. This design philosophy permits an exacting control over resource utilization and system call overhead, which is crucial in environments characterized by high-throughput and low-latency requirements.

Design Principles of Non-Blocking Sockets

The architecture of non-blocking sockets within the Mio framework is underpinned by principles that prioritize efficiency and scalability. Sockets configured in non-blocking mode operate under the

premise that system calls will return immediately, thereby eliminating the delays incurred by blocking operations. This paradigm
requires that the application continuously monitor socket descriptors for readiness indications. The fundamental approach ensures
that the programmer retains explicit control over the scheduling
and processing of I/O events. By decoupling the management of
connection states from the actual data transmission, the design
yields a streamlined mechanism that efficiently addresses the inherent challenges posed by asynchronous communication.

Event Loop Mechanisms and the Reactor Pattern

Central to Mio's operation is the implementation of an event loop
that embodies the reactor pattern. In this mechanism, a singular
loop orchestrates the registration, demultiplexing, and dispatching of I/O events. Mio's reactor is responsible for polling socket
descriptors and identifying those that become ready for reading,
writing, or error handling. The framework relies on an iterative
process where each cycle of the event loop processes a batch of
pending events before reinitiating the polling phase. This structured approach minimizes latency by reducing the frequency of
blocking system calls and enables a systematic approach to re-
schedule tasks based on their readiness. The event loop mechanism
is therefore pivotal in maintaining an efficient, scalable I/O model
in environments where high volumes of events must be processed
concurrently.

Managing Concurrency in High-Throughput Environments

Scalability in network applications is achieved through the adept
handling of concurrent I/O events. Mio facilitates this by enabling
a design in which multiple socket channels are monitored and acted
upon in parallel. The non-blocking configuration allows the event
loop to service a large number of simultaneous connections without dedicating individual threads to each socket. This concurrency
model leverages the operating system's native multiplexing capabilities, thereby reducing overhead associated with context switching and synchronization. Complex scenarios, including handling

rapid bursts of network traffic, benefit from this fine-tuned control over event distribution and prioritization. The ability to distinctively process discrete operations while maintaining a shared event management loop is intrinsic to the success of high-throughput architectures.

Performance Considerations and Optimization Strategies

Achieving optimal performance in scalable socket programming under Mio necessitates a meticulous analysis of both system-level and application-specific factors. A core aspect of this analysis involves minimizing the latency introduced by repetitive system calls and ensuring that event notifications are processed with minimal computational overhead. Performance optimization strategies include aggregating multiple events into single processing cycles and leveraging zero-copy techniques to reduce the memory overhead associated with data movement. Additionally, careful management of buffer lifecycles and dynamic allocation can lead to significant improvements in throughput. The interplay between the operating system's scheduling and Mio's event processing loop requires that both theoretical and empirical evaluations be conducted to fine-tune the overall I/O efficiency. By employing these optimization strategies, systems utilizing Mio are capable of sustaining high data rates and maintaining responsiveness in demanding network environments.

Rust Code Snippet

```
use std::collections::HashMap;
use std::io::{self, Read, Write};
use std::time::Duration;
use mio::net::{TcpListener, TcpStream};
use mio::{Events, Interest, Poll, Token};

// Constant token for the server listener.
const SERVER: Token = Token(0);

fn main() -> io::Result<()> {
    // Bind the TCP listener to the local address.
    let addr = "127.0.0.1:9000".parse().expect("Invalid address");
    let mut server = TcpListener::bind(addr)?;
```

```rust
// Create a new poll instance to monitor events.
let mut poll = Poll::new()?;
// Register the server with interest in read events.
poll.registry().register(&mut server, SERVER,
↪   Interest::READABLE)?;

// A HashMap to manage client connections using unique tokens.
let mut connections = HashMap::new();
// Token counter starting after SERVER for client connections.
let mut unique_token = Token(SERVER.0 + 1);

// Allocate a buffer for reading data.
let mut buffer = [0u8; 4096];

// Create an events container with a capacity for batching
↪   events.
let mut events = Events::with_capacity(128);

// Main event loop based on the reactor pattern.
loop {
    // Poll for events with a timeout of 1 second.
    poll.poll(&mut events, Some(Duration::from_secs(1)))?;

    // Performance Insight (in comments):
    //   Let T_cycle be the duration of one polling cycle.
    //   Throughput (Number of bytes processed) / T_cycle.
    //   For example, if 4096 bytes are processed in 10ms, then:
    //   Throughput = 4096 / 0.01 = 409600 bytes/sec.
    //
    // Also, latency can be approximated as:
    //   Latency T_cycle - T_processing,
    // where T_processing is the time spent handling each event.

    // If no events occurred, continue the loop (could be used
    ↪   to adjust scheduling).
    if events.is_empty() {
        continue;
    }

    // Process each event received in this cycle.
    for event in events.iter() {
        let token = event.token();

        if token == SERVER {
            // Accept any pending connections.
            loop {
                match server.accept() {
                    Ok((mut connection, address)) => {
                        println!("Accepted connection from: {}",
                        ↪   address);
```

```rust
            // Register the new connection for both
            ↪   reading and writing.
            poll.registry().register(
                &mut connection,
                unique_token,

                ↪   Interest::READABLE.add(Interest::WRITABLE)
            )?;

            // Store the connection in our HashMap.
            connections.insert(unique_token,
            ↪   connection);

            // Increment the token for the next
            ↪   connection.
            unique_token = Token(unique_token.0 +
            ↪   1);
        }
        Err(ref e) if e.kind() ==
        ↪   io::ErrorKind::WouldBlock => {
            // No more connections are available to
            ↪   accept at the moment.
            break;
        }
        Err(e) => {
            eprintln!("Error accepting connection:
            ↪   {}", e);
            break;
        }
    }
}
} else {
    // Process events related to an existing client.
    if let Some(connection) =
    ↪   connections.get_mut(&token) {
        if event.is_readable() {
            // Read data from the connection.
            match connection.read(&mut buffer) {
                Ok(0) => {
                    // Reading 0 bytes implies the
                    ↪   connection closed.
                    println!("Connection {:?} closed by
                    ↪   peer.", token);
                    connections.remove(&token);
                }
                Ok(n) => {
                    println!("Read {} bytes from
                    ↪   connection {:?}", n, token);

                    // Echo the received data back to
                    ↪   the client.
                    let mut total_written = 0;
                    while total_written < n {
```

70

```rust
                    match connection.write(&buffer[
                    total_written..n]) {
                        Ok(0) => {
                            // If no bytes were
                            ↪  written, break to
                            ↪  avoid tight loop.
                            println!("Write returned
                            ↪  0, closing
                            ↪  connection {:?}",
                            ↪  token);
                            connections.remove(
                            &token);
                            break;
                        }
                        Ok(written) => {
                            total_written +=
                            ↪  written;
                        }
                        Err(ref e) if e.kind() ==
                        ↪  io::ErrorKind::WouldBlock
                        ↪  => {
                            // If the socket is not
                            ↪  ready for writing,
                            ↪  break the inner
                            ↪  loop.
                            break;
                        }
                        Err(e) => {
                            eprintln!("Error writing
                            ↪  to connection {:?}:
                            ↪  {}", token, e);
                            connections.remove(
                            &token);
                            break;
                        }
                    }
                }
            }
            Err(ref e) if e.kind() ==
            ↪  io::ErrorKind::WouldBlock => {
                // No data ready to be read.
            }
            Err(e) => {
                eprintln!("Error reading from
                ↪  connection {:?}: {}", token, e);
                connections.remove(&token);
            }
        }
    }
}
    // Additional handling for writable events might
    ↪  be added here.
    }
}
```

```
    }

    // Adaptive Event Batching (illustrative algorithm):
    //   Let N be the number of events processed in the current
    ↪  loop.
    //   If N exceeds a certain threshold (e.g., 50 events), the
    ↪  poll timeout
    //   can be reduced to allow quicker responsiveness:
    //     if N > 50 { next_timeout = max(1, default_timeout /
    ↪  2) }
    //   This strategy minimizes latency during high traffic and
    ↪  maximizes throughput.
  }
}
```

Chapter 10

Efficient HTTP Parsing and Request Handling

Fundamental Concepts in HTTP Message Structure

HTTP messages consist of a start-line, a sequence of header fields, an empty line, and an optional message body. The start-line encapsulates the method, request-target, and protocol version, while subsequent header fields convey metadata and control parameters. The inherent variability of field order, optional inclusion of certain headers, and the presence of transfer encoding schemes impose significant challenges on parser design. A rigorous interpretation of the formal grammar, as delineated in the relevant RFCs, is imperative for the accurate and efficient extraction of semantic information from raw byte streams. The parser must accommodate both well-formed requests and inputs that deviate from the normative syntactic structure, ensuring resilience against malformed data while maintaining high throughput.

Parsing Methodologies and Algorithmic Constructs

The development of a high-performance HTTP parser demands the integration of advanced parsing algorithms and efficient computational models. In this context, the primary goal is to minimize the per-byte processing overhead while ensuring that the syntactic structure of HTTP requests is faithfully reproduced in the output. Two principal approaches are typically applied: the use of deterministic finite state machines and the incorporation of grammar-based parsing techniques. Each approach offers distinct advantages in terms of error detection, recovery, and computational determinism.

1   Finite State Machines for Lexical Analysis

A deterministic finite state machine (DFSM) provides a robust framework for the lexical analysis of HTTP messages. The DFSM traverses the input stream, transitioning among a set of predefined states that correspond to tokens such as methods, pseudo-headers, delimiters, and content boundaries. Owing to their linear time complexity, these automata facilitate the conversion of raw byte streams to token sequences in an operation that is proportional to the input size. The design of the state machine is optimized for low-level byte processing and is instrumental in detecting token boundaries, managing escape sequences, and handling inter-field separators, all while operating with minimal memory overhead.

2   Grammar-Based Parsing Techniques

In conjunction with state-based lexing, grammar-based parsing techniques introduce an additional layer of syntactic verification. By modeling the HTTP protocol using a context-free grammar, the parser enforces structural rules that guide the interpretation of header fields and content bodies. This formalism enables the early detection of deviations from the expected syntax, thereby facilitating robust error reporting and recovery. The integration of grammar-driven methods into the parsing pipeline ensures that both lexical and syntactic aspects of the HTTP protocol are validated concurrently, contributing to a resilient and self-correcting parsing system.

Memory-Efficient Byte-Level Processing

Achieving optimal throughput in HTTP parsing requires meticulous management of byte-level data in memory. The parser is designed to operate directly on input buffers, thereby obviating the need for extraneous memory allocations and data copying. Techniques such as zero-copy processing and in-place tokenization are employed to maintain a parsimonious memory footprint. By parsing the raw data with minimal transformations, the system effectively reduces cache misses and minimizes the processing latency per request. These strategies are quantified by a throughput metric defined as

$$\mathcal{T} = \frac{\text{Total bytes processed}}{T_{\text{cycle}}},$$

where T_{cycle} represents the duration of a complete processing cycle. The deliberate orchestration of buffer management and careful reuse of memory segments are pivotal in sustaining high processing rates under load.

Pipelined Architecture for Request Decoding and Handling

The architecture of the request handling pipeline is constructed to decouple the parsing phase from subsequent stages of request processing. The pipeline initiates with the rapid conversion of raw data into a structured request object, which is then disseminated to specialized modules responsible for authentication, routing, and business logic execution. The design leverages asynchronous processing paradigms to permit concurrent handling of multiple HTTP requests. This separation of concerns not only improves overall system responsiveness but also facilitates independent scaling of the parsing and processing layers.

1 Decoupling Parsing from Subsequent Processing

The modular architecture adopted within the pipeline ensures that the output of the parser serves as a self-contained descriptor for each HTTP request. Such a descriptor encapsulates all necessary information regarding the request-line, header fields, and payload, thereby enabling downstream components to operate without reparsing the original input. This decoupling is achieved through a layered approach wherein the parser and the request handler communicate via well-defined interfaces. The delineation of responsibilities minimizes inter-component dependencies and enhances maintainability, while also enabling each layer to be optimized for its specific function.

2   Throughput Optimization and Scalability Considerations

The design of the processing pipeline is governed by stringent performance requirements, demanding that both the parsing and subsequent handling stages operate in concert to maximize system throughput. The architecture employs concurrency control mechanisms and asynchronous event handling strategies to mitigate bottlenecks. Scalability is further enhanced by adopting a modular design that supports parallel processing across multiple execution threads or cores. Analytical models have been formulated to capture the relationship between the processing latency $T_{\text{processing}}$, the number of parsed requests, and the aggregate throughput. These models guide the iterative refinement of buffering strategies and scheduling policies, ensuring that the pipeline sustains high performance even under extreme load conditions.

Rust Code Snippet

```rust
use std::time::{Duration, Instant};
use std::str;

/// Represents the different states in the HTTP parsing finite state
↪    machine.
#[derive(Debug)]
enum ParserState {
    StartLine,
    Headers,
    Body,
    Finished,
    Error,
}

/// Structure to hold the parsed HTTP request information.
#[derive(Debug)]
struct HttpRequest {
    method: String,
    uri: String,
    version: String,
    headers: Vec<(String, String)>,
    body: Option<String>,
}
```

```rust
/// Parses a raw HTTP request using a finite state machine approach
///     combined with
/// grammar based verification. This function demonstrates zero-copy
///     techniques by
/// processing byte slices directly and uses a simple DFSM to
///     tokenize input.
fn parse_http(request: &[u8]) -> Result<HttpRequest, String> {
    // Initial parser state.
    let mut state = ParserState::StartLine;
    let mut pos = 0;
    let len = request.len();

    // Helper function to extract the next line from the input
    //     buffer based on CRLF.
    fn get_next_line(request: &[u8], pos: &mut usize) ->
        Option<&[u8]> {
        if *pos >= request.len() {
            return None;
        }
        // Search for the CRLF delimiter.
        if let Some(newline_pos) =
            request[*pos..].windows(2).position(|w| w == b"\r\n") {
            let line = &request[*pos..*pos + newline_pos];
            *pos += newline_pos + 2; // Advance past CRLF.
            Some(line)
        } else {
            // If no CRLF is found, return the rest of the buffer.
            let line = &request[*pos..];
            *pos = request.len();
            Some(line)
        }
    }

    // Parse the start-line which should be in the format: METHOD SP
    //     URI SP VERSION.
    let start_line = get_next_line(request, &mut pos)
        .ok_or("Failed to read the start line; request is empty")?;
    let start_line_str = str::from_utf8(start_line)
        .map_err(|_| "Invalid UTF-8 in start line")?;
    let parts: Vec<&str> =
        start_line_str.split_whitespace().collect();
    if parts.len() != 3 {
        return Err("Malformed start line: expected 3
            parts".to_string());
    }
    let method = parts[0].to_string();
    let uri = parts[1].to_string();
    let version = parts[2].to_string();
    state = ParserState::Headers;

    // Parse header fields until an empty line is encountered.
    let mut headers = Vec::new();
    loop {
```

77

```rust
        let line = get_next_line(request, &mut pos)
            .ok_or("Unexpected end of headers")?;
        if line.is_empty() {
            // An empty line indicates the termination of headers.
            break;
        }
        let line_str = str::from_utf8(line)
            .map_err(|_| "Invalid UTF-8 sequence in header")?;
        if let Some(colon_index) = line_str.find(':') {
            let key = line_str[..colon_index].trim().to_string();
            let value = line_str[colon_index +
            ↪   1..].trim().to_string();
            headers.push((key, value));
        } else {
            return Err("Malformed header: missing
            ↪   colon".to_string());
        }
    }

    state = ParserState::Body;
    // Everything after the header section is treated as the body
    ↪   (if any).
    let body = if pos < len {
        let body_bytes = &request[pos..];
        Some(str::from_utf8(body_bytes)
            .map_err(|_| "Invalid UTF-8 sequence in
            ↪   body")?.to_string())
    } else {
        None
    };

    state = ParserState::Finished;
    Ok(HttpRequest { method, uri, version, headers, body })
}

/// Calculates the throughput metric using the formula:
///     = (Total bytes processed) / (Processing cycle duration)
fn calculate_throughput(total_bytes: usize, duration: Duration) ->
↪   f64 {
    total_bytes as f64 / duration.as_secs_f64()
}

/// Simulates an asynchronous processing pipeline for HTTP requests.
↪   In a real-world
/// scenario, non-blocking I/O operations and further processing
↪   (e.g., authentication,
/// routing) would be integrated. Here, the parser is invoked and
↪   its output returned.
async fn process_request(request: &[u8]) -> Result<HttpRequest,
↪   String> {
    // For demonstration, we call the synchronous parser within an
    ↪   async context.
    let parsed_request = parse_http(request)?;
```

78

```rust
    // Further asynchronous processing components could be
    ⌙  integrated here.
    Ok(parsed_request)
}


/// The main function demonstrates the full processing pipeline:
/// 1. It defines a sample raw HTTP request.
/// 2. It measures the processing cycle time.
/// 3. It computes the throughput using the provided formula.
/// 4. It prints the parsed HTTP request and performance metrics.
#[tokio::main]
async fn main() {
    // Sample HTTP request (using CRLF as line delimiters).
    let raw_request = b"GET /index.html HTTP/1.1\r\n\
Host: example.com\r\n\
User-Agent: RustClient/1.0\r\n\
Accept: */*\r\n\
\r\n\
This is the body of the request.";

    // Begin time measurement for throughput evaluation.
    let start_time = Instant::now();

    // Process the request asynchronously through the parsing
    ⌙  pipeline.
    match process_request(raw_request).await {
        Ok(http_request) => {
            println!("Parsed HTTP request:\n{:#?}", http_request);
        },
        Err(e) => {
            eprintln!("Error while parsing HTTP request: {}", e);
        },
    };

    // Complete the time measurement cycle.
    let cycle_duration = start_time.elapsed();
    let total_bytes = raw_request.len();

    // Compute throughput using the formula:
    //     = Total bytes processed / T_cycle
    let throughput = calculate_throughput(total_bytes,
    ⌙  cycle_duration);

    println!(
        "Processed {} bytes in {:.6} seconds.",
        total_bytes,
        cycle_duration.as_secs_f64()
    );
    println!("Throughput: {:.2} bytes/second", throughput);
}
```

Chapter 11

Extending Hyper for Custom HTTP Services

Architectural Foundations for Hyper Customizations

Hyper is a high-performance HTTP library that exhibits a modular architecture designed to facilitate both client and server implementations with high concurrency and low latency. At its core, Hyper leverages asynchronous I/O paradigms and is built upon a state-of-the-art event loop. The internal structure of Hyper is segmented into discrete layers, each responsible for specific aspects of HTTP processing, including request parsing, header management, and response generation. This layered design permits granular customizations without deviating from the core HTTP protocol specifications. In this context, the library's modularity is exploited to insert bespoke behavior into the processing pipeline. Each component, from the low-level socket handling to the high-level service trait interfaces, is architected with extensibility in mind, thereby allowing domain-specific adjustments without sacrificing the inherent performance of the asynchronous runtime.

Customization Mechanisms for Bespoke Server Behavior

Bespoke server behavior within Hyper is achieved through deliberate alterations to the service abstraction. Hyper employs a well-defined service model where a service is conceptualized as a function mapping an incoming HTTP request to a corresponding future that resolves to a response. Customization efforts center on redefining this mapping function, formally denoted as f : Request $\rightarrow$ Future $<$ Response $>$, in order to integrate specialized processing logic. Enhancements may include tailored authentication procedures, dynamic content generation, or request routing logic that diverges from standard implementations. The customization process involves interfacing with Hyper's request handling lifecycle, which encompasses connection establishment, header parsing, and response buffering. By modifying the service layer, it becomes feasible to intercept and modify the default control flow, leading to the injection of application-specific protocols and policies. Such modifications require an intricate understanding of asynchronous control structures and the interplay between I/O-bound operations and CPU-bound processing.

Techniques for Extending Protocol Handling

Extending protocol handling in Hyper necessitates a rigorous examination of both syntactic and semantic aspects of HTTP. Hyper's default behavior adheres to the conventions established by RFCs, yet certain applications demand protocol-level adjustments to handle custom header fields, alternate method semantics, or non-standard content encodings. These extensions are realized by embedding additional processing steps into the parsing and serialization routines that underlie the library. In practice, this entails overriding certain core routines to inspect and manipulate the HTTP message components prior to the invocation of the service logic. A prototypical extension involves reinterpreting the header credit, wherein data is restructured according to custom delimiters or tokenization schemes. Moreover, the extension process may incorporate middleware-style components that perform early validation and enrichment of the request context; such middleware is seamlessly integrated into the Hyper pipeline, yielding a custom protocol handler that preserves both efficiency and compliance with established security practices. The modifications are often quantitatively analyzed through performance metrics such as throughput $\mathcal{T}$, defined as the ratio of the total number of bytes processed to the execution duration, ensuring that enhancements do not introduce prohibitive latency.

Implementation Considerations and Performance Implications

The implementation of custom HTTP services using an extended Hyper library demands careful consideration of concurrency, memory management, and error propagation. At the implementation level, specific attention is directed toward minimizing synchronization overhead while preserving state consistency across asynchronous tasks. The intrinsic use of non-blocking I/O techniques and the zero-copy design paradigm in Hyper forms the foundation for high-throughput server operations. When extending Hyper, it is essential to maintain compatibility with these performance optimizations. This involves ensuring that custom logic does not violate the invariant that critical paths remain highly optimized. Developers are encouraged to integrate profiling tools to measure the impact of modifications and to adjust the design by balancing abstraction overhead against the benefits of bespoke functionality. Furthermore, the extended components must adhere to the rigorous error-handling semantics that characterize Hyper's design philosophy. In practice, this involves the propagation of errors in a controlled manner that allows for graceful degradation of service. Such considerations are paramount when scaling to environments where the server is expected to handle a vast number of concurrent connections without incurring significant penalties in latency or resource utilization.

Rust Code Snippet

```
use std::convert::Infallible;
use std::net::SocketAddr;
use std::time::Instant;

use hyper::{Body, Request, Response, Server};
```

```rust
use hyper::service::{make_service_fn, service_fn};
use hyper::header::HeaderValue;

/// This function represents the core mapping function:
///     f: Request -> Future<Response>
/// Here, we perform custom header inspection, protocol handling,
↪    and throughput
/// calculation based on processing time and number of bytes in the
↪    response.
async fn custom_handler(req: Request<Body>) ->
↪    Result<Response<Body>, Infallible> {
    // Begin measuring processing time for throughput calculation.
    let start = Instant::now();

    // Extract a custom header value (e.g., "x-custom-header") to
    ↪    customize behavior.
    let custom_value = req.headers()
        .get("x-custom-header")
        .and_then(|hv| hv.to_str().ok())
        .unwrap_or("default");

    // Custom protocol extension: modify request handling based on
    ↪    header contents.
    // For example, one could integrate bespoke authentication,
    ↪    dynamic routing,
    // or even modified serialization steps here.
    let response_text = format!("Processed request with
    ↪    x-custom-header: {}", custom_value);

    // Create a basic HTTP response using the computed text.
    // This mirrors the mapping: f(Request) -> Future<Response>.
    let mut response =
    ↪    Response::new(Body::from(response_text.clone()));

    // Calculate throughput metric (), defined as:
    //      = (total bytes processed) / (elapsed time in seconds)
    // In this simplified example, total_bytes is the length of the
    ↪    response text.
    let total_bytes = response_text.len() as f64;
    let elapsed = start.elapsed().as_secs_f64();
    let throughput = if elapsed > 0.0 { total_bytes / elapsed } else
    ↪    { 0.0 };

    // Insert the computed throughput into the response headers for
    ↪    diagnostics.
    response.headers_mut().insert("x-throughput",
        HeaderValue::from_str(&format!("{:.2}",
        ↪    throughput)).unwrap());

    Ok(response)
}

#[tokio::main]
```

```rust
async fn main() {
    // Define the address on which the server will listen.
    let addr = SocketAddr::from(([127, 0, 0, 1], 3000));

    // The make_service closure instantiates a new service (i.e.,
    ↪   the custom_handler)
    // for each incoming connection. This reinforces the modular
    ↪   architecture that allows
    // for custom behavior in Hyper's execution pipeline.
    let make_service = make_service_fn(|_conn| async {
        Ok::<_, Infallible>(service_fn(custom_handler))
    });

    // Build and run the Hyper server with the custom service.
    let server = Server::bind(&addr).serve(make_service);

    println!("Custom Hyper server running on http://{}", addr);

    // Await the server future and report any errors.
    if let Err(e) = server.await {
        eprintln!("Server error: {}", e);
    }
}
```

84

Chapter 12

Composable Middleware with Tower Service

Architectural Foundations for Tower Middleware

The design of middleware within the Tower framework is predicated upon the establishment of clearly delineated service abstractions. At its core, the Tower framework defines a contract in which a service is modeled as an entity that maps an HTTP request to an asynchronous future representing a response. Formally, the service interface may be represented as

$$S :: call(\text{Request}) \rightarrow \text{Future<Response>},$$

thereby encapsulating the non-blocking transformation inherent to modern network services. This abstraction reinforces the decoupling of core business logic from ancillary cross-cutting concerns. The architectural segmentation afforded by Tower allows each middleware component to be developed as a distinct, composable layer, enabling specialized operations such as validation, transformation, or logging to be introduced without disturbing the foundational service behavior. Central to this design is the preservation of modularity and the facilitation of independent evolution of each component, ensuring that modifications and optimizations can be applied

85

with minimal impact on the overall system stability.

Middleware Composition and Integration Strategies

Middleware in Tower is composed by sequentially aggregating multiple service transformations to form a composite processing pipeline. Each individual layer within this pipeline is responsible for intercepting and potentially modifying an HTTP request or response prior to its delivery to subsequent layers. Formally, the overall processing pipeline may be represented as

$$S_{\text{composite}} = M_n \circ M_{n-1} \circ \cdots \circ M_1 \circ S_{\text{base}},$$

where S_{base} denotes the underlying service, and each M_i represents a distinct middleware layer. This functional composition invites a clear stratification of responsibilities, whereby middleware layers may be individually designed to enforce security policies, introduce diagnostic tracing, or dynamically modify HTTP headers. The integration strategy necessitates that each layer adheres to strict interface contracts, thereby ensuring consistency in asynchronous behavior and in the propagation of errors. The self-contained nature of each middleware component facilitates streamlined testing and validation, while the composition model guarantees that the collective behavior of the middleware stack is both predictable and scalable.

Interception and Modification of HTTP Requests and Responses

Within the Tower service model, middleware layers are endowed with the capability to act as interceptors at critical junctures in the HTTP processing sequence. This interception mechanism allows middleware to effectuate modifications prior to and subsequent to the core service invocation. In the pre-service phase, middleware may inspect and transform incoming requests through operations such as URL rewriting, header augmentation, or payload inspection. Mathematically, these operations can be expressed as transformation functions

$$T : \text{Request} \to \text{Request}',$$

which adjust the original request to meet specific application criteria. In a corresponding post-service phase, responses are subjected to further processing. Here, middleware components may perform content filtering, enrich response headers with diagnostic metadata, or modify response bodies based on dynamic policy rules. This transformation is formally depicted as

$$T' : \text{Response} \rightarrow \text{Response}',$$

exemplifying the capacity to seamlessly modify behavior at both ingress and egress points. The middleware layers implement these transformation functions while ensuring that the asynchronous execution context is preserved and that the overall processing latency remains minimal. The interception strategy is pivotal for integrating cross-cutting concerns such as security enforcement and performance monitoring into the HTTP lifecycle.

Design Considerations and Performance Implications

The implementation of composable middleware using Tower abstractions involves a series of design considerations that are essential to maintaining system performance and robust error handling. Each middleware layer is required to introduce minimal overhead in the service pipeline, thus preserving the high concurrency and low latency characteristics inherent to asynchronous network services. Critical design factors include the management of context propagation, the careful orchestration of memory allocation, and the adherence to non-blocking paradigms. Furthermore, error propagation mechanisms must be meticulously engineered so that exceptions within any middleware layer are contained and propagated in a controlled manner, ensuring that the integrity of the composite service is maintained. Quantitative metrics, such as throughput and response latency, serve as guides for iterative refinement, as each middleware component is evaluated for its impact on the overall performance. The Tower architecture thereby provides an elegant framework that harmonizes the introduction of sophisticated middleware functionality with the exigencies of high-performance asynchronous processing.

Rust Code Snippet

```rust
use tower::Service;
use std::task::{Context, Poll};
use std::future::Future;
use std::pin::Pin;
use futures::task::noop_waker_ref;

// Define Request and Response types used throughout the service
//    chain.
#[derive(Debug, Clone)]
pub struct Request {
    pub url: String,
    pub headers: Vec<(String, String)>,
    pub body: Vec<u8>,
}

#[derive(Debug, Clone)]
pub struct Response {
    pub status_code: u16,
    pub headers: Vec<(String, String)>,
    pub body: Vec<u8>,
}

// BaseService: The core service implementing the S::call(Request)
//    -> Future<Response> interface.
pub struct BaseService;

impl Service<Request> for BaseService {
    type Response = Response;
    type Error = ();
    // The Future returned is boxed and must be Send.
    type Future = Pin<Box<dyn Future<Output = Result<Response, ()>>
        + Send>>;

    fn poll_ready(&mut self, _cx: &mut Context<'_>) ->
        Poll<Result<(), ()>> {
        // Base service is always ready in this example.
        Poll::Ready(Ok(()))
    }

    fn call(&mut self, req: Request) -> Self::Future {
        Box::pin(async move {
            // Simulate asynchronous processing.
            println!("BaseService: Processing request for {}",
                req.url);
            Ok(Response {
                status_code: 200,
                headers: vec![("Content-Type".to_string(),
                    "text/plain".to_string())],
                body: b"Response from BaseService".to_vec(),
            })
```

```
        })
    }
}

// LoggingMiddleware: A middleware layer that intercepts requests
↪    and responses for logging,
// exemplifying a cross-cutting concern.
pub struct LoggingMiddleware<S> {
    inner: S,
}

impl<S> LoggingMiddleware<S> {
    pub fn new(inner: S) -> Self {
        Self { inner }
    }
}

impl<S> Service<Request> for LoggingMiddleware<S>
where
    S: Service<Request, Error = ()> + Send,
    S::Future: Send + 'static,
{
    type Response = S::Response;
    type Error = ();
    type Future = Pin<Box<dyn Future<Output = Result<Self::Response,
↪    ()>> + Send>>;

    fn poll_ready(&mut self, cx: &mut Context<'_>) ->
↪    Poll<Result<(), ()>> {
        self.inner.poll_ready(cx)
    }

    fn call(&mut self, req: Request) -> Self::Future {
        println!("LoggingMiddleware: Received request for {}",
↪    req.url);
        let fut = self.inner.call(req);
        Box::pin(async move {
            let res = fut.await?;
            println!("LoggingMiddleware: Sending response with
↪    status code {}", res.status_code);
            Ok(res)
        })
    }
}

// TransformMiddleware: A middleware layer that applies
↪    transformation functions
// to both the request (T: Request -> Request') and the response
↪    (T': Response -> Response').
// This reflects the formal transformation functions presented in
↪    the chapter.
pub struct TransformMiddleware<S> {
    inner: S,
```

```rust
}

impl<S> TransformMiddleware<S> {
    pub fn new(inner: S) -> Self {
        Self { inner }
    }

    // Transformation function for the incoming Request.
    // (T: Request -> Request')
    pub fn transform_request(req: Request) -> Request {
        let mut req = req;
        req.headers.push(("X-Transformed".to_string(),
        ↪    "true".to_string()));
        req
    }

    // Transformation function for the outgoing Response.
    // (T': Response -> Response')
    pub fn transform_response(mut res: Response) -> Response {
        let footer = b"\n-- Transformed by Middleware".to_vec();
        res.body.extend(footer);
        res
    }
}

impl<S> Service<Request> for TransformMiddleware<S>
where
    S: Service<Request, Error = ()> + Send,
    S::Future: Send + 'static,
{
    type Response = Response;
    type Error = ();
    type Future = Pin<Box<dyn Future<Output = Result<Response, ()>>
    ↪    + Send>>;

    fn poll_ready(&mut self, cx: &mut Context<'_>) ->
    ↪    Poll<Result<(), ()>> {
        self.inner.poll_ready(cx)
    }

    fn call(&mut self, req: Request) -> Self::Future {
        // Apply the request transformation T: Request -> Request'
        let req = Self::transform_request(req);
        let fut = self.inner.call(req);
        Box::pin(async move {
            let res = fut.await?;
            // Apply the response transformation T': Response ->
            ↪    Response'
            Ok(Self::transform_response(res))
        })
    }
}
```

```rust
// Main function demonstrating middleware composition mimicking the
↪  formula:
// S_composite = M_n  M_{n-1}  ...  M_1  S_base
#[tokio::main]
async fn main() {
    // Compose middleware layers with BaseService at the core.
    let base_service = BaseService;
    let logging_service = LoggingMiddleware::new(base_service);
    // TransformMiddleware wraps LoggingMiddleware.
    let mut composite_service =
    ↪  TransformMiddleware::new(logging_service);

    // Create a sample HTTP request.
    let request = Request {
        url: "http://example.com".to_string(),
        headers: vec![],
        body: b"Sample payload".to_vec(),
    };

    // Ensure the composed service is ready.
    let waker = noop_waker_ref();
    let mut cx = Context::from_waker(waker);
    composite_service.poll_ready(&mut cx).expect("Service not
    ↪  ready");

    // Invoke the composite service. This represents
    ↪  S::call(request) -> Future<Response>
    match composite_service.call(request).await {
        Ok(response) => {
            println!("Final Response: {:?}", response);
        }
        Err(_) => {
            println!("An error occurred while processing the
            ↪  request.");
        }
    }
}
```

Chapter 13

Fluent Routing Mechanisms in Rust

Type-Level Abstractions in Routing

The design of routing systems in Rust benefits from the stringent guarantees provided by its type system. By leveraging concepts such as parametric polymorphism, trait bounds, and algebraic data types, routes can be modeled as first-class entities with well-defined interfaces. In this framework, each route is associated with a distinct type, ensuring that the space of valid requests is partitioned and that only those inputs which conform to predetermined specifications are admitted. Consider a routing function represented as

$$f : R \to H,$$

where R denotes the set of valid requests and H the corresponding handler outcomes. Such a formulation enables the compiler to enforce correctness properties at compile time, thereby eliminating a class of runtime errors associated with ambiguous or ill-formed route definitions.

The utilization of exhaustive type matching further reinforces the reliability of the routing mechanism. By expressing routes in terms of enums or other sum types, every potential branch of the request space is accounted for. This static guarantee facilitates not only error detection during compilation but also enables downstream optimizations that can remove redundant checks, leading to efficient code generation. The synergy between static type verification and dynamic routing logic forms the foundational basis upon which fluent routing is constructed.

Advanced Pattern Matching and Route Decomposition

Rust's pattern matching constructs provide a powerful mechanism for decomposing complex route definitions into simpler, well-understood components. The language's intrinsic support for nested patterns, guards, and exhaustive matching allows for the precise classification of incoming requests. In this context, the match construct serves as a formal tool to determine the appropriate routing path based on the structure of the request.

The abstraction of route decomposition can be conceptualized through a function

$$g : R \to \{H_1, H_2, \ldots, H_n\},$$

where each H_i represents a distinct handler corresponding to a particular route pattern. This mathematical formulation mirrors the syntactic and semantic properties of pattern matching in Rust, ensuring that every valid case is scrutinized. The inherent ability of Rust to perform compile-time checks on these match expressions further guarantees that exhaustive routing logic is maintained without the overhead of runtime conditionals. As a result, the complex interplay of nested routes and conditional branches is managed with both clarity and efficiency.

Expressiveness in Route Composition

The fluent routing paradigm in Rust is marked by its ability to capture intricate routing policies through elegant, composable constructs. Route composition is achieved by chaining modular transformations and filters, each represented by discrete layers that operate on request and response types. The composition operator, denoted by

$$\circ,$$

embodies the functional paradigm of route concatenation, ensuring that the application of one transformation seamlessly feeds into the subsequent stage. This operator is mathematically analogous to the classical function composition defined by

$$f \circ g(x) = f(g(x)).$$

In this architectural design, each modular component adheres to a clearly defined contract, thereby facilitating the independent verification of each routing layer. The expressiveness of the fluent interface is further enhanced by method chaining and closure-based transformations, which together condense verbose routing logic into succinct, declarative statements. The resulting structure not only improves readability but also enables maintainable routing definitions that can be easily refactored or extended without compromising the integrity of the overall system.

Static Analysis, Efficiency, and Zero-Cost Abstractions

A central consideration in the construction of fluent routing mechanisms is the assurance of runtime efficiency while preserving static guarantees. Rust's philosophy of zero-cost abstractions manifests in the routing layer, where compile-time constructs are employed to eliminate unnecessary runtime overhead. The rigorous integration of static analysis into the routing apparatus permits the early detection of unreachable patterns and redundancies, thereby ensuring that only the most optimized routing paths are compiled.

Monomorphization and aggressive inlining are instrumental in transforming high-level routing abstractions into code that rivals the performance of hand-tuned implementations. The compiler's ability to analyze and optimize pattern matching constructs further contributes to the generation of efficient jump tables or branch predictions for well-structured enums. In this environment, the collaborative effect of pattern matching and static verification underpins a routing mechanism where the elegance of expressive design is harmonized with uncompromised performance characteristics. The result is a routing framework that embodies both theoretical rigor and practical efficiency, driven by the advanced capabilities of Rust's type system and pattern matching semantics.

Rust Code Snippet

```rust
// The code snippet below demonstrates a type-safe, fluent routing
↪    mechanism in Rust,
// inspired by the mathematical abstractions discussed in this
↪    chapter.
// We model the routing function as f: R -> H, where R is a Request
↪    and H is a Handler outcome.
// Additionally, we use exhaustive pattern matching and function
↪    composition (f  g) to
// illustrate route decomposition and transformation.

// Define basic data structures for a simplified HTTP
↪    request/response.
#[derive(Debug)]
struct Request {
    path: String,
    method: HttpMethod,
}

#[derive(Debug, PartialEq)]
enum HttpMethod {
    GET,
    POST,
}

#[derive(Debug)]
struct Response {
    status: u16,
    body: String,
}

// Trait representing a handler for a given route.
trait Handler {
    fn handle(&self, req: &Request) -> Response;
}

// Implementation of a handler for the home route.
struct HomeHandler;
impl Handler for HomeHandler {
    fn handle(&self, req: &Request) -> Response {
        Response {
            status: 200,
            body: format!("Welcome to the Home Page at path: {}",
            ↪    req.path),
        }
    }
}

// Implementation of a handler for the about route.
struct AboutHandler;
impl Handler for AboutHandler {
```

95

```rust
    fn handle(&self, _req: &Request) -> Response {
        Response {
            status: 200,
            body: "About Rust Routing".to_string(),
        }
    }
}

// Handler for unmatched routes.
struct NotFoundHandler;
impl Handler for NotFoundHandler {
    fn handle(&self, _req: &Request) -> Response {
        Response {
            status: 404,
            body: "404 Not Found".to_string(),
        }
    }
}

// Enum representing the set of valid routes.
// This mirrors the formulation: g : R -> {H, H, ..., H} where each
↪ variant corresponds to a handler.
enum Route {
    Home(HomeHandler),
    About(AboutHandler),
    NotFound(NotFoundHandler),
}

impl Route {
    // Resolve a Request into a Route using advanced pattern
    ↪ matching.
    fn resolve(req: &Request) -> Self {
        match req.path.as_str() {
            "/" => Route::Home(HomeHandler),
            "/about" => Route::About(AboutHandler),
            _ => Route::NotFound(NotFoundHandler),
        }
    }

    // Execute the appropriate handler based on the resolved Route.
    fn execute(&self, req: &Request) -> Response {
        match self {
            Route::Home(handler) => handler.handle(req),
            Route::About(handler) => handler.handle(req),
            Route::NotFound(handler) => handler.handle(req),
        }
    }
}

// Function composition operator for chaining route transformations.
// This is analogous to the mathematical definition: (f  g)(x) =
↪  f(g(x)).
fn compose<F, G>(f: F, g: G) -> impl Fn(&Request) -> Response
```

```rust
where
    F: Fn(Response) -> Response,
    G: Fn(&Request) -> Response,
{
    move |req: &Request| f(g(req))
}

// Middleware function that transforms a Response by appending a
↪   footer.
// This simulates additional processing on the result of the routing
↪   function.
fn middleware_add_footer(mut res: Response) -> Response {
    res.body.push_str("\n-- Footer: Rust Routing Engine --");
    res
}

// Core routing function f: R -> H.
// It resolves a Request into a Route and executes its handler.
fn route_request(req: &Request) -> Response {
    let route = Route::resolve(req);
    route.execute(req)
}

// Main function demonstrating the complete routing mechanism with
↪   function composition.
fn main() {
    // Sample requests.
    let req_home = Request {
        path: "/".to_string(),
        method: HttpMethod::GET,
    };

    let req_about = Request {
        path: "/about".to_string(),
        method: HttpMethod::GET,
    };

    let req_unknown = Request {
        path: "/contact".to_string(),
        method: HttpMethod::GET,
    };

    // Compose the route_request function with the middleware
    ↪   transformation.
    let composed_handler = compose(middleware_add_footer,
    ↪   route_request);

    // Process each request and obtain a Response.
    let res_home = composed_handler(&req_home);
    let res_about = composed_handler(&req_about);
    let res_unknown = composed_handler(&req_unknown);

    // Output the results.
```

```
    println!("Response for Home: {:?}", res_home);
    println!("Response for About: {:?}", res_about);
    println!("Response for Unknown: {:?}", res_unknown);
}
```

Chapter 14

Asynchronous JSON Serialization and Deserialization

Fundamentals of Asynchronous JSON Conversion in Rust

The conversion between JSON and native Rust data structures is an essential component in the implementation of modern API payloads. In asynchronous environments, the process of serialization and deserialization must be adapted to non-blocking paradigms to meet the demands of high throughput and low latency. The JSON format, characterized by its hierarchical data representation with objects, arrays, numbers, strings, and booleans, requires a robust mechanism for translating this flexible schema into strictly typed Rust constructs. The mathematical abstraction of this transformation can be represented as a function $f : D \rightarrow J$, where D denotes the domain of Rust data types and J the set of valid JSON representations. Efficiency in this context is achieved by minimizing extraneous computational overhead and ensuring that the conversion process integrates seamlessly with asynchronous I/O operations.

Integration of Serde in Asynchronous Contexts

Serde serves as a cornerstone library for managing the intricacies of JSON serialization and deserialization within the Rust ecosystem. It accomplishes this by leveraging Rust's trait system, specifically through the implementation of the *Serialize* and *Deserialize* traits. In asynchronous applications, where operations are often executed concurrently and require non-blocking behavior, the design of Serde facilitates conversion routines that are both predictable and efficient. A critical aspect of this integration involves the coordination between asynchronous runtimes, such as those based on event-driven architectures, and Serde's statically derived routines. The conversion process can be theoretically modeled by a composition of functions, for example, $g : R \to D$ followed by the transformation $f : D \to J$, where R represents the raw input from an asynchronous stream. The outcome is a seamless translation that exploits Rust's stringent type checks while maintaining low-latency processing.

Design Considerations and Efficiency in Async Environments

The adoption of asynchronous JSON serialization and deserialization necessitates careful architectural decisions to uphold both performance and reliability. The use of Serde in these contexts is coupled with design patterns that ensure zero-cost abstractions at runtime. This is enabled by aggressive monomorphization and inlining strategies performed by the Rust compiler. Such techniques guarantee that the high-level abstractions provided by Serde impose negligible overhead during execution. Moreover, the asynchronous processing framework mandates that the conversion routines be structured to avoid blocking calls, thereby enabling continuous processing of incoming API payloads. The dual focus on compile-time verification and dynamic efficiency is underscored by the assurance that each transformation, expressed as $h : J \to D$, incurs minimal runtime cost. The synergy between static analysis and dynamic scheduling culminates in an architecture that robustly handles high-volume data streams with optimal resource utilization.

Error Propagation and Robustness in Asynchronous JSON Operations

Robust error handling is critical when performing JSON serialization and deserialization in asynchronous systems. In these environments, error propagation must be managed gracefully to prevent the disruption of concurrent operations. The error management model typically involves the use of a result type, encapsulated as $Result < T, E >$, where T represents the successful output of a conversion process and E encapsulates potential errors that may arise during serialization or deserialization. This model allows the asynchronous pipeline to detect, report, and recover from anomalies without compromising the overall system integrity. Semantically, error propagation is analogous to the mathematical treatment of partial functions, wherein a function $f : D \rightarrow J$ is extended to a function $f' : D \rightarrow Result(J, E)$, thereby explicitly handling exceptional conditions. Such a strategy ensures that the asynchronous mechanisms are both resilient and maintainable, fulfilling the rigorous demands of modern network services.

Performance Implications and Zero-Cost Abstractions

Achieving high-performance asynchronous JSON conversion requires a fine balance between abstraction and low-level efficiency. The integration of Serde within asynchronous contexts is informed by the philosophy of zero-cost abstractions, a core tenet of Rust's design. This paradigm ensures that the abstractions provided for JSON serialization and deserialization translate into machine code that is as performant as hand-optimized implementations. The process emphasizes eliminating unnecessary runtime indirection, thereby directly mapping high-level constructs to efficient low-level routines. In practical terms, the compilation process exploits optimizations such as inlining and static dispatch, which guarantee that the operations associated with the conversion functions, denoted abstractly as $f : D \rightarrow J$, execute without incurring dynamic penalty. The deliberate design choices in both the Serde library and the asynchronous runtime underscore a commitment to achieving optimal throughput while preserving strict type safety and reliability in API payload handling.

Rust Code Snippet

```rust
use serde::{Deserialize, Serialize};
use tokio::fs::File;
use tokio::io::{AsyncReadExt, AsyncWriteExt};
use std::error::Error;

// Define a data structure representing the API payload.
// This corresponds to our domain D.
#[derive(Debug, Serialize, Deserialize)]
struct ApiPayload {
    id: u32,
    name: String,
    values: Vec<f64>,
}

// "g: R -> D"
// Converts a raw JSON string (from an asynchronous stream) to the
//   Rust data structure.
async fn raw_to_data(raw_input: &str) -> Result<ApiPayload,
    serde_json::Error> {
    let data: ApiPayload = serde_json::from_str(raw_input)?;
    Ok(data)
}

// "f: D -> J"
// Converts the Rust data structure to its JSON representation.
fn data_to_json(data: &ApiPayload) -> Result<String,
    serde_json::Error> {
    let json_str = serde_json::to_string(data)?;
    Ok(json_str)
}

// Compose functions to complete the transformation from raw input
//   (R) to JSON (J)
// This demonstrates f   g which is extended to handle errors as f':
//   D -> Result<J, E>
async fn process_payload(raw_input: &str) -> Result<String, Box<dyn
    Error>> {
    let data = raw_to_data(raw_input).await?;
    let json_out = data_to_json(&data)?;
    Ok(json_out)
}

// Asynchronous demonstration using Tokio runtime.
#[tokio::main]
async fn main() {
    // Example raw JSON input
    let input = r#"{"id": 42, "name": "Test", "values": [3.14,
        2.718]}"#;

    // Process the payload by composing the conversion functions.
```

102

```rust
    match process_payload(input).await {
        Ok(json_result) => println!("Processed JSON: {}",
        ↪ json_result),
        Err(e) => eprintln!("Error processing payload: {:?}", e),
    }

    // Demonstrate asynchronous file I/O operations
    if let Err(e) = async_file_demo().await {
        eprintln!("File I/O error: {:?}", e);
    }
}

// An asynchronous function demonstrating non-blocking file reading
↪ and writing.
// This further applies the conversion process (f  g) within an
↪ async I/O context.
async fn async_file_demo() -> Result<(), Box<dyn Error>> {
    // Open and read the file asynchronously.
    let filepath = "data.json";
    let mut file = File::open(filepath).await?;
    let mut contents = Vec::new();
    file.read_to_end(&mut contents).await?;

    // Convert the file content to a string (raw input R).
    let content_str = String::from_utf8(contents)?;

    // Process the raw JSON data, converting using our composition
    ↪ of functions.
    let processed = process_payload(&content_str).await?;
    println!("File processed JSON: {}", processed);

    // Write the processed JSON back to an output file
    ↪ asynchronously.
    let mut out_file = File::create("out_data.json").await?;
    out_file.write_all(processed.as_bytes()).await?;

    Ok(())
}
```

Chapter 15

Streaming Large Payloads over HTTP

Fundamental Principles of Chunked Transfer Encoding

Chunked transfer encoding constitutes a mechanism within the HTTP/1.1 protocol that permits the segmentation of an arbitrarily large data payload into a sequence of manageable chunks. In this paradigm, a complete payload D is partitioned into a collection of chunks $C_1, C_2, \ldots, C_n$, so that

$$D = \bigcup_{i=1}^{n} C_i.$$

Each chunk is transmitted with a preceding header that encodes its length in hexadecimal form, followed by a delineation that marks the termination of that segment. The conclusion of the payload is signified by a zero-length chunk, which acts as an unambiguous end-of-data marker. This structured approach enables the efficient handling of large data transfers by obviating the need to determine the full payload size a priori, while ensuring that memory and processing demands are distributed over time in a non-blocking manner.

Architectural Integration of Asynchronous HTTP Responses

The deployment of chunked transfer encoding within asynchronous HTTP responses is predicated on the integration of event-driven I/O frameworks and the decoupling of data production from its network transmission. In an asynchronous environment, each operation concerning the generation and dispatching of data chunks is scheduled independently, thereby circumventing potential blocking delays. This design is encapsulated by the transformation function

$$f : S \to T,$$

where S represents the continuous stream of raw data from the source, and T symbolizes the target stream configured in compliance with HTTP protocols. The function f abstracts the conversion process, ensuring that the raw input is methodically segmented, encoded, and transmitted in adherence with both protocol specifications and resource constraints inherent in high-concurrency settings.

Buffering Strategies and Flow Control Mechanisms

Efficient streaming of large payloads mandates the implementation of advanced buffering strategies coupled with robust flow control mechanisms. Buffer management is essential to temporarily store segmented data prior to its transmission, thereby mitigating the risks of congestion and excessive memory utilization. This buffering process can be mathematically depicted as a mapping

$$B : \mathcal{C} \to \mathcal{M},$$

where $\mathcal{C}$ is the set of generated data chunks and $\mathcal{M}$ denotes the allocated memory resources. Concurrently, flow control mechanisms operate to synchronize the pace at which data is produced with the corresponding rate permitted by the consuming network endpoints. This synchronization is typically achieved via back pressure techniques that dynamically adjust the injection of data into the transmission pipeline. Consequently, the interplay between buffering and flow control ensures that latency is minimized and throughput is maintained at a level commensurate with network capacity.

Mathematical Formalization of Chunked Data Transmission

The process of transmitting a large payload using chunked encoding admits a rigorous mathematical formalization. Let a payload D be partitioned into chunks $C_1, C_2, \ldots, C_n$, and consider an encoding function

$$\phi : C_i \to E(C_i),$$

which transforms a raw chunk C_i into its corresponding encoded representation $E(C_i)$. The complete transmission can then be represented as a composition of these encoding operations:

$$T(D) = \phi(C_n) \circ \phi(C_{n-1}) \circ \cdots \circ \phi(C_1).$$

This compositional model ensures that the aggregated conversion and transmission of chunks preserves the integrity of the original payload. When combined with an asynchronous runtime, each encoded chunk $E(C_i)$ is dispatched as an individual, non-blocking operation, thereby facilitating concurrent processing and minimizing the overall latency imposed by sequential data transfer.

Implications for Resource Utilization in Asynchronous Streams

The adoption of chunked encoding and streaming techniques in asynchronous HTTP responses has a profound impact on resource utilization and system performance. By decomposing a large payload into discrete chunks, the system achieves a high degree of parallelism, which in turn permits fine-grained control over memory allocation and CPU scheduling. Performance metrics in this context can be abstractly modeled by a function

$$P(\omega, L, B) = \alpha \cdot \omega - \beta \cdot L + \gamma \cdot B,$$

where ω denotes the workload intensity, L represents the network latency, B is the effective I/O bandwidth, and α, β, and γ are system-specific parameters. This quantitative framework encapsulates the trade-offs between throughput, latency, and resource consumption. Moreover, the dynamic adjustment of buffer sizes and transmission intervals—driven by real-time network conditions—ensures that the system maintains an optimal equilibrium between high-volume data transfers and the efficient utilization of computational resources.

Rust Code Snippet

```rust
use tokio::io::{self, AsyncWriteExt};
use tokio::net::{TcpListener, TcpStream};
use tokio::time::{sleep, Duration};
use std::error::Error;

/// This function implements the encoding of a raw data chunk C_i to
↪   its HTTP
/// chunked transfer encoding representation, denoted by (C_i).
/// It prepends the chunk's length in hexadecimal followed by CRLF,
↪   appends
/// the chunk data, and then adds a terminating CRLF.
/// Example: for a chunk with 16 bytes, the header will be "10\r\n"
↪   in hex.
fn encode_chunk(chunk: &[u8]) -> Vec<u8> {
    let len_hex = format!("{:X}", chunk.len());
    let mut encoded = Vec::new();
    // Append header: hexadecimal length of the chunk + CRLF
    encoded.extend_from_slice(len_hex.as_bytes());
    encoded.extend_from_slice(b"\r\n");
    // Append the raw chunk data
    encoded.extend_from_slice(chunk);
    // Append CRLF to mark the end of this chunk
    encoded.extend_from_slice(b"\r\n");
    encoded
}

/// This function splits the entire payload D into smaller chunks
↪   (C_1, C_2, ..., C_n),
/// and then applies the encoding transformation  on each chunk.
↪   This represents
/// the conversion function f: S -> T, where S is the unformatted
↪   stream and T is the
/// HTTP protocol compliant stream.
/// The payload D is segmented into parts, each being processed
↪   individually.
fn encode_payload(payload: &[u8], chunk_size: usize) -> Vec<Vec<u8>>
↪   {
    payload.chunks(chunk_size)
          .map(|chunk| encode_chunk(chunk))
          .collect()
}

/// Function to simulate a performance metric calculation based on:
/// P(, L, B) =  *  -  * L +  * B.
```

```rust
/// Here:
///     is the workload intensity,
///     L is network latency,
///     B is the I/O bandwidth,
/// and , ,  are system-specific parameters.
fn performance_metric(workload: u32, latency: u32, bandwidth: u32)
↪  -> f32 {
    let alpha: f32 = 1.0;
    let beta: f32 = 1.0;
    let gamma: f32 = 1.0;
    alpha * workload as f32 - beta * latency as f32 + gamma *
    ↪  bandwidth as f32
}


/// Asynchronous function to handle an individual client connection.
/// It simulates the sending of an HTTP response using chunked
↪  encoding.
/// For each connection, it writes the HTTP header and then streams
↪  each encoded chunk.
/// The composition of all these steps models the formula:
///     T(D) = (C_n) (C_{n-1})  ...  (C_1)
/// Additionally, a delay is introduced between chunks to simulate
↪  buffering and flow control.
async fn handle_connection(mut socket: TcpStream, chunks:
↪  Vec<Vec<u8>>) -> io::Result<()> {
    // Write HTTP response header with Transfer-Encoding declared as
    ↪  chunked.
    socket.write_all(b"HTTP/1.1 200 OK\r\nTransfer-Encoding:
    ↪  chunked\r\n\r\n").await?;

    // Stream each encoded chunk asynchronously.
    for encoded_chunk in chunks.iter() {
        socket.write_all(encoded_chunk).await?;
        // Simulate back-pressure and buffering using a delay.
        sleep(Duration::from_millis(50)).await;
    }

    // Write the final zero-length chunk to signal end of the data
    ↪  stream.
    socket.write_all(b"0\r\n\r\n").await?;
    Ok(())
}


#[tokio::main]
async fn main() -> Result<(), Box<dyn Error>> {
    // Generate a simulated large payload.
    // The large payload D is represented as a repeated sentence.
    let payload = "The quick brown fox jumps over the lazy dog.
    ↪  ".repeat(50);
    let payload_bytes = payload.as_bytes();

    // Set the chunk size - determining the granularity for each
    ↪  C_i.
```

108

```rust
let chunk_size = 32;
let chunks = encode_payload(payload_bytes, chunk_size);

println!("Starting chunked transmission simulation...");

// Bind a TCP listener to simulate an HTTP server.
let listener = TcpListener::bind("127.0.0.1:8080").await?;
println!("Server listening on 127.0.0.1:8080");

// Accept incoming connections indefinitely.
loop {
    let (socket, addr) = listener.accept().await?;
    println!("Accepted connection from: {}", addr);

    // Clone the encoded chunks to pass into the asynchronous
    ↪   task.
    let chunks_clone = chunks.clone();

    // Spawn a new asynchronous task for each connection.
    tokio::spawn(async move {
        if let Err(e) = handle_connection(socket,
        ↪   chunks_clone).await {
            eprintln!("Error handling connection with {}: {}",
            ↪   addr, e);
        }
        // Simulate the calculation of a performance metric
        ↪   after completing the response.
        let perf = performance_metric(100, 50, 200);
        println!("Performance metric for connection {}: {}",
        ↪   addr, perf);
    });
}
}
```

Chapter 16

Type-Safe HTTP Header Management

Motivation and Overview

The management of HTTP headers represents a critical component in the design of network services, where the correctness of header semantics directly influences the reliability, security, and interoperability of communication protocols. Within the domain of type-safe programming, ensuring that header values conform to a predetermined schema is essential. This chapter delineates the principles underlying the parsing, validation, and generation of HTTP headers by leveraging Rust's robust type system. The approach emphasizes a compile-time enforcement of invariants, thereby reducing the potential for runtime errors and facilitating the development of high-assurance network applications.

Parsing Strategies in Type-Safe Environments

In a type-safe framework, the extraction of HTTP headers from raw input entails a systematic process of lexical analysis and syntactic validation. Consider a set $H = \{h_1, h_2, \ldots, h_n\}$, where each header h_i is defined as a key-value pair satisfying specific protocol constraints. The parsing strategy employs a decomposition of the input stream into constituent tokens, which are then mapped to their corresponding header representations. This process is governed by the function

$$\psi : I \to H,$$

where I denotes the collection of input characters, and ψ encapsulates the transformation from raw bytes to well-structured header objects. The rigorous assignment of types to header fields ensures that only syntactically correct and semantically meaningful constructs are produced, thereby preventing the propagation of malformed data through the subsequent stages of the application.

Validation Techniques for HTTP Headers

The validation of HTTP headers is a multifaceted process that involves verifying the adherence of header components to established protocol standards. Each header field is associated with a set of invariants, denoted by

$$\mathcal{I}(h_i) = \{\iota_1, \iota_2, \ldots, \iota_m\},$$

which must be satisfied to consider a header valid. The invariants may include restrictions on character sets, pattern conformance, numerical ranges, and length limits. The type system in Rust facilitates the construction of smart constructors and refinements that guarantee compliance with these invariants at the moment of instantiation. By enforcing these checks at compile time, the design reduces the possibility of runtime discrepancies and streamlines the error-handling mechanisms in the system. Formal validations, such as verifying that a header name matches the regular expression $[A-Za-z][A-Za-z0-9]*$ or that a header value does not contain forbidden characters, are systematically integrated into the type definitions.

Generation of HTTP Headers with Type Guarantees

The formation of HTTP headers is executed through a generation process that utilizes transitional abstractions to construct headers conformant to the pre-established type invariants. This process is modeled by the function

$$\gamma : D \to H,$$

where D represents a domain of raw data or header fragments, and γ embodies the conversion into a header structure that guarantees type safety. An effective generation strategy relies on compositional patterns that allow for the incremental assembly of header fields. Each component is built with an assurance that it adheres to the syntactic and semantic rules articulated during the parsing phase. The use of Rust's strong type system ensures that the aggregated output, formed through combinatory functions, remains consistent with the desired header format, thereby facilitating reliable client-server interactions.

Leveraging Rust's Type System for Compile-Time Guarantees

Rust's type system offers a unique advantage in the realm of network programming by enabling the early detection of potential errors. This chapter illustrates that the use of advanced type theoretic constructs—such as enumerated types, tuple structs, and phantom data markers—can effectively encode the semantics of HTTP headers. The process can be formally viewed as the establishment of a type invariant

$$\tau : H \to \{\text{Valid}, \text{Invalid}\},$$

which deterministically categorizes header objects based on their adherence to the prescribed rules. This paradigm shifts the validation burden from runtime to compilation, contributing to a reduction in error-prone code paths and enforcing robust programming practices. Furthermore, static analysis benefits ensue from this approach, as the invariants encoded within the type system facilitate comprehensive verification of header management logic, thereby bolstering system resilience and performance in concurrent environments.

Rust Code Snippet

```
use regex::Regex;
use std::collections::HashMap;
use std::fmt;

/// Represents an HTTP header name with type-level invariants.
```

112

```rust
/// According to RFC specifications, a valid header name must match
↪   the regex: [A-Za-z][A-Za-z0-9\-]*
#[derive(Debug, Clone, PartialEq, Eq, Hash)]
pub struct HeaderName(String);

impl HeaderName {
    /// Smart constructor that validates the header name using a
    ↪   regular expression.
    pub fn new(name: &str) -> Result<Self, String> {
        let pattern = r"^[A-Za-z][A-Za-z0-9\-]*$";
        let re = Regex::new(pattern)
            .map_err(|e| format!("Failed to compile regex: {}",
            ↪   e))?;
        if re.is_match(name) {
            Ok(HeaderName(name.to_string()))
        } else {
            Err(format!("Invalid header name: '{}'", name))
        }
    }

    /// Returns the inner string slice.
    pub fn as_str(&self) -> &str {
        &self.0
    }
}

impl fmt::Display for HeaderName {
    fn fmt(&self, f: &mut fmt::Formatter<'_>) -> fmt::Result {
        write!(f, "{}", self.0)
    }
}

/// Represents an HTTP header value with basic validation to ensure
↪   forbidden characters
/// (such as CR and LF) are not present.
#[derive(Debug, Clone, PartialEq, Eq)]
pub struct HeaderValue(String);

impl HeaderValue {
    /// Smart constructor that validates the header value.
    /// Disallows carriage return ('\r') and line feed ('\n')
    ↪   characters.
    pub fn new(value: &str) -> Result<Self, String> {
        if value.contains('\r') || value.contains('\n') {
            Err("Header value contains forbidden characters (CR or
            ↪   LF)".to_string())
        } else {
            Ok(HeaderValue(value.to_string()))
        }
    }

    /// Returns the inner string slice.
    pub fn as_str(&self) -> &str {
```

113

```rust
            &self.0
    }
}

impl fmt::Display for HeaderValue {
    fn fmt(&self, f: &mut fmt::Formatter<'_>) -> fmt::Result {
        write!(f, "{}", self.0)
    }
}

/// A complete header consisting of a validated name and value.
#[derive(Debug, Clone)]
pub struct Header {
    pub name: HeaderName,
    pub value: HeaderValue,
}

impl Header {
    /// Creates a new Header by validating the provided name and
    ↪   value.
    pub fn new(name: &str, value: &str) -> Result<Self, String> {
        Ok(Header {
            name: HeaderName::new(name)?,
            value: HeaderValue::new(value)?,
        })
    }

    /// Converts the header into a formatted string following the
    ↪   pattern: "Name: Value".
    pub fn to_string(&self) -> String {
        format!("{}: {}", self.name, self.value)
    }
}

/// Parsing function: models the mathematical function  : I → H,
/// where I is a raw input string and H is a collection of
↪   well-structured headers.
///
/// It splits the raw header input by newlines and processes each
↪   line to extract key-value pairs.
///
/// # Errors
/// Returns an error if any header fails validation or if the format
↪   is incorrect.
pub fn parse_headers(input: &str) -> Result<HashMap<HeaderName,
↪   HeaderValue>, String> {
    let mut headers = HashMap::new();

    // Process each non-empty line from the input.
    for line in input.lines() {
        let trimmed = line.trim();
        if trimmed.is_empty() {
            continue;
```

114

```
        }
        if let Some(index) = trimmed.find(':') {
            let (name_part, value_part) = trimmed.split_at(index);
            let name = name_part.trim();
            let value = value_part.trim_start_matches(':').trim();

            let header_name = HeaderName::new(name)?;
            let header_value = HeaderValue::new(value)?;

            headers.insert(header_name, header_value);
        } else {
            return Err(format!("Invalid header format: '{}'",
            ↪   line));
        }
    }
    Ok(headers)
}

/// Generation function: models the mathematical function  : D → H,
/// where D is a domain of raw (name, value) data and H is a vector
↪   of validated Header objects.
///
/// It takes a vector of tuple slices and returns a vector of
↪   Headers.
pub fn generate_headers(data: Vec<(&str, &str)>) ->
↪   Result<Vec<Header>, String> {
    data
        .into_iter()
        .map(|(n, v)| Header::new(n, v))
        .collect()
}

#[cfg(test)]
mod tests {
    use super::*;

    #[test]
    fn test_valid_header_name() {
        let name = "Content-Type";
        let header_name = HeaderName::new(name).unwrap();
        assert_eq!(header_name.as_str(), name);
    }

    #[test]
    fn test_invalid_header_name() {
        assert!(HeaderName::new("1Invalid").is_err());
        assert!(HeaderName::new("Invalid Header").is_err());
    }

    #[test]
    fn test_valid_header_value() {
        let value = "text/html; charset=UTF-8";
        let header_value = HeaderValue::new(value).unwrap();
```

```rust
            assert_eq!(header_value.as_str(), value);
    }

    #[test]
    fn test_invalid_header_value() {
        // Using CRLF in the value must trigger a validation error.
        assert!(HeaderValue::new("line1\r\nline2").is_err());
    }

    #[test]
    fn test_parse_headers() {
        let raw_headers = "Content-Type: text/html
Content-Length: 1234
X-Custom-Header: custom-value";
        let headers = parse_headers(raw_headers).unwrap();
        assert_eq!(
            headers.get(&HeaderName::new(
            "Content-Type").unwrap()).unwrap().as_str(),
            "text/html"
        );
        assert_eq!(
            headers.get(&HeaderName::new(
            "Content-Length").unwrap()).unwrap().as_str(),
            "1234"
        );
        assert_eq!(
            headers.get(&HeaderName::new(
            "X-Custom-Header").unwrap()).unwrap().as_str(),
            "custom-value"
        );
    }

    #[test]
    fn test_generate_headers() {
        let data = vec![
            ("Accept", "application/json"),
            ("User-Agent", "RustClient/1.0"),
        ];
        let headers = generate_headers(data).unwrap();
        assert_eq!(headers.len(), 2);
        assert_eq!(headers[0].name.as_str(), "Accept");
        assert_eq!(headers[0].value.as_str(), "application/json");
    }
}

fn main() {
    // Demonstrates parsing raw HTTP headers into a type-safe
    ↪   structure.
    let raw_headers = "Host: example.com\r\nConnection:
    ↪   keep-alive\r\nAccept: */*\r\n";
    match parse_headers(raw_headers) {
        Ok(headers_map) => {
            println!("Parsed Headers:");
```

116

```rust
            for (name, value) in headers_map.iter() {
                println!("{}: {}", name, value);
            }
        },
        Err(e) => {
            eprintln!("Error parsing headers: {}", e);
        }
    }

    // Demonstrates generating HTTP headers from raw key-value
    ↪  pairs.
    let header_data = vec![
        ("Content-Type", "application/json"),
        ("Cache-Control", "no-cache"),
    ];
    match generate_headers(header_data) {
        Ok(headers_vec) => {
            println!("\nGenerated Headers:");
            for header in headers_vec {
                println!("{}", header.to_string());
            }
        },
        Err(e) => {
            eprintln!("Error generating headers: {}", e);
        }
    }
}
```

Chapter 17

Designing High-Throughput RESTful APIs

Architectural Foundations of RESTful API Design

The construction of RESTful endpoints is predicated on a set of well-defined architectural principles that emphasize stateless interactions, resource identification, and uniform interface constraints. These principles facilitate an environment within which each request is processed as an independent transaction, enabling the efficient routing and handling of network messages. In such an architecture, resource representations are exchanged via standardized protocols, and the system is designed to decouple client and server state. This decoupling is essential in high-load environments where the preservation of statelessness minimizes overhead and sustains consistent performance across disparate computational units.

The formalization of these design principles is further supported by an abstraction that maps requests to resource operations. Each request is treated quantitatively as an element in a set R, wherein the transformation function $f : R \rightarrow S$ reliably translates raw inputs into structured outputs in a resource space S. The imposition of such mathematical rigor ensures that uniformity is maintained across endpoints while enabling systematic validation of request semantics. The combination of these foundational strategies underpins a robust system architecture capable of scaling to meet high-throughput demands.

High-Performance Coding Patterns

The optimization of RESTful endpoints for high throughput necessitates the adoption of coding patterns that inherently reduce latency and computational overhead. Among these strategies, asynchronous non-blocking input/output (I/O) operations are pivotal. By decoupling request processing from thread-bound execution, asynchronous paradigms enable the system to manage multiple network connections concurrently without the penalties associated with thread contention. This design pattern allows for the overlapping of I/O and computational tasks such that resource utilization is maximized.

Complementary to asynchronous operations are techniques that focus on the minimization of serialization and deserialization overhead. The conversion of data between object representations and byte streams embodies a critical performance bottleneck when executed suboptimally. High-performance patterns in this realm advocate for the use of optimized parsing routines that exploit invariants of the data format to achieve linear time complexity, denoted as $O(n)$ with respect to the size of the payload. When combined with the judicious use of memory buffers and data streaming techniques, these patterns form the backbone of a system that is both resilient and efficient under heavy load.

Scalability Strategies and Concurrency Control

The scalability of RESTful APIs is intrinsically linked to the manner in which concurrent requests are managed and executed. In scenarios characterized by high request volumes, it is imperative that the system distributes workload across multiple processing units in a manner that precludes the formation of bottlenecks. This is accomplished through a concurrency control model that integrates event-driven mechanisms and fine-grained task scheduling. The resulting architecture benefits from a multiplicative increase in throughput as the number of processing cores, denoted by N, is scaled dynamically to match incoming request rates.

A mathematical model of the scalability paradigm can be expressed by the function $D(r, N)$, where r represents the inflow rate of requests and N denotes available computing threads. The function D models the load distribution and is constructed to ensure that performance remains optimal provided that $r \leq \beta N$, where β represents the system-specific threshold for efficient processing. The application of asynchronous programming models, combined with robust thread-pooling and resource contention mitigation mechanisms, enables RESTful endpoints to process simultaneous operations in parallel. Such an arrangement guarantees that the system sustains consistent performance even under extreme load conditions.

Efficient Data Transformation and Resource Management

Central to the operation of high-throughput RESTful APIs is the efficient transformation of data. The conversion of raw input into meaningful resource representations and the inverse process is performed under stringent performance constraints. Techniques such as memory pooling, reuse of buffer allocations, and zero-copy strategies are employed to minimize the overhead of data manipulation. This ensures that the conversion pipelines operate with time complexities that remain proportional to the size of the input, typically exhibiting $O(n)$ behavior, where n quantifies the number of bytes processed.

Resource management in this context involves maintaining a delicate balance between memory usage and processing speed. Efficient caching of frequently accessed resources and the elimination of redundant data transformations contribute significantly to reducing latency. Each transformation is designed to adhere rigidly to type invariants and resource schemas, thereby ensuring that the integrity of data is preserved throughout its lifecycle. The integration of these strategies forms a cohesive framework that undergirds the overall performance of RESTful endpoints by ensuring that every phase of data processing is optimized for speed and reliability.

Load Balancing and Caching Mechanisms

In high-throughput network architectures, the proficient management of load balancing and caching emerges as a critical factor in sustaining throughput and minimizing response times. Load balancing strategies serve to distribute incoming requests evenly across multiple service nodes, thereby averting the overutilization of any single computational resource. These strategies often utilize algorithms based on consistent hashing or round-robin scheduling to achieve an equitable distribution of workload. The formal performance metric in such scenarios is represented by the reduction in average processing time T_{avg} as the request load is distributed across multiple servers.

Caching mechanisms complement load balancing by storing the results of frequently executed operations, thus obviating the need for repeated computation. The effectiveness of caching can be quantified by the cache hit ratio $H = \frac{h}{t}$, where h represents the number of successful cache retrievals and t denotes the total number of requests processed. High cache hit ratios directly correlate with reduced latency and improved throughput, as cached responses are typically delivered with minimal delay. The synergistic application of load balancing and caching mechanisms ensures that RESTful endpoints remain performant even when subjected to heavy, unpredictable loads, thereby fulfilling the stringent demands of high-throughput systems.

Rust Code Snippet

```rust
use std::collections::HashMap;
use std::sync::{Arc, Mutex};
use std::sync::atomic::{AtomicUsize, Ordering};
use tokio::time::{sleep, Duration};

/// A resource representation resulting from processing a request.
/// This simulates the mapping f: R -> S, where R is a Request and S
↪  is a Resource.
#[derive(Clone, Debug)]
struct Resource {
    content: String,
}

/// A simple request structure with an identifier and payload.
struct Request {
    id: u64,
```

```rust
    payload: String,
}

/// Transform a raw Request into a Resource.
/// This function exemplifies an O(n) linear-time processing routine
↪   where n is the length of the payload.
fn transform_request(req: &Request) -> Resource {
    // Example transformation: convert payload to uppercase.
    let processed = req.payload.to_uppercase();
    Resource {
        content: processed,
    }
}

/// API server that handles requests, implements caching, and
↪   records processing metrics.
struct ApiServer {
    cache: Mutex<HashMap<u64, Resource>>,
    total_requests: AtomicUsize,
    cache_hits: AtomicUsize,
}

impl ApiServer {
    /// Create a new ApiServer instance.
    fn new() -> Self {
        ApiServer {
            cache: Mutex::new(HashMap::new()),
            total_requests: AtomicUsize::new(0),
            cache_hits: AtomicUsize::new(0),
        }
    }

    /// Asynchronously process a request.
    /// This method demonstrates non-blocking I/O via a simulated
    ↪   delay and applies the transformation function.
    async fn handle_request(&self, req: Request) -> Resource {
        // Increment total number of processed requests.
        self.total_requests.fetch_add(1, Ordering::SeqCst);

        // Check if the result for this request is already cached.
        {
            let cache = self.cache.lock().unwrap();
            if let Some(cached) = cache.get(&req.id) {
                // Increment cache hit counter if found.
                self.cache_hits.fetch_add(1, Ordering::SeqCst);
                return cached.clone();
            }
        }

        // Simulate an asynchronous non-blocking I/O delay.
        sleep(Duration::from_millis(10)).await;

        // Process the request using function f: R -> S.
```

```rust
    let res = transform_request(&req);

    // Insert the new result into the cache.
    {
        let mut cache = self.cache.lock().unwrap();
        cache.insert(req.id, res.clone());
    }

    res
}

/// Compute the cache hit ratio H = h / t, where h is the number
/// of hits and t is the total requests.
fn cache_hit_ratio(&self) -> f64 {
    let hits = self.cache_hits.load(Ordering::SeqCst) as f64;
    let total = self.total_requests.load(Ordering::SeqCst) as
        f64;
    if total == 0.0 { 0.0 } else { hits / total }
}
}

/// Check if the current load (request_rate) is within the scalable
/// threshold given available threads (N)
/// and a system-specific factor (beta) as defined by the inequality
/// r <= beta * N.
fn is_load_within_threshold(request_rate: usize, available_threads:
    usize, beta: usize) -> bool {
    request_rate <= beta * available_threads
}

#[tokio::main]
async fn main() {
    // Initialize the API server wrapped in an Arc for shared
    //   ownership across tasks.
    let server = Arc::new(ApiServer::new());

    // Simulation parameters:
    // available_threads (N) represent processing cores, beta is the
    //   scaling threshold,
    // and simulated_request_rate (r) is the inflow rate of
    //   requests.
    let available_threads = 4;
    let beta = 10;
    let simulated_request_rate = 30;

    // Validate the load distribution using the scalability function
    //   D(r, N).
    if !is_load_within_threshold(simulated_request_rate,
        available_threads, beta) {
        println!("Warning: Request rate exceeds threshold! Potential
            bottlenecks may occur.");
    }
```

123

```rust
    // Vector to hold task handles for concurrent processing.
    let mut handles = Vec::new();

    // Simulate processing multiple requests concurrently.
    for i in 0..simulated_request_rate {
        let server_clone = Arc::clone(&server);
        let req = Request {
            id: i as u64,
            payload: format!("request_payload_{}", i),
        };

        // Spawn an asynchronous task to handle the request.
        let handle = tokio::spawn(async move {
            let res = server_clone.handle_request(req).await;
            println!("Processed response: {}", res.content);
        });
        handles.push(handle);
    }

    // Await all spawned tasks to complete.
    for handle in handles {
        let _ = handle.await;
    }

    // Print the cache hit ratio calculated from the processed
    ↪   requests.
    println!("Cache Hit Ratio: {:.2}", server.cache_hit_ratio());
}
```

Chapter 18

Secure Session and Cookie Handling

Foundations of Session Integrity and Confidentiality

A rigorous approach to session management necessitates the formalization of both the integrity and confidentiality attributes of transient application states. This section delineates the theoretical constructs underlying secure session handling. In typical web services, a session is represented as an ephemeral state, denoted by a token T, whose lifecycle is bounded by predefined temporal constraints. The secure transformation of a request into an authenticated session state is captured by a mapping function $\Phi : R \to T$, where R corresponds to the incoming request details. An essential requirement is that the transformation process preserves the cryptographic properties of the data, ensuring that any subsequent session representation cannot be tampered with. The use of cryptographic hash functions and keyed-hash message authentication codes (HMACs), represented symbolically as $H(k, m)$ with key k and message m, reinforces the assurance of data integrity and origin authentication.

Cookie Attributes as Security Enablers

Cookies serve as the primary vehicle for persisting session identifiers across stateless HTTP interactions. The security of these tokens is enhanced by a judicious selection of cookie attributes, each of which contributes to mitigating common attack vectors such as session hijacking and cross-site scripting. The designation of a cookie as *Secure* ensures that it is transmitted exclusively over encrypted channels, while the *HttpOnly* attribute restricts client-side script access, thereby reducing exposure to injection-based exploits. Furthermore, the implementation of the *SameSite* attribute enforces a policy that confines cookie transmission to first-party contexts, thus limiting the risk associated with cross-origin requests. The interplay between these attributes and the underlying session token supports a comprehensive security model, where the aggregated effect is a reduction in the attack surface inherent in distributed web architectures.

Code-Level Techniques for Session and Cookie Management

Implementing secure session and cookie handling at the code level involves a multifaceted strategy aimed at managing state transitions and enforcing policy constraints. The initiation of a session typically involves the generation of a cryptographically random token, which is then associated with a unique user identifier in a secure database. The encapsulation of session data must adhere to stringent invariants; for example, each session must be assigned a time-to-live parameter, expressed as Δt, to automatically invalidate long-lived sessions. During the session's operation, periodic revalidation and token rotation protocols are employed. These protocols involve recalculating verification hashes and ensuring that the session token remains synchronized with client-side cookies. Moreover, cryptographic signing of session data ensures that any modification can be detected through the computed signature $\sigma = H(k, T)$, thereby reinforcing the integrity of the session state throughout its lifetime.

Mechanisms for Robust Data Validation and Confidentiality Assurance

Ensuring the robustness of session and cookie handling extends to the meticulous validation of inbound and outbound session data. Each session token must be rigorously verified against a stored signature, thereby mitigating risks stemming from data corruption or unauthorized manipulation. This verification process is mathematically characterized by the condition $\sigma' = H(k, T')$, where σ' indicates the computed signature of the received token T' and k represents a securely stored cryptographic key. In parallel, the confidentiality of sensitive session information is maintained through encryption mechanisms that transform plaintext session data into secure ciphertext, adhering to the relation $C = E_k(P)$ for a given plaintext P and encryption key k. The decryption process, described by $P = D_k(C)$, ensures that only authorized entities can access the original session data. These mechanisms, implemented with a focus on precise data handling and strict policy enforcement, form the technical backbone that safeguards session and cookie integrity within high-performance web services.

Rust Code Snippet

```rust
use std::time::{SystemTime, Duration};
use rand::Rng;
use rand::rngs::OsRng;
use rand::RngCore;
use hmac::{Hmac, Mac};
use sha2::Sha256;
use aes::Aes256;
use block_modes::{BlockMode, Cbc};
use block_modes::block_padding::Pkcs7;
use hex;

// Alias for HMAC-SHA256
type HmacSha256 = Hmac<Sha256>;
// Alias for AES-256 CBC mode with PKCS7 padding
type Aes256Cbc = Cbc<Aes256, Pkcs7>;

/// Generates a cryptographically secure random token of the given
↪  length.
fn generate_random_token(len: usize) -> Vec<u8> {
    let mut token = vec![0u8; len];
    OsRng.fill(&mut token[..]);
    token
```

```rust
}

/// Signs the given token using HMAC-SHA256 with the provided key.
/// This corresponds to computing the signature = H(k, T).
fn sign_token(key: &[u8], token: &[u8]) -> Vec<u8> {
    let mut mac = HmacSha256::new_from_slice(key)
        .expect("HMAC can take key of any size");
    mac.update(token);
    let result = mac.finalize();
    let code_bytes = result.into_bytes();
    code_bytes.to_vec()
}

/// Verifies the provided signature against the token using
↪    HMAC-SHA256.
fn verify_token(key: &[u8], token: &[u8], signature: &[u8]) -> bool
↪    {
    let mut mac = HmacSha256::new_from_slice(key)
        .expect("HMAC can take key of any size");
    mac.update(token);
    mac.verify_slice(signature).is_ok()
}

/// Encrypts the plaintext using AES-256 in CBC mode.
/// Returns the initialization vector (IV) and the ciphertext.
/// This demonstrates the equation C = E_k(P).
fn encrypt_data(key: &[u8], plaintext: &[u8]) -> (Vec<u8>, Vec<u8>)
↪    {
    // AES-256 expects a 32-byte key and CBC mode requires a 16-byte
    ↪    IV.
    let mut iv = [0u8; 16];
    OsRng.fill_bytes(&mut iv);
    let cipher = Aes256Cbc::new_from_slices(key, &iv)
        .expect("Invalid key/IV length");
    let ciphertext = cipher.encrypt_vec(plaintext);
    (iv.to_vec(), ciphertext)
}

/// Decrypts the ciphertext using AES-256 in CBC mode.
/// This follows the decryption relation P = D_k(C).
fn decrypt_data(key: &[u8], iv: &[u8], ciphertext: &[u8]) -> Vec<u8>
↪    {
    let cipher = Aes256Cbc::new_from_slices(key, iv)
        .expect("Invalid key/IV length");
    cipher.decrypt_vec(ciphertext)
        .expect("Decryption error")
}

/// Represents a user session with an associated token, its
↪    cryptographic signature,
/// and a time-to-live (TTL) to automatically invalidate long-lived
↪    sessions.
struct Session {
```

```rust
        token: Vec<u8>,
        signature: Vec<u8>,
        ttl: Duration,
        created_at: SystemTime,
    }

    impl Session {
        /// Creates a new session by generating a random token and
        ↪   signing it.
        /// The mapping function : R → T is conceptually represented as
        ↪   this process.
        fn new(key: &[u8], ttl: Duration) -> Self {
            let token = generate_random_token(32); // 256-bit token
            let signature = sign_token(key, &token);
            Self {
                token,
                signature,
                ttl,
                created_at: SystemTime::now(),
            }
        }

        /// Validates the session by ensuring it has not expired (TTL
        ↪   check) and that the token's signature is valid.
        fn is_valid(&self, key: &[u8]) -> bool {
            if self.created_at.elapsed().unwrap() > self.ttl {
                return false;
            }
            verify_token(key, &self.token, &self.signature)
        }

        /// Rotates (refreshes) the token and its signature, resetting
        ↪   the session state.
        fn rotate(&mut self, key: &[u8]) {
            self.token = generate_random_token(32);
            self.signature = sign_token(key, &self.token);
            self.created_at = SystemTime::now();
        }
    }

    fn main() {
        // In production, ensure that the secret_key is securely
        ↪   generated and managed.
        // The secret_key here is used for both HMAC signing and AES
        ↪   encryption.
        let secret_key: [u8; 32] = [0x01; 32];

        // Create a new session with a TTL of 5 minutes.
        let session_ttl = Duration::new(300, 0);
        let mut session = Session::new(&secret_key, session_ttl);

        println!("Session token: {}", hex::encode(&session.token));
```

129

```rust
    println!("Session signature: {}",
        hex::encode(&session.signature));

    // Validate the session by checking its signature and TTL.
    if session.is_valid(&secret_key) {
        println!("Session is valid");
    } else {
        println!("Session is invalid or expired");
    }

    // Rotate the session token to simulate token refresh protocols.
    session.rotate(&secret_key);
    println!("Rotated session token: {}",
        hex::encode(&session.token));
    println!("Rotated session signature: {}",
        hex::encode(&session.signature));

    // Demonstrate encryption of sensitive session data.
    let plaintext = b"Sensitive session data";
    let (iv, ciphertext) = encrypt_data(&secret_key, plaintext);
    println!("IV: {}", hex::encode(&iv));
    println!("Ciphertext: {}", hex::encode(&ciphertext));

    // Decrypt the ciphertext to retrieve the original plaintext.
    let decrypted = decrypt_data(&secret_key, &iv, &ciphertext);
    println!("Decrypted text: {}", String::from_utf8(decrypted)
        .expect("Invalid UTF-8"));
}
```

Chapter 19

Robust API Request Validation

Foundations of Rust's Type Safety in Input Processing

Within the domain of API request handling, Rust's static type system plays a central role in expressing and enforcing the invariants that characterize valid data. Each incoming request is encapsulated by an explicitly defined type, which formalizes the structure and semantic expectations of the payload. This rigorous demarcation establishes an unambiguous contract between the data producer and consumer, such that any deviation from the predefined format is detected during compilation. The type system thereby precludes the emergence of vague or ambiguous representations, ensuring that only data conforming to the specified schema is admitted into the processing pipeline. The adherence to precise type signatures allows the compiler to perform extensive checks, significantly reducing the likelihood of runtime anomalies and preserving the integrity of downstream processing.

Declarative Data Decomposition via Pattern Matching

Rust's pattern matching capability provides a powerful mechanism for decomposing complex data types into their constituent components. Through exhaustive match expressions, each variant of an incoming request is isolated and scrutinized against detailed patterns. These patterns serve to both destructure nested constructs and impose fine-grained conditions that must be satisfied for a branch to be executed. Formally, if an incoming request is denoted by r, then a match expression partitions the set of possible representations into mutually exclusive cases, each corresponding to a concrete pattern. This operation is analogous to defining a function

$$f : \mathcal{R} \to \{\text{case}_1, \text{case}_2, \ldots, \text{case}_k\},$$

where $\mathcal{R}$ represents the universe of possible requests. In each branch, specific invariants and assumptions regarding the structure of r are validated, thereby ensuring that only those variants meeting all criteria propagate for further processing.

Integrated Mechanisms for API Request Verification

The synthesis of Rust's type system and its pattern matching facility leads to a robust framework for API request validation. By leveraging explicit type annotations, every field and potential variant is accompanied by a predefined range of acceptable values, thereby reducing the ambiguity present in loosely typed environments. Concurrently, the match construct affords a declarative modality to dissect and verify the incoming data. Each branch of the match statement is effectively a guard that scrutinizes critical elements such as format, field presence, and value ranges. If any component fails to satisfy the stipulated criteria, the associated branch directs the execution to a controlled error-handling pathway. The combined effect of these mechanisms is a validation process that is both intricate and resilient. Through meticulous case analysis, every possible state is accounted for; the integration of these checks ensures that the system validates the entirety of an API request against multiple levels of invariants before such a request is processed further.

Mathematical Characterization of Validation Invariants

The validation protocol can be rigorously characterized through a formal mapping of an incoming API request to a binary outcome. Let $r \in \mathcal{R}$ denote an arbitrary incoming request, where $\mathcal{R}$ is the set of all requests. The validation function $V : \mathcal{R} \to \{0, 1\}$ is defined such that $V(r) = 1$ if r adheres to every internal invariant and $V(r) = 0$ otherwise. Let the property P encapsulate a conjunction of n distinct predicates, $P_1, P_2, \ldots, P_n$, which represent criteria such as structural integrity, field presence, and semantic consistency. The validity of a request r is then expressed as

$$V(r) = 1 \quad \text{if and only if} \quad P(r) = P_1(r) \wedge P_2(r) \wedge \cdots \wedge P_n(r).$$

In this formulation, the invariant $P(r)$ is intimately connected to the specific patterns evaluated within the match expression. Rust's compiler, in concert with these declarative constructs, enforces that all possible instances of r are subject to validation, thereby eliminating potential vulnerabilities that may arise from unchecked conditions. This mathematical characterization underpins a methodical approach to API request validation, ensuring that every request is rigorously examined and appropriately classified before it enters the primary processing flow.

Rust Code Snippet

```
//! This example implements a robust API request validation system
↪   inspired by
//! the chapter's discussion on Rust's type safety and pattern
↪   matching. The
//! validation function follows a mathematical formulation:
//!
//!      V(r) = 1 if and only if P(r) = P1(r) && P2(r) && P3(r)
//!
//! where each predicate (P1, P2, P3) corresponds to:
//!   - P1: URL validity (non-empty)
//!   - P2: Body requirements (none for GET / required for POST)
//!   - P3: Required headers (e.g., "Content-Type" exists for POST)
//!
//! Only if all predicates succeed does the request get classified
↪   as valid.

use std::collections::HashMap;
```

```rust
// Define the types of HTTP methods supported.
#[derive(Debug)]
enum RequestMethod {
    Get,
    Post,
    // Add more methods (PUT, DELETE, etc.) as needed.
}

// APIRequest struct encapsulates the structure of an incoming API
↪   request.
#[derive(Debug)]
struct APIRequest {
    method: RequestMethod,
    url: String,
    headers: HashMap<String, String>,
    body: Option<String>,
}

impl APIRequest {
    /// Validate the API request against a series of safety and
    ↪   structural invariants.
    /// This function implements the mapping:
    ///   V(r) = 1  if and only if  all predicates P1, P2, ..., Pn
    ↪   hold true;
    /// otherwise, V(r) = 0.
    fn validate(&self) -> bool {
        // Predicate P1: URL must be non-empty.
        if !Self::is_url_valid(&self.url) {
            return false;
        }

        // Predicate P2: Validate request body based on HTTP method.
        if !Self::is_body_valid(&self.method, &self.body) {
            return false;
        }

        // Predicate P3: Check for required "Content-Type" header
        ↪   for POST requests.
        if !Self::has_valid_content_type(&self.method,
        ↪   &self.headers) {
            return false;
        }

        // All predicates have passed, so the request is valid.
        true
    }

    /// Check if the URL field is non-empty.
    fn is_url_valid(url: &str) -> bool {
        !url.trim().is_empty()
    }
```

```rust
/// Validate the body based on request method:
///  - GET requests must not have a body.
///  - POST requests must have a non-empty body.
fn is_body_valid(method: &RequestMethod, body: &Option<String>)
↪  -> bool {
    match method {
        RequestMethod::Get => body.is_none(),
        RequestMethod::Post => {
            if let Some(content) = body {
                // For POST, body should not be empty.
                !content.trim().is_empty()
            } else {
                false
            }
        }
    }
}

/// For POST requests, a valid "Content-Type" header is
↪  required.
/// GET requests bypass this check.
fn has_valid_content_type(method: &RequestMethod, headers:
↪  &HashMap<String, String>) -> bool {
    match method {
        RequestMethod::Post => {
            // Check headers for a key matching "Content-Type"
            ↪  (case-insensitive).
            headers.iter().any(|(key, value)| {
                key.to_lowercase() == "content-type" &&
                ↪  !value.trim().is_empty()
            })
        }
        _ => true,
    }
}

fn main() {
    // Example usage of the API request validation system.

    // Create a valid POST request.
    let mut post_headers = HashMap::new();
    post_headers.insert("Content-Type".to_string(),
    ↪  "application/json".to_string());
    let post_request = APIRequest {
        method: RequestMethod::Post,
        url: "/api/data".to_string(),
        headers: post_headers,
        body: Some("{\"key\": \"value\"}".to_string()),
    };

    // Create a valid GET request.
    let get_request = APIRequest {
```

135

```rust
        method: RequestMethod::Get,
        url: "/api/info".to_string(),
        headers: HashMap::new(),
        body: None,
    };

    // Create an invalid POST request (empty URL and missing
    ↪   header).
    let invalid_request = APIRequest {
        method: RequestMethod::Post,
        url: "".to_string(), // Invalid: URL is empty.
        headers: HashMap::new(),
        body: Some("Invalid content".to_string()),
    };

    // Validate and print the results.
    println!("Post request is valid: {}", post_request.validate());
    println!("Get request is valid: {}", get_request.validate());
    println!("Invalid request is valid: {}",
    ↪   invalid_request.validate());
}
```

Chapter 20

Declarative URL Routing with Macros

Foundations of Macro-Based URL Routing

Declarative URL routing systems are predicated on the abstraction of route definitions by means of syntactic transformations executed at compile time. In statically typed languages that emphasize rigorous invariants, a macro-based approach enables the specification of routing structures in a concise and precise manner. Declarative annotations serve to describe URL patterns as high-level specifications, the semantics of which are enforced by the language's type system. The core idea is to transform these high-level representations into low-level routing tables without compromising correctness or violating predefined invariants. This transformation can be conceptualized as a mapping $f : S \to T$, where S denotes the set of declarative specifications and T represents the resulting routing constructs that are further manipulated by the compiler.

Procedural Macros in URL Routing

Procedural macros operate by accepting input token streams and generating modified token sequences that adhere to the desired routing specifications. This process is analogous to a functional transformation $g : \mathcal{T} \to \mathcal{T}'$, where $\mathcal{T}$ and $\mathcal{T}'$ are the domains of input and output token streams, respectively. The algebraic properties of such transformations guarantee that the structural integrity of the routing definitions is maintained throughout expansion. In practice, these macros perform syntactic analyses to ensure that all instances of route annotations satisfy predetermined patterns. As a result, compile-time errors are raised for malformed specifications, thereby precluding runtime inconsistencies. The transformation provided by a procedural macro encapsulates both the reduction of boilerplate code and the preservation of domain-specific invariants embedded in the routing constructs.

Attribute Macros and Their Declarative Syntax

Attribute macros afford a syntactic ribbon that is attached directly to function and type declarations. This annotation mechanism introduces metadata that is semantically significant for the routing framework. When an attribute macro is applied, it performs a declarative mapping $\pi : \rho \to \mathcal{R}$, where ρ represents the annotated metadata and $\mathcal{R}$ corresponds to the set of routable endpoints. The operational semantics of attribute macros involve verifying that the annotated elements are consistent with the expectations of the routing framework. Such verifications include the examination of URL patterns, the match between HTTP methods and route parameters, and the enforcement of naming conventions critical for disambiguation. This declarative approach encapsulates the dual objectives of conciseness and observability, as the macro system automatically validates the structure and intent of annotated components at compile time.

Mathematical Characterization of Routing Transformations

The interplay between procedural and attribute macros in the construction of routing tables can be formalized through a compositional framework. Define a macro transformation function $\mathcal{M}$ such that for any well-formed specification $S \in \Sigma$, the expansion is given by

$$S' = \mathcal{M}(S),$$

where Σ is the domain of legal URL routing specifications and S' is the resultant internal representation. The correctness of the transformation is ensured by the predicate

$$I(S) : \Sigma \to \{0, 1\},$$

where $I(S) = 1$ if and only if S satisfies all invariants required for safe and efficient dispatching. In this context, $\mathcal{M}$ acts as a bijective mapping on Σ, such that the composition with any well-defined attribute macro results in a routing definition that is both complete and free of ambiguities. This formal characterization supports the assertion that declarative macros engender a high level of confidence in the correctness of URL routing mechanisms by subjecting every specification to a rigorous transformation process.

Advantages of a Declarative Routing Paradigm

The paradigm advantages of utilizing a declarative macro system in URL routing lie primarily in its capacity to foster code clarity, reduce redundancy, and ensure compile-time validation of routing invariants. By abstracting the intricacies of route matching and dispatching into declarative annotations, the macro system significantly diminishes the propensity for human error. The transformation process guarantees that every route specification is transformed into a routable entity that faithfully adheres to the predetermined layout. Furthermore, the separation between route declaration and implementation logic allows for an enhanced modularity, drawing a clear boundary between high-level intent and low-level behavior. The resulting framework not only streamlines development procedures but also bolsters the static guarantees provided by the underlying type system, solidifying the correctness and efficiency of the compiled routing infrastructure.

Rust Code Snippet

```
//! This example demonstrates a simplified declarative URL routing
↪    system using Rust.
//!
//! Mathematical concepts mentioned in the chapter:
//!
```

```
//! 1. Transformation: S' = (S)
//!    - Here, a route specification S (with fields like method,
↪   path, and handler)
//!      is transformed into an internal routing entry S' via ,
↪   provided that the
//!      invariant I(S) holds true, i.e., I(S)=1.
//!
//! 2. Invariant check predicate: I(S):  → {0,1}
//!    - For a given RouteSpec S  , I(S) returns 1 (true) only if
↪   all safety
//!      and formatting invariants are met.
//!
//! 3. Procedural mapping simulation:
//!    - We simulate a procedural macro transformation by using a
↪   declarative macro
//!      'declare_routes!' that internally calls a transformation
↪   function.
//!
//! The following code defines:
//! - A RouteSpec struct representing a high-level specification
↪   (S).
//! - A transform_route() function to map S to S' after verifying
↪   I(S).
//! - A RoutingTable that stores the mapping, representing the
↪   target routing
//!   construct T.
//! - A macro 'declare_routes!' to declaratively create a routing
↪   table.
//!

use std::collections::HashMap;

/// Trait to validate that a given route specification satisfies
↪   required invariants.
trait Invariant {
    /// Returns true if the invariants (I(S)==1) are met.
    fn validate(&self) -> bool;
}

/// High-level route specification (S)
#[derive(Debug)]
struct RouteSpec {
    path: &'static str,
    method: &'static str,
    handler: fn(),
}

/// Implementation of invariant check for RouteSpec
impl Invariant for RouteSpec {
    fn validate(&self) -> bool {
        // Invariant I(S): The path must start with '/'
        self.path.starts_with('/')
    }
```

```
}

/// Transformation function representing : S → S'
/// It takes a RouteSpec and returns the transformed tuple to be
↪    stored in the routing table.
/// This simulates the mapping:
///     S' = (S)    subject to I(S) == true.
fn transform_route(spec: &RouteSpec) -> (&'static str, &'static str,
↪    fn()) {
    if !spec.validate() {
        panic!("RouteSpec does not satisfy invariants (I(S)==0):
        ↪    {:?}", spec);
    }
    (spec.method, spec.path, spec.handler)
}

/// Internal representation of routing table (T)
struct RoutingTable {
    // Mapping from (HTTP method, URL path) to a handler function.
    routes: HashMap<(&'static str, &'static str), fn()>,
}

impl RoutingTable {
    /// Creates a new, empty routing table.
    fn new() -> Self {
        RoutingTable {
            routes: HashMap::new(),
        }
    }

    /// Adds a route specification to the table after
    ↪    transformation.
    fn add_route(&mut self, spec: RouteSpec) {
        // Transformation: S' = (S)
        let (method, path, handler) = transform_route(&spec);
        // Store in the routing table.
        self.routes.insert((method, path), handler);
    }

    /// Dispatches a request based on method and path.
    fn dispatch(&self, method: &'static str, path: &'static str) {
        if let Some(&handler) = self.routes.get(&(method, path)) {
            println!("Dispatching to handler for {} {}", method,
            ↪    path);
            handler();
        } else {
            println!("No matching route for {} {}", method, path);
        }
    }
}

/// Declarative macro to define routes akin to attribute macros in
↪    procedural systems.
```

```
///
/// This macro simulates the mapping from high-level specifications
↪  S to the routing table.
/// Usage example:
/// declare_routes! {
///     GET "/index" => index_handler,
///     POST "/contact" => contact_handler,
/// }
macro_rules! declare_routes {
    ( $( $method:ident $path:expr => $handler:ident ),* $(,)? ) =>
    ↪  {
        {
            let mut table = RoutingTable::new();
            $(
                // Create a RouteSpec instance (S)
                let spec = RouteSpec {
                    path: $path,
                    method: stringify!($method), // Converts method
                    ↪  identifier to string literal.
                    handler: $handler,
                };
                // Add transformed route (S') to the routing table.
                table.add_route(spec);
            )*
            table
        }
    };
}

// --- Example Handlers ---

fn index_handler() {
    println!("Executing index_handler: rendering index page.");
}

fn about_handler() {
    println!("Executing about_handler: displaying about
    ↪  information.");
}

fn contact_handler() {
    println!("Executing contact_handler: processing contact form.");
}

// --- Main Function Demonstrating the Routing System ---
fn main() {
    // Build the routing table using the declarative macro.
    let routing_table = declare_routes! {
        GET "/index"   => index_handler,
        GET "/about"   => about_handler,
        POST "/contact" => contact_handler,
    };
```

```
  // Test dispatching to various routes.
  routing_table.dispatch("GET", "/index");        // Expected: calls
  ↪   index_handler.
  routing_table.dispatch("GET", "/nonexistent");  // Expected: no
  ↪   matching route.
  routing_table.dispatch("POST", "/contact");     // Expected:
  ↪   calls contact_handler.
}
```

Chapter 21

Integrating TLS for Secure Communications

TLS Protocol Architecture

Transport Layer Security (TLS) is a protocol suite that provides a robust framework for securing communications over computer networks. The protocol operates by orchestrating a sequence of interactions, commonly known as the handshake, in which negotiating parties establish shared cryptographic parameters. Under this regime, asymmetric cryptographic operations are employed to exchange or derive a symmetric key, which subsequently encrypts the data. The handshake can be formally modeled by considering a state transition system, where an initial state s_0 is transformed via a function T, such that $T(s_0)$ yields a state representative of a secure session. Integral to the protocol are certificate-based authentication and the selection of cipher suites, which are chosen based on both policy constraints and mutual capability. These processes ensure that confidentiality, integrity, and authenticity are maintained through the establishment of secure connections.

Incorporating TLS Libraries in Network Services

The integration of TLS libraries within network service architectures requires a systematic abstraction over lower-level cryptographic primitives. TLS libraries encapsulate the complexity of establishing and maintaining a secure channel, thereby presenting a high-level interface for initiating TLS sessions, managing negotiation parameters, and handling session renegotiation or termination. In this context, a library serves as a mapping function $L : I \to S$, where I denotes the set of interface calls made by the network application and S represents the corresponding secure session states. The modular design provided by such libraries facilitates the separation between the secure transport layer and the application's business logic. This decoupling not only aids in maintaining code clarity and reusability but also enforces the security invariants that are critical to the operation of network services.

Certificate Verification and Trust Models

Establishing secure TLS connections depends critically on the verification of digital certificates, which underpin the trust model of the protocol. Certificates are issued according to a hierarchical structure, forming a chain from a trusted root authority to the end entity. Formally, a certificate chain may be represented as a sequence $\langle c_1, c_2, \ldots, c_n \rangle$, wherein each certificate c_i is validated by its successor c_{i+1}. The validity of such a chain is predicated on satisfying the condition

$$\bigwedge_{i=1}^{n-1} V(c_i, c_{i+1}) = 1,$$

where $V(c_i, c_{i+1})$ is a validation function that confirms the integrity and authenticity of the linking certificates. Robust certificate verification mechanisms incorporate the evaluation of certificate revocation states via mechanisms such as Certificate Revocation Lists (CRLs) or Online Certificate Status Protocol (OCSP) responses. Such meticulous validation is indispensable in establishing a secure channel, as it ensures that communications occur solely with authenticated and trusted endpoints.

Algorithmic and Cryptographic Foundations

TLS relies on a suite of cryptographic algorithms to deliver mutually authenticated and confidential communication channels. The key exchange process may employ various algorithms such as RSA, Diffie-Hellman (DH), or Elliptic Curve Diffie-Hellman (ECDH), each predicated on well-established computational hardness assumptions. Following the establishment of a shared secret, symmetric encryption algorithms—typically variants of the Advanced Encryption Standard (AES) in modes such as Galois/Counter Mode (GCM)—are utilized to encrypt bulk data traffic. Additionally, integrity verification is conducted using hash-based message authentication codes (HMACs). The overall encryption-decryption process can be abstractly represented by a function

$$F : M \times K \to C,$$

where M is the message space, K is the space of cryptographic keys, and C is the space of ciphertexts; the decryption function F^{-1} satisfies the equation $F^{-1}(C, K) = M$. This union of asymmetric exchanges, symmetric encryption, and cryptographic hash functions ensures that the integrity and confidentiality of data remain intact throughout transmission.

Performance and Security Trade-offs

The deployment of TLS within network services introduces a non-trivial overhead that must be judiciously balanced against the concurrent imperative for robust security. The computational demands of asymmetric key exchanges, symmetric encryption, and certificate verifications incur additional latency that is particularly evident in high-throughput environments. In formal terms, the performance impact can be modeled by a degradation function $P(D)$, where D represents data volume or connection concurrency; the goal is to minimize $P(D)$ while upholding stringent security constraints. Optimization strategies involve the selective use of hardware acceleration, careful configuration of cipher suites, and effective session reuse mechanisms that amortize the cost of the TLS handshake over multiple data exchanges. Such considerations are essential to ensure that the integration of TLS not only fortifies the network service against adversarial threats but also sustains operational efficiency under varying load conditions.

Rust Code Snippet

```rust
use std::fmt;

// Enumeration representing the TLS state machine.
// This models the state transition: s --T(·)→ s.
#[derive(Debug, Clone)]
enum TlsState {
    Init,
    Handshake,
    Established,
    Terminated,
}

impl fmt::Display for TlsState {
    fn fmt(&self, f: &mut fmt::Formatter) -> fmt::Result {
        match self {
            TlsState::Init => write!(f, "Init"),
            TlsState::Handshake => write!(f, "Handshake"),
            TlsState::Established => write!(f, "Established"),
            TlsState::Terminated => write!(f, "Terminated"),
        }
    }
}

// Representation of a TLS session, holding the current state,
// selected cipher suite, and an optional shared secret resulting
↪   from key exchange.
#[derive(Debug, Clone)]
struct TlsSession {
    state: TlsState,
    cipher_suite: String,
    shared_secret: Option<Vec<u8>>,
}

impl TlsSession {
    fn new() -> Self {
        TlsSession {
            state: TlsState::Init,
            cipher_suite: String::from("TLS_AES_128_GCM_SHA256"),
            shared_secret: None,
        }
    }

    // Function to update the session state, representing the
    ↪   transition T(s)→s.
    fn transform_state(&mut self, new_state: TlsState) {
```

```rust
        self.state = new_state;
    }
}

// A simulated digital certificate.
#[derive(Debug, Clone)]
struct Certificate {
    subject: String,
    issuer: String,
    data: Vec<u8>, // Simulated binary data for the certificate.
}

impl Certificate {
    // Verification function V(c, c) that checks if this certificate
    // ↪ is properly issued.
    // For the simulation, if the issuer of the current certificate
    // ↪ matches the subject
    // of the next certificate, then the link is considered valid.
    fn verify_with(&self, issuer_cert: &Certificate) -> bool {
        self.issuer == issuer_cert.subject
    }
}

// Validate a certificate chain represented as (c, c, ..., c).
// The chain is valid if for each consecutive pair, V(c, c) == true.
fn verify_certificate_chain(chain: &[Certificate]) -> bool {
    if chain.len() < 2 {
        return false;
    }
    for i in 0..chain.len() - 1 {
        if !chain[i].verify_with(&chain[i + 1]) {
            return false;
        }
    }
    true
}

// Simulated Diffie-Hellman key exchange.
// This dummy implementation mimics the generation of a shared
// ↪ secret
// using basic arithmetic. In practice, DH or ECDH would be used.
fn diffie_hellman_key_exchange(client_private: u32, server_public:
↪ u32) -> Vec<u8> {
    let prime: u32 = 23; // A small prime number for demonstration
    // ↪ purposes.
    let shared = (client_private * server_public) % prime;
    // Convert the u32 shared secret to bytes.
    shared.to_le_bytes().to_vec()
}

// Simulated encryption function F: M × K → C.
// For demonstration, we apply a simple XOR between the message and
// ↪ key (repeating key if needed).
```

148

```rust
fn encrypt(message: &[u8], key: &[u8]) -> Vec<u8> {
    message
        .iter()
        .enumerate()
        .map(|(i, &byte)| byte ^ key[i % key.len()])
        .collect()
}

// Simulated decryption function F'(C, K) = M.
// Using XOR, encryption is symmetric, so decryption is identical to
↪    encryption.
fn decrypt(ciphertext: &[u8], key: &[u8]) -> Vec<u8> {
    encrypt(ciphertext, key)
}

// Simulated TLS handshake process.
// This function represents the state transition T(s) and session
↪    establishment workflow.
// It derives a shared secret using a dummy Diffie-Hellman key
↪    exchange.
fn tls_handshake(mut session: TlsSession, client_private: u32,
↪    server_public: u32) -> TlsSession {
    println!("Initial state: {}", session.state);

    // Transition: Init → Handshake
    session.transform_state(TlsState::Handshake);
    println!("State after handshake initiation: {}", session.state);

    // Perform (simulated) Diffie-Hellman key exchange.
    let shared_secret = diffie_hellman_key_exchange(client_private,
↪    server_public);
    session.shared_secret = Some(shared_secret);

    // Transition: Handshake → Established (secure session
↪    established).
    session.transform_state(TlsState::Established);
    println!("State after establishing secure session: {}",
↪    session.state);

    session
}

fn main() {
    // Create a new TLS session (initial state s).
    let mut session = TlsSession::new();

    // Construct a dummy certificate chain:
    // Certificate chain: (cert, cert, cert) with the property that
    // V(cert, cert)  V(cert, cert) must be true.
    let cert1 = Certificate {
        subject: String::from("www.example.com"),
        issuer: String::from("Intermediate CA"),
        data: vec![1, 2, 3],
```

149

```rust
    };
    let cert2 = Certificate {
        subject: String::from("Intermediate CA"),
        issuer: String::from("Root CA"),
        data: vec![4, 5, 6],
    };
    let cert3 = Certificate {
        subject: String::from("Root CA"),
        issuer: String::from("Root CA"),
        data: vec![7, 8, 9],
    };
    let cert_chain = vec![cert1, cert2, cert3];
    if verify_certificate_chain(&cert_chain) {
        println!("Certificate chain is valid.");
    } else {
        println!("Certificate chain is invalid.");
    }

    // Simulate TLS handshake with dummy Diffie-Hellman parameters.
    // Here, client's private key and server's public key are
    // ↪ represented by u32 values.
    let client_private: u32 = 6;
    let server_public: u32 = 15;
    session = tls_handshake(session, client_private, server_public);

    // Simulate data exchange using the encryption function F: M × K
    // ↪ → C.
    let message = b"Hello, TLS!";
    let key = session.shared_secret.as_ref().unwrap();

    let ciphertext = encrypt(message, key);
    println!("Encrypted message: {:?}", ciphertext);

    let decrypted = decrypt(&ciphertext, key);
    println!(
        "Decrypted message: {}",
        String::from_utf8_lossy(&decrypted)
    );
}
```

Chapter 22

Asynchronous TLS Handshake Implementation

Conceptual Foundation

The Transport Layer Security handshake, as traditionally implemented, involves a series of blocking exchanges that negotiate cryptographic parameters and authenticate the communicating parties. In a non-blocking architecture, these exchanges are reformulated to accommodate asynchronous control flow, thereby decoupling cryptographic computations and message transmissions from the execution thread. The handshake process is viewed as the progression of an abstract state, where an initial state s_0 transitions through a predefined sequence until a secure session is established. Such an abstraction facilitates the reengineering of the protocol to support high concurrency and efficient resource utilization in environments demanding scalable network services.

Asynchronous State Transition Model

The handshake is modeled by a state machine in which each state represents a distinct phase of the TLS negotiation. Let the set S denote all possible states such that the handshake is characterized by a sequence $\{s_0, s_1, s_2, \ldots, s_k\}$, where s_0 is the initial state and s_k

151

represents a fully established secure session. The state transitions are governed by a function $T : S \to S$, wherein each invocation of T corresponds to the successful processing of handshake messages or cryptographic computations. The asynchronous setting is achieved by encapsulating each transition as a non-blocking operation that returns a future. With this design, the completion of $T(s)$ for a given state s is contingent on the arrival of requisite network events and the fulfillment of cryptographic verification tasks, thereby obviating any blocking I/O calls.

Integration with Async Runtimes

The implementation of a non-blocking TLS handshake is inherently intertwined with the asynchronous runtime environment. These runtimes provide an event-driven framework where input/output operations and computational tasks are scheduled independently of the main execution thread. Within this paradigm, each stage of the TLS handshake is expressed as an asynchronous task that is dispatched upon the receipt of network messages or the conclusion of cryptographic processing. The underlying asynchronous libraries leverage system primitives such as *epoll*, *kqueue*, or equivalent mechanisms, ensuring that the handshake tasks are activated based on the readiness of the underlying file descriptors. This integration allows the secure connection setup to operate concurrently with other network operations while adhering to the stringent requirements of non-blocking execution.

Concurrency Control and Message Sequencing

In the context of an asynchronous handshake, the ordering of protocol messages and the preservation of session integrity are critical considerations. The concurrent processing of handshake steps demands robust mechanisms that enforce the correct sequence of state transitions and prevent race conditions. To address these challenges, asynchronous message queues and task schedulers manage the incidence and ordering of events, ensuring that each handshake message is processed according to the protocol's specifications. Let Q represent the function that maps incoming messages to their designated protocol step; the integrity of the handshake is maintained only if Q preserves the invariant sequence of transitions. Such an ordering is typically achieved through the use of atomic operations and lock-free data structures that secure shared state across multiple asynchronous tasks, thereby ensuring that the processing order is consistent with the expected handshake progression.

Security Implications in Non-Blocking Handshake

The redesign of the TLS handshake to operate in a non-blocking environment introduces additional security considerations. Each state transition must be subject to rigorous verification to uphold the cryptographic assurances of the protocol. Non-blocking operations inherently introduce the possibility of interleaved execution, necessitating measures to guard against timing attacks and race conditions. Cryptographic functions, such as those abstracted by $F : M \times K \to C$, are implemented with constant-time execution considerations to mitigate side-channel leakage arising from asynchronous scheduling. The isolation of cryptographic operations from the I/O event loop ensures that sensitive key material and session parameters remain secure despite the concurrent processing environment. In this model, error handling routines are closely integrated with the state machine, detecting deviations and aborting the handshake if any anomaly is observed, thereby preserving the overall security and robustness of the secure connection setup.

Rust Code Snippet

```rust
use tokio::sync::mpsc;
use tokio::time::{sleep, Duration};
use std::error::Error;

/// Enum representing the distinct states of the TLS handshake.
#[derive(Debug)]
enum TlsState {
    Init,
    ClientHello,    // Sent ClientHello, waiting for ServerHello.
    ServerHello,    // Received ServerHello, waiting for Certificate.
    Certificate,    // Received Certificate, waiting for KeyExchange.
    KeyExchange,    // Received KeyExchange, waiting for Finished.
    Established,    // Handshake complete, secure session
    ↪   established.
```

153

```rust
        Error,          // Error state.
}

/// Struct representing the TLS handshaker state machine.
struct TlsHandshaker {
    state: TlsState,
}

impl TlsHandshaker {
    /// Create a new TlsHandshaker with the initial state.
    pub fn new() -> Self {
        Self {
            state: TlsState::Init,
        }
    }

    /// Transition the handshake state based on an incoming protocol
    ↪   message.
    ///
    /// This function emulates the transition function T: S -> S,
    /// where each asynchronous call may yield a new state after
    ↪   handling a message.
    async fn transition_state(&mut self, incoming: &str) ->
    ↪   Result<(), &'static str> {
        match self.state {
            TlsState::Init => {
                // Initiate handshake by sending ClientHello.
                // Here, we simulate sending by immediately
                ↪   transitioning to ClientHello.
                println!("State: {:?} -> Sending ClientHello",
                ↪   self.state);
                self.state = TlsState::ClientHello;
                Ok(())
            },
            TlsState::ClientHello => {
                if incoming == "ServerHello" {
                    println!("Received ServerHello. Transitioning to
                    ↪   ServerHello state.");
                    self.state = TlsState::ServerHello;
                    Ok(())
                } else {
                    self.state = TlsState::Error;
                    Err("Expected 'ServerHello' in ClientHello
                    ↪   state")
                }
            },
            TlsState::ServerHello => {
                if incoming == "Certificate" {
                    println!("Received Certificate. Transitioning to
                    ↪   Certificate state.");
                    self.state = TlsState::Certificate;
                    Ok(())
                } else {
```

154

```rust
                self.state = TlsState::Error;
                Err("Expected 'Certificate' in ServerHello
                ↪   state")
            }
        },
        TlsState::Certificate => {
            if incoming == "KeyExchange" {
                println!("Received KeyExchange. Transitioning to
                ↪   KeyExchange state.");
                self.state = TlsState::KeyExchange;
                Ok(())
            } else {
                self.state = TlsState::Error;
                Err("Expected 'KeyExchange' in Certificate
                ↪   state")
            }
        },
        TlsState::KeyExchange => {
            if incoming == "Finished" {
                println!("Received Finished. Handshake
                ↪   complete.");
                self.state = TlsState::Established;
                Ok(())
            } else {
                self.state = TlsState::Error;
                Err("Expected 'Finished' in KeyExchange state")
            }
        },
        _ => Err("Invalid state encountered during handshake"),
    }
}

/// Perform the asynchronous TLS handshake by processing
↪   incoming messages.
///
/// Each processed message represents an atomic state
↪   transition,
/// and the asynchronous runtime ensures that I/O events do not
↪   block the main thread.
async fn perform_handshake(&mut self, mut rx:
↪   mpsc::Receiver<String>) -> Result<(), &'static str> {
    // Start the handshake by initiating ClientHello.
    self.transition_state("ClientHello").await?;

    // Process incoming messages sequentially.
    while let Some(raw_msg) = rx.recv().await {
        // Simulate mapping raw network data to protocol
        ↪   messages Q(raw) = message.
        let message = map_message(&raw_msg);
        println!("Processing mapped message: {}", message);
        self.transition_state(&message).await?;
        if let TlsState::Established = self.state {
            println!("TLS Handshake established successfully.");
```

155

```rust
                return Ok(());
            }
            // Simulate non-blocking I/O delay.
            sleep(Duration::from_millis(100)).await;
        }
        Err("Handshake incomplete: message channel closed
        ↪ unexpectedly")
    }
}


/// Simulated cryptographic function F : M x K -> C implemented
↪ asynchronously.
///
/// This function performs a dummy constant-time XOR operation to
↪ mimic cryptographic processing.
/// In real-world scenarios, this would be a robust cryptographic
↪ algorithm ensuring constant-time execution.
async fn constant_time_crypto(message: &[u8], key: &[u8]) -> Vec<u8>
↪ {
    // Force a constant delay, independent of input, to mitigate
    ↪ timing attacks.
    sleep(Duration::from_millis(50)).await;
    // Dummy implementation: XOR each byte of the message with the
    ↪ key (cycling through key bytes).
    message.iter()
        .zip(key.iter().cycle())
        .map(|(m_byte, k_byte)| m_byte ^ k_byte)
        .collect()
}


/// Function to simulate mapping of raw network data to protocol
↪ messages.
///
/// In a fully implemented system, this function would perform
↪ comprehensive parsing
/// and validation of incoming data. Here, it directly returns the
↪ trimmed string.
fn map_message(raw: &str) -> String {
    raw.trim().to_string()
}


/// Main entry point for the asynchronous TLS handshake simulation.
///
/// This function sets up the asynchronous runtime, spawns a task to
↪ send simulated handshake messages,
/// and then drives the TLS handshake state machine.
#[tokio::main]
async fn main() -> Result<(), Box<dyn Error>> {
    // Create an asynchronous channel to simulate incoming TLS
    ↪ handshake messages.
    let (tx, rx) = mpsc::channel(10);
```

```rust
    // Spawn a task that simulates the server-side sending handshake
    ↪ messages.
    tokio::spawn(async move {
        let simulated_messages = vec!["ServerHello", "Certificate",
        ↪ "KeyExchange", "Finished"];
        for msg in simulated_messages {
            println!("Simulated sending of message: {}", msg);
            if let Err(e) = tx.send(msg.to_string()).await {
                eprintln!("Failed to send message: {}", e);
                break;
            }
            sleep(Duration::from_millis(100)).await;
        }
    });

    // Initialize the TLS handshaker.
    let mut handshaker = TlsHandshaker::new();

    // Perform the TLS handshake asynchronously.
    match handshaker.perform_handshake(rx).await {
        Ok(()) => println!("Handshake process completed
        ↪ successfully."),
        Err(e) => eprintln!("Handshake failed with error: {}", e),
    }

    // Demonstrate the simulated constant-time cryptographic
    ↪ function.
    let message = b"plaintext message";
    let key = b"secretkey";
    let encrypted = constant_time_crypto(message, key).await;
    println!("Encrypted message (dummy XOR): {:?}", encrypted);

    Ok(())
}
```

Chapter 23

Cryptographic Operations in Network Services

Foundations of Cryptographic Integration

The integration of cryptographic libraries into network services is predicated on a rigorous understanding of both theoretical and practical cryptographic principles. At its core, cryptographic integration involves the deployment of well-established mathematical functions that map plaintext messages and cryptographic keys to ciphertext, as expressed by the function

$$E : M \times K \to C,$$

and its inverse operation,

$$D : C \times K \to M.$$

In these expressions, M denotes the message space, K represents the key space, and C is the set of ciphertexts. Such a formulation creates a formal environment in which the properties of confidentiality, integrity, and authenticity can be systematically analyzed and assured. The selection of cryptographic libraries is guided by the need for proven security guarantees as well as by performance considerations inherent to high-throughput network services.

Encryption and Decryption Mechanisms

Encryption and decryption operations serve as the fundamental mechanisms for protecting data in network communications. Symmetric encryption algorithms rely on a single key to perform both encryption and decryption, and they are conventionally represented by the mapping

$$C = E_K(M),$$

where the secrecy of the key K is paramount. Asymmetric encryption, by contrast, employs a pair of keys—one public and one private, denoted by $(K_{\text{pub}}, K_{\text{priv}})$—to enable not only confidentiality but also authenticity and non-repudiation. The mathematical underpinnings of such algorithms often involve modular arithmetic, finite field computations, or elliptic curve operations, and their effectiveness is predicated on the computational intractability of problems such as prime factorization or the discrete logarithm. Integration of these operations into network services necessitates that the implementation be both efficient and secure, with considerations for optimal data block size, padding schemes, and the use of appropriate modes of operation to mitigate vulnerabilities.

Secure Key Exchange Protocols

The establishment of shared secrets over potentially untrusted networks is critical for maintaining secure communications between disparate entities. Key exchange protocols facilitate this process by enabling the derivation of common cryptographic keys without prior secure channels. The classical Diffie-Hellman protocol exemplifies this approach through the exchange of public components that are subsequently combined with private inputs to yield a shared secret. Formally, the protocol may be characterized by computations such as

$$g^a \mod p$$

and

$$g^b \mod p,$$

where g is a generator of a cyclic group and p is a large prime number. The resultant shared key is derived from the relation

$$K_{\text{shared}} = (g^b)^a \mod p = (g^a)^b \mod p.$$

More recent advances, such as Elliptic Curve Diffie-Hellman (ECDH), exploit the algebraic structure of elliptic curves to achieve comparable security with reduced computational overhead. The integration of key exchange protocols within a network service framework leverages cryptographic libraries that provide robust implementations of these protocols, ensuring that the exchange process adheres to established security assumptions and is resilient to a variety of cryptanalytic attacks.

Integration Strategies and System Considerations

The successful deployment of cryptographic operations within network services demands a careful orchestration between low-level cryptographic routines and high-level service architectures. In environments that mandate high concurrency and non-blocking behavior, it is essential that cryptographic functions are integrated in a manner that minimizes impact on throughput and latency. This integration is achieved by encapsulating cryptographic operations in modular components that interface seamlessly with asynchronous I/O frameworks. Such components are designed to operate in constant time where required, thus mitigating the risk of timing attacks and side-channel leaks. In addition, the integration strategy must account for the rigorous synchronization of cryptographic state across distributed systems, ensuring that secure key distribution, storage, and destruction are managed per established best practices. Performance optimizations, including hardware acceleration and parallel processing, are frequently employed to offset the computational cost of cryptographic operations while preserving the overall responsiveness of the network service.

Rust Code Snippet

```
//! This example demonstrates key cryptographic concepts from the
↪   chapter:
//! 1. Formal encryption/decryption mappings: E : M × K → C and D :
↪   C × K → M.
//!    Here, a simple XOR (symmetric) cipher is used for
↪   demonstration.
//!
//! 2. Diffie-Hellman key exchange protocol, where:
```

160

```
//!    - Public key computations: A = g^a mod p, B = g^b mod p
//!    - Shared secret derivation: K_shared = (g^a)^b mod p =
↪   (g^b)^a mod p
//!
//! Although the operations here are simplified (and use small
↪   numbers / a basic XOR cipher),
//! they illustrate the core equations and ideas discussed in the
↪   chapter.

extern crate rand;

use rand::Rng;

/// Performs modular exponentiation using the binary (exponentiation
↪   by squaring) algorithm.
/// This function computes (base^exp) mod modulus.
///
/// # Arguments
/// * `base` - The base number in the exponentiation.
/// * `exp` - The exponent.
/// * `modulus` - The modulus for the operation.
///
/// # Returns
/// * A u64 representing (base^exp) mod modulus.
fn mod_exp(mut base: u64, mut exp: u64, modulus: u64) -> u64 {
    let mut result: u64 = 1;
    base %= modulus;
    while exp > 0 {
        if exp & 1 == 1 {
            result = (result * base) % modulus;
        }
        exp >>= 1;
        base = (base * base) % modulus;
    }
    result
}

/// Symmetric encryption function that maps:
///    E : M × K → C
/// using a simple XOR cipher for demonstration.
/// In practice, use a robust algorithm like AES for
↪   confidentiality.
///
/// # Arguments
/// * `plaintext` - A slice of bytes representing the message M.
/// * `key` - A single byte key K.
///
/// # Returns
/// * A Vec<u8> containing the ciphertext C.
fn symmetric_encrypt(plaintext: &[u8], key: u8) -> Vec<u8> {
    // Each byte is XOR-ed with the key. (NOT SECURE, demo only)
    plaintext.iter().map(|byte| byte ^ key).collect()
}
```

161

```rust
/// Symmetric decryption function that maps:
///     D : C × K → M
/// using the same XOR cipher. Since XOR is its own inverse, the
/// ↪ operation is identical.
///
/// # Arguments
/// * `ciphertext` - A slice of bytes representing encrypted data C.
/// * `key` - The same key used for encryption K.
///
/// # Returns
/// * A Vec<u8> with the decrypted plaintext M.
fn symmetric_decrypt(ciphertext: &[u8], key: u8) -> Vec<u8> {
    ciphertext.iter().map(|byte| byte ^ key).collect()
}

fn main() {
    // Diffie-Hellman parameters.
    // NOTE: In real applications, p should be a large prime (e.g.,
    // ↪ 2048+ bits) and g a primitive root modulo p.
    const P: u64 = 23; // A small prime for demonstration purposes.
    const G: u64 = 5;  // A primitive root modulo P for
    // ↪ demonstration.

    let mut rng = rand::thread_rng();

    // Each party selects a private key: a and b, where 1 < key < P.
    let alice_private: u64 = rng.gen_range(2..P);
    let bob_private: u64 = rng.gen_range(2..P);

    // Compute public keys:
    // Alice computes A = g^a mod p.
    // Bob computes B = g^b mod p.
    let alice_public = mod_exp(G, alice_private, P);
    let bob_public = mod_exp(G, bob_private, P);

    // Both parties compute the shared secret.
    // Alice computes shared = B^a mod p.
    // Bob computes shared = A^b mod p.
    let alice_shared = mod_exp(bob_public, alice_private, P);
    let bob_shared = mod_exp(alice_public, bob_private, P);

    println!("Diffie-Hellman Key Exchange Demonstration:");
    println!("--------------------------------------------");
    println!("Global Parameters: p = {}, g = {}", P, G);
    println!("Alice's Private Key (a): {}", alice_private);
    println!("Bob's Private Key (b): {}", bob_private);
    println!("Alice's Public Key (A): {}", alice_public);
    println!("Bob's Public Key (B): {}", bob_public);
    println!("Alice's Computed Shared Secret: {}", alice_shared);
    println!("Bob's Computed Shared Secret: {}", bob_shared);

    // Ensure both computed the same shared secret.
```

162

```rust
    assert_eq!(alice_shared, bob_shared);
    let shared_secret = alice_shared;

    // For demonstration of symmetric encryption/decryption,
    // derive a simple 8-bit key from the shared secret.
    // In practice, use a key derivation function to obtain a key
    ↪    for AES or another cipher.
    let symmetric_key: u8 = (shared_secret % 256) as u8;
    println!("\nDerived symmetric key (8-bit): {}", symmetric_key);

    // Define a plaintext message.
    let plaintext = b"Hello, secure world! This message uses
    ↪    Cryptographic Operations.";

    // Encrypt the message.
    let ciphertext = symmetric_encrypt(plaintext, symmetric_key);
    // Decrypt the message.
    let decrypted = symmetric_decrypt(&ciphertext, symmetric_key);

    println!("\nSymmetric Encryption Demonstration:");
    println!("Plaintext: {}", String::from_utf8_lossy(plaintext));
    println!("Ciphertext (in hex):");
    for byte in &ciphertext {
        print!("{:02X} ", byte);
    }
    println!("\nDecrypted: {}",
    ↪    String::from_utf8_lossy(&decrypted));

    // Ensure decryption recovers the original plaintext.
    assert_eq!(plaintext.to_vec(), decrypted);
}
```

Chapter 24

Building Secure WebSocket Servers

Secure Handshake Protocols

The initiation of a WebSocket connection is realized through a handshake protocol that commences over an HTTP channel. This process is characterized by an HTTP request that includes specific headers such as $Upgrade : websocket$ and $Connection : Upgrade$, as well as a unique client-generated key encapsulated in the Sec-$WebSocket$-Key header. The server, upon receipt of this request, concatenates the provided key with the globally defined identifier $258EAFA5$-$E914$-$47DA$-$95CA$-$C5AB0DC85B11$, and subjects the resultant value to a cryptographic hash function, typically employing the SHA-1 algorithm. The hash output is then encoded using Base64 and returned within the Sec-$WebSocket$-$Accept$ header, thereby validating the continuity of the handshake process. This protocol is designed to serve as a mutual verification mechanism that reinforces the integrity of the upgrade procedure and ensures that any transient or injected messages are promptly identifiable. The handshake mechanism, when executed in conjunction with transport layer security, provides robust protection against a variety of network-based adversarial techniques.

Connection Upgrade Mechanisms

The transition from an HTTP connection to a persistent Web-Socket communication channel is governed by a stringent upgrade mechanism. Upon successful validation of the handshake, the server responds with an HTTP status code 101 (Switching Protocols), signifying its agreement to supplant the original HTTP semantics with the full-duplex, bidirectional messaging model stipulated by the WebSocket protocol. This transition is predicated on a precise adherence to the specifications detailed in RFC 6455, where the accurate parsing and verification of HTTP headers are of paramount importance. The server must validate not only the syntactic correctness of the upgrade request but also implement temporal constraints to mitigate the risk of replay or injection attacks. The establishment of this upgraded connection implicitly assumes that the integrity of the prior handshake has been uncompromised and that a secure exchange of cryptographic parameters has been achieved, thereby setting the stage for sustained, secure communication.

Persistent Communication and Session Integrity

Once the connection upgrade is successfully executed, the resulting persistent communication channel assumes critical importance. Long-lived WebSocket connections are inherently vulnerable to a spectrum of security challenges, necessitating continuous, in-depth monitoring and management of session state. In this regard, the persistent channel is maintained securely through the exchange of control frames—such as ping and pong messages—which serve to verify the ongoing integrity of the connection. These control frames are instrumental in the detection of any anomalies that might indicate an attempted session hijack or data injection. Moreover, substantial emphasis is placed on the periodic rotation of cryptographic keys and the revalidation of session parameters to prevent the temporal degradation of data confidentiality and integrity. The server must apply rigorous authentication protocols during the lifecycle of the connection, ensuring that any deviation from established security norms, including unauthorized frame injection or protocol deviation, is promptly identified and isolated. The overall strategy encapsulates a disciplined approach to stateful session management, where formalized cryptographic primitives are sustained through continuous monitoring and systematic re-negotiation of session parameters, thereby preserving a secure and resilient communication channel.

Rust Code Snippet

```rust
use tokio::net::{TcpListener, TcpStream};
use tokio::io::{AsyncReadExt, AsyncWriteExt};
use tokio::time::{sleep, Duration};
use sha1::{Sha1, Digest};
use base64::{engine::general_purpose, Engine as _};
use std::str;

// The constant magic string as defined in RFC 6455.
const MAGIC_STRING: &str = "258EAFA5-E914-47DA-95CA-C5AB0DC85B11";

/// Compute the Sec-WebSocket-Accept header value.
/// It implements the algorithm:
///    accept_key = base64( SHA1( sec_websocket_key + MAGIC_STRING) )
fn compute_accept_key(sec_websocket_key: &str) -> String {
    // Concatenate the client's key with the magic string.
    let concatenated = format!("{}{}", sec_websocket_key.trim(),
    ↪ MAGIC_STRING);
    // Create a SHA-1 hasher instance and process the concatenated
    ↪ string.
    let mut hasher = Sha1::new();
    hasher.update(concatenated.as_bytes());
    let hash = hasher.finalize();
    // Encode the resulting hash using Base64.
    general_purpose::STANDARD.encode(hash)
}

/// Perform the WebSocket handshake by parsing the client's HTTP
↪ request,
/// computing the Sec-WebSocket-Accept value, and sending the
↪ corresponding
/// HTTP 101 Switching Protocols response.
async fn perform_handshake(stream: &mut TcpStream) -> Result<String,
↪ Box<dyn std::error::Error>> {
    // Create a buffer to read the client's handshake request.
    let mut buffer = [0u8; 1024];
    let n = stream.read(&mut buffer).await?;
    let request = str::from_utf8(&buffer[..n])?;

    // Extract the Sec-WebSocket-Key header value.
    let sec_key_line = request.lines()
        .find(|line| line.starts_with("Sec-WebSocket-Key:"))
        .ok_or("Missing Sec-WebSocket-Key header")?;
    let sec_key = sec_key_line.split(':').nth(1)
                    .ok_or("Invalid Sec-WebSocket-Key header")?
```

```
            .trim();

    // Compute the accept key using the provided key.
    let accept_key = compute_accept_key(sec_key);

    // Build the HTTP response to complete the handshake.
    let response = format!(
        "HTTP/1.1 101 Switching Protocols\r\n\
         Upgrade: websocket\r\n\
         Connection: Upgrade\r\n\
         Sec-WebSocket-Accept: {}\r\n\r\n",
        accept_key
    );
    stream.write_all(response.as_bytes()).await?;
    Ok(accept_key)
}

/// Handle the persistent communication with the client after a
↪   successful handshake.
/// This includes processing basic WebSocket control frames (e.g.,
↪   ping/pong)
/// to maintain session integrity.
async fn handle_connection(mut stream: TcpStream) -> Result<(),
↪   Box<dyn std::error::Error>> {
    // Perform the handshake procedure.
    let accept_key = perform_handshake(&mut stream).await?;
    println!("Handshake completed. Computed Sec-WebSocket-Accept:
↪   {}", accept_key);

    // Enter a loop to simulate persistent connection handling.
    loop {
        // Allocate a small buffer to receive a potential ping
        ↪   frame.
        let mut frame_buffer = [0u8; 2];
        let n = stream.read(&mut frame_buffer).await?;
        if n == 0 {
            // Connection has been closed by the client.
            println!("Client closed the connection.");
            break;
        }

        // For demonstration purposes, we assume that a ping message
        ↪   is represented
        // by the byte sequence [0x89, 0x00] (where 0x89 is the
        ↪   opcode for Ping).
        if frame_buffer == [0x89, 0x00] {
            println!("Received Ping; replying with Pong.");
            // A Pong frame is represented with opcode 0x8A.
            let pong_frame = [0x8A, 0x00];
            stream.write_all(&pong_frame).await?;
        }
```

```rust
        // Periodically send a Ping frame to the client to verify
        ↪   session integrity.
        // In a production system, this would be scheduled
        ↪   independently.
        sleep(Duration::from_secs(30)).await;
        println!("Sending periodic Ping to client.");
        let ping_frame = [0x89, 0x00];
        stream.write_all(&ping_frame).await?;
    }
    Ok(())
}

#[tokio::main]
async fn main() -> Result<(), Box<dyn std::error::Error>> {
    // Bind the server to a local address.
    let listener = TcpListener::bind("127.0.0.1:9001").await?;
    println!("WebSocket server is running at ws://127.0.0.1:9001");

    // Accept incoming connections in an infinite loop.
    loop {
        let (stream, addr) = listener.accept().await?;
        println!("New connection established from: {}", addr);
        // Spawn a new asynchronous task to handle the connection.
        tokio::spawn(async move {
            if let Err(e) = handle_connection(stream).await {
                eprintln!("Error handling connection from {}: {}",
                ↪   addr, e);
            }
        });
    }
}
```

168

Chapter 25

Frame Processing and Async Messaging in WebSockets

Efficient Frame Parsing in WebSocket Communication

The WebSocket protocol defines a binary framing format that necessitates a rigorous approach to frame parsing. At the outset, each frame is composed of a fixed header segment followed by an optional extended payload length field, a masking key, and the payload data. The first byte of the header encodes the FIN flag, which indicates whether the frame is the final fragment in a message (1 for final, 0 otherwise), as well as reserved bits that are typically set to 0 unless negotiated extensions are in place. The second byte includes the masking indicator and a payload length value, where the presence of a value equal to 126 or 127 serves as an indicator that additional bytes must be interpreted as the payload length. In scenarios where the masking bit is active, a subsequent four-byte masking key is employed to obfuscate the payload, and the unmasking process requires a bitwise operation between the key and the payload data. This parsing procedure must be executed with utmost efficiency, minimizing buffer copies and redundant computations, while accurately interpreting the structure defined by the protocol. Each step—ranging from header extraction and extended length evaluation to payload decoding—is critical for maintaining low latency and high throughput in real-time communication systems.

Message Buffering and Data Integrity

Robust message buffering mechanisms form the backbone of reliable WebSocket communication, particularly in environments where frame fragmentation is common. Due to the transport characteristics of the underlying network, data may be received in segments that do not necessarily correspond to complete messages. Buffering strategies must thus accommodate partial frames and seamlessly reassemble them according to the sequence delineated by the frame headers. The buffering subsystem maintains a mutable data store into which incoming frame fragments are deposited until a complete message can be reconstructed. This process involves tracking frame boundaries, verifying completeness by examining flagged indicators such as the FIN bit, and ensuring that control frames do not disrupt the logical consistency of message sequence reassembly. In parallel, integrity checks such as checksum validations or parity assessments may be applied during the buffering stage to detect transmission errors, thereby safeguarding the data stream from accidental corruption and malicious injection. The interplay between the buffering layer and the frame parser demands a high degree of coordination to ensure that the aggregated data reflects the precise semantics intended by the sender.

Asynchronous Handling and Processing Pipeline

The processing of WebSocket frames in high-concurrency applications benefits from an asynchronous handling paradigm that decouples the reception of data from its subsequent processing. Asynchronous models allow incoming frames to be enqueued within a task-based processing pipeline, where each stage of the pipeline undertakes a specific role—from initial frame parsing to detailed message assembly and control frame management. The asynchronous pipeline is typically orchestrated by an event loop that schedules non-blocking tasks, thereby facilitating concurrent processing of multiple connections with minimal context switching overhead.

Within this architecture, the frame parser operates as an independent module that extracts header details and payload data before dispatching the resulting message fragments to a buffering subsystem. Concurrently, dedicated controllers monitor the state of each connection, managing control frames such as ping and pong signals to uphold session integrity and ensure timely communication. The design of such an asynchronous processing framework mandates careful consideration of synchronization primitives and resource allocation tactics to prevent race conditions and ensure that the overall system scales effectively under heavy loads. The modular structure of the processing pipeline enables fine-grained optimization, where each component can be refined independently to maximize the efficiency of the entire WebSocket communication system.

Rust Code Snippet

```rust
use tokio::sync::mpsc;
use tokio::time::{sleep, Duration};
use std::error::Error;

/// Representation of a parsed WebSocket frame.
#[derive(Debug)]
pub struct WebSocketFrame {
    pub fin: bool,          // true if this is the final frame in a
                            // message.
    pub opcode: u8,         // operation code (e.g., 1 for text, 2
                            // for binary).
    pub mask: bool,         // true if the payload is masked.
    pub payload_len: u64,   // length of the payload.
    pub mask_key: Option<[u8; 4]>, // present only if `mask` is
                            // true.
    pub payload: Vec<u8>,   // actual payload data.
}

/// Parses a slice of bytes into a WebSocket frame according to the
/// RFC.
/// Returns the parsed frame and the number of bytes consumed from
/// the buffer.
pub fn parse_frame(buffer: &[u8]) -> Result<(WebSocketFrame, usize),
    String> {
    if buffer.len() < 2 {
        return Err("Buffer too short to contain
            header".to_string());
    }
    let byte1 = buffer[0];
    let byte2 = buffer[1];
```

171

```rust
// First byte: FIN flag and opcode.
let fin = (byte1 & 0x80) != 0;
let opcode = byte1 & 0x0F;

// Second byte: Mask bit and initial payload length.
let mask = (byte2 & 0x80) != 0;
let mut payload_len = (byte2 & 0x7F) as u64;
let mut pos = 2;

// Extended payload length (16 or 64-bit) if necessary.
if payload_len == 126 {
    if buffer.len() < pos + 2 {
        return Err("Buffer too short for 16-bit extended payload
        ↪  length".to_string());
    }
    payload_len = u16::from_be_bytes([buffer[pos], buffer[pos +
    ↪  1]]) as u64;
    pos += 2;
} else if payload_len == 127 {
    if buffer.len() < pos + 8 {
        return Err("Buffer too short for 64-bit extended payload
        ↪  length".to_string());
    }
    payload_len = u64::from_be_bytes([
        buffer[pos], buffer[pos + 1], buffer[pos + 2],
        ↪  buffer[pos + 3],
        buffer[pos + 4], buffer[pos + 5], buffer[pos + 6],
        ↪  buffer[pos + 7],
    ]);
    pos += 8;
}

// Read masking key if present.
let mask_key = if mask {
    if buffer.len() < pos + 4 {
        return Err("Buffer too short for masking
        ↪  key".to_string());
    }
    let key = [buffer[pos], buffer[pos + 1], buffer[pos + 2],
    ↪  buffer[pos + 3]];
    pos += 4;
    Some(key)
} else {
    None
};

// Check if buffer has the complete payload data.
if buffer.len() < pos + payload_len as usize {
    return Err("Buffer does not contain complete payload
    ↪  data".to_string());
}
```

172

```rust
    let mut payload = buffer[pos..pos + payload_len as
    ↪    usize].to_vec();
    // If payload is masked, unmask it by XOR-ing every byte with
    ↪    the mask key (cycling over 4 bytes).
    if let Some(key) = mask_key {
        for i in 0..payload.len() {
            payload[i] ^= key[i % 4];
        }
    }
    pos += payload_len as usize;

    Ok((WebSocketFrame { fin, opcode, mask, payload_len, mask_key,
    ↪    payload }, pos))
}

/// A simple buffering mechanism to accumulate payload fragments
↪    from potentially
/// fragmented WebSocket frames. When a frame with FIN=true is
↪    received, the
/// complete message is returned.
pub struct MessageBuffer {
    data: Vec<u8>,
}

impl MessageBuffer {
    pub fn new() -> Self {
        Self { data: Vec::new() }
    }

    /// Append the payload of the given frame to the buffer.
    /// If the FIN flag is set, returns the complete reassembled
    ↪    message.
    pub fn append_frame(&mut self, frame: &WebSocketFrame) ->
    ↪    Option<Vec<u8>> {
        self.data.extend(&frame.payload);
        if frame.fin {
            let complete_message = self.data.clone();
            self.data.clear();
            Some(complete_message)
        } else {
            None
        }
    }
}

/// Asynchronous consumer that processes complete messages received
↪    through
/// a Tokio channel. In a real application, further validation and
↪    processing could be done.
async fn process_messages(mut rx: mpsc::Receiver<Vec<u8>>) {
    while let Some(message) = rx.recv().await {
        println!("Received complete message: {:?}",
        ↪    String::from_utf8_lossy(&message));
```

173

```
        }
    }

/// Simulates receiving connection data in fragments, parsing
↪   WebSocket frames,
/// buffering incomplete messages, and publishing complete messages
↪   to a channel.
async fn simulate_connection(mut tx: mpsc::Sender<Vec<u8>>) {
    // Simulated raw data of a complete masked WebSocket frame
    ↪   carrying the text "Hello".
    //
    // Frame breakdown:
    //   Byte 0: 0x81 -> FIN=1, opcode=1 (text frame)
    //   Byte 1: 0x85 -> MASK=1, payload length=5
    //   Bytes 2-5: Masking key [0x01, 0x02, 0x03, 0x04]
    //   Bytes 6-10: Masked payload where each byte is:
    //       original XOR mask_key[i % 4]
    //   For "Hello": [0x48, 0x65, 0x6C, 0x6C, 0x6F] are the
    ↪   original bytes.
    //   Masked payload:
    //       0x48 ^ 0x01, 0x65 ^ 0x02, 0x6C ^ 0x03, 0x6C ^ 0x04,
    ↪   0x6F ^ 0x01
    //   This yields the following masked bytes.
    let raw_frame: Vec<u8> = vec![
        0x81, 0x85,                 // FIN+opcode, MASK+payload length
        0x01, 0x02, 0x03, 0x04,     // Masking key
        0x48 ^ 0x01,                // 'H' masked
        0x65 ^ 0x02,                // 'e' masked
        0x6C ^ 0x03,                // 'l' masked
        0x6C ^ 0x04,                // 'l' masked
        0x6F ^ 0x01,                // 'o' masked (key cycles back)
    ];

    // To simulate network conditions, split the frame into two
    ↪   fragments.
    let chunks = vec![
        raw_frame[..4].to_vec(),  // First part: header + part of
        ↪   masking key.
        raw_frame[4..].to_vec(),  // Second part: remainder of
        ↪   masking key and payload.
    ];

    let mut buffer = Vec::new();
    let mut msg_buffer = MessageBuffer::new();

    // Process each chunk with an artificial delay.
    for chunk in chunks {
        sleep(Duration::from_millis(100)).await;
        buffer.extend(chunk);

        // Attempt to parse and process as many complete frames as
        ↪   possible.
        loop {
```

174

```
        match parse_frame(&buffer) {
            Ok((frame, consumed)) => {
                // Remove the processed bytes from buffer.
                buffer.drain(0..consumed);
                if let Some(message) =
                ↪  msg_buffer.append_frame(&frame) {
                    // When a complete message is reassembled,
                    ↪  send it to the consumer.
                    if let Err(e) = tx.send(message).await {
                        eprintln!("Failed to send complete
                        ↪  message: {}", e);
                        return;
                    }
                }
            }
            Err(_) => {
                // Likely due to incomplete data. Wait for more
                ↪  data.
                break;
            }
        }
    }
  }
}

#[tokio::main]
async fn main() -> Result<(), Box<dyn Error>> {
    // Create a channel for passing complete messages between the
    ↪  parsing pipeline and processing task.
    let (tx, rx) = mpsc::channel(10);

    // Spawn the asynchronous tasks.
    let processor = tokio::spawn(process_messages(rx));
    let simulator = tokio::spawn(simulate_connection(tx));

    // Wait for the simulator to finish feeding data.
    simulator.await?;
    // Allow some extra time for any remaining messages to be
    ↪  processed.
    sleep(Duration::from_millis(500)).await;
    // Ensure the processor task completes (in a real server, main
    ↪  might run indefinitely).
    processor.await?;
    Ok(())
}
```

Chapter 26

Real-Time Bi-Directional Communication

Duplex Channel Architecture

The conceptual framework underlying duplex communication in WebSocket-based systems is predicated on the establishment of symmetric data paths that concurrently support message initiation and reception. A persistent connection, typically underpinned by the reliable, ordered delivery semantics of TCP, serves as the foundational transport layer for these channels. The WebSocket protocol encapsulates data into frames that are interleaved with control signals, thereby enabling the transmission of both application-specific and protocol-level messages. Each frame comprises header elements that demarcate the boundaries of a message, including a FIN flag to indicate finality, and length indicators that accommodate variable payload sizes. The resulting architecture permits the parallel exchange of messages in both directions, effectively partitioning the communication link into independent ingress and egress streams. This duality is critical for sustaining real-time interactions, wherein the rapid propagation of updates in either direction is essential for preserving system responsiveness.

Asynchronous Data Flow and Synchronization Mechanisms

An asynchronous paradigm is instrumental in managing the concurrent processing demands inherent in real-time duplex communication. The system's operation is orchestrated by an event loop that schedules non-blocking operations across multiple execution contexts. In this environment, the reception and emission of frames are decoupled to prevent contention between the two channels. Incoming frame fragments are aggregated in dedicated buffers that employ well-defined synchronization protocols, ensuring that the reassembly of fragmented messages proceeds in an orderly and consistent manner. Mathematical constructs governing this reassembly process, such as the balance between the rates of message production and consumption, are characterized by parameters like the maximum allowable delay Δt. These mechanisms are precisely calibrated to inhibit race conditions and prevent data corruption, as they enforce a strict ordering of events without incurring excessive locking overhead. The outcome is a robust asynchronous data flow model that inherently accommodates the complexity of bidirectional message scheduling and stateful connection management.

Performance Optimization and Robustness in Real-Time Communication

Optimizing performance in the context of real-time bi-directional communication requires a comprehensive examination of latency sources and throughput limitations. Critical to this analysis is the minimization of overhead associated with frame parsing, buffer management, and context switching between concurrent tasks. The architectural design leverages techniques such as zero-copy data processing and in situ message handling to reduce redundant memory operations. These measures serve to curtail the time spent on data marshalling and ensure that the delay induced by internal processing remains bounded. Quantitative models, wherein throughput T is maximized while keeping delay D within stringent limits, guide the fine-tuning of system parameters. Robustness is further enhanced by incorporating adaptive buffering strategies that dynamically adjust to variations in network conditions, thereby mitigating the impact of transient congestion or jitter. The integrated

177

design emphasizes minimal interference between simultaneous data flows, ensuring that the duplex channel maintains high fidelity under diverse operational stresses.

Rust Code Snippet

```
/*
    Simulation of a duplex channel for real-time bi-directional
    ↪  communication,
    demonstrating key equations and algorithms discussed in the
    ↪  chapter.

    Key Equations and Metrics:
      - Throughput (T) = N / t, where N is the number of messages
    ↪  processed and t is the elapsed time.
      - Maximum allowable delay (MAX_DELAY) is set to 50
    ↪  milliseconds (example value).
      - Round-trip delay is computed to ensure that processing
    ↪  delays do not exceed MAX_DELAY.

    Algorithm Overview:
      1. A client task asynchronously sends messages to a server
    ↪  task through a channel.
      2. The server task receives and processes each message,
    ↪  simulating a processing delay,
         and then returns an acknowledgment via a separate channel.
      3. The client collects acknowledgments and calculates
    ↪  performance metrics (throughput and delays).
      4. Warnings are printed if processing or round-trip delays
    ↪  exceed the specified MAX_DELAY.
*/

use tokio::sync::mpsc;
use tokio::time::{sleep, Duration, Instant};

#[derive(Debug)]
struct Message {
    id: u32,
    // Timestamp when the message was created or sent.
    sent: Instant,
}

#[tokio::main]
async fn main() {
    // Number of messages to be exchanged.
    const NUM_MESSAGES: u32 = 100;
    // Maximum allowable delay for processing or round-trip (t).
    const MAX_DELAY: Duration = Duration::from_millis(50);

    // Channel from client to server.
```

```rust
let (client_to_server_tx, mut client_to_server_rx) =
    mpsc::channel::<Message>(NUM_MESSAGES as usize);
// Channel from server to client (acknowledgments).
let (server_to_client_tx, mut server_to_client_rx) =
    mpsc::channel::<Message>(NUM_MESSAGES as usize);

// Spawn the server task.
let server_handle = tokio::spawn(async move {
    while let Some(msg) = client_to_server_rx.recv().await {
        // Calculate processing delay.
        let processing_delay =
        ↪   Instant::now().duration_since(msg.sent);
        if processing_delay > MAX_DELAY {
            println!("Server: Warning, processing delay {:?}
            ↪   exceeds MAX_DELAY", processing_delay);
        }
        // Simulate server-side processing delay (e.g.,
        ↪   zero-copy handling).
        sleep(Duration::from_millis(10)).await;
        // Prepare acknowledgment message.
        let ack = Message {
            id: msg.id,
            // Record the time at which the ack is sent.
            sent: Instant::now(),
        };
        server_to_client_tx.send(ack).await.unwrap();
    }
});

// Spawn the client task.
let client_handle = tokio::spawn(async move {
    let mut sent_count: u32 = 0;
    let start_time = Instant::now();

    // Send messages asynchronously.
    for i in 0..NUM_MESSAGES {
        let msg = Message {
            id: i,
            sent: Instant::now(),
        };
        client_to_server_tx.send(msg).await.unwrap();
        sent_count += 1;
        // Introduce a small delay between sends to mimic
        ↪   non-blocking event scheduling.
        sleep(Duration::from_millis(5)).await;
    }

    // Process acknowledgments from the server.
    let mut ack_count = 0;
    while ack_count < NUM_MESSAGES {
        if let Some(response) = server_to_client_rx.recv().await
        ↪   {
```

179

```rust
            // Compute round-trip delay (note: this is
            ↪  approximated with the ack's timestamp).
            let round_trip =
            ↪  Instant::now().duration_since(response.sent);
            if round_trip > MAX_DELAY {
                println!("Client: Warning, round-trip delay {:?}
                ↪  exceeds MAX_DELAY", round_trip);
            }
            ack_count += 1;
        }
    }

    // Calculate the total elapsed time.
    let elapsed = Instant::now().duration_since(start_time);
    // Compute throughput T = N / t.
    let throughput = sent_count as f64 / elapsed.as_secs_f64();
    println!(
        "Client: Throughput (T) = {:.2} messages/sec, Total
        ↪  messages: {}, Elapsed time: {:?}",
        throughput, sent_count, elapsed
    );
});

// Await the completion of both server and client tasks.
let _ = tokio::join!(server_handle, client_handle);
}
```

Chapter 27

Leveraging Async Channels for Intra-Service Communication

System Architecture of Asynchronous Messaging

Intra-service communication within modern distributed systems is frequently architected around asynchronous channels that facilitate decoupled message propagation between service components. This design paradigm emphasizes the segregation of message-producing and message-consuming agents, thereby creating a non-blocking conduit for event notifications and data transfers. The temporal dynamics of messaging can be modeled by the relation $T = N/\Delta t$, where N represents the number of messages transmitted over a time interval Δt and T denotes the resultant throughput. Such formulations underscore the inherent scalability of asynchronous communication by abstracting message flow into quantifiable performance metrics. The underlying architecture is meticulously engineered to eliminate resource contention, ensuring that internal message exchanges do not impede parallel processing nor degrade system responsiveness under high-load conditions.

Design and Properties of Tokio Channels and Asynchronous Primitives

Tokio channels constitute a core component of the asynchronous primitives employed for internal messaging in Rust-based systems. These channels are designed with rigorous attention to memory safety and concurrency correctness, offering both bounded and unbounded configurations that cater to varying operational constraints. The bounded variant introduces a natural back-pressure mechanism that limits the queue length, while the unbounded channels allow for unrestricted message accumulation in scenarios where throughput considerations prevail over memory constraints. In each case, the channels enforce strict first-in-first-out (FIFO) semantics. The inherent scheduling of message transmission is governed by an event-driven runtime that optimizes non-blocking operations, ensuring that channel operations incur minimal overhead. This deliberate design not only guarantees reliable message ordering but also facilitates high-fidelity intra-service communication by harmonizing asynchronous execution with deterministic processing behavior.

Performance Considerations and Latency Analysis

Performance evaluation of asynchronous channels requires careful analysis of both latency and throughput parameters. The operational efficiency of these channels is critically dependent on minimizing the delays incurred during message enqueuing, transmission, and dequeueing. The processing delay, denoted by δ, must be maintained well below the latency threshold to prevent performance degradation. Analytical models characterize system performance by evaluating the balance between channel capacity and the frequency of asynchronous task scheduling. Such models capture the cost of context switching and message buffering, thereby delineating the conditions under which optimal throughput is achieved. By employing non-blocking, lock-free data structures as the basis for message queuing, Tokio channels significantly reduce the computational overhead associated with data marshalling. This leads to a proportional improvement in throughput, as the system is capable of sustaining high volumes of messages while keeping the average latency within a tightly constrained bound.

Robustness, Synchronization, and Error Resilience in Asynchronous Communication

The robustness of intra-service messaging is underpinned by a synthesis of advanced synchronization techniques and error-resilient design patterns. Async channels integrate atomic operations and lock-free algorithms to synchronize concurrent activities, thereby precluding race conditions and ensuring data consistency. In scenarios where transient inconsistencies or network-induced anomalies occur, error signaling is executed through non-blocking protocols that enable rapid detection and remediation. The synchronization mechanisms embedded in these channels are designed to uphold strict protocol invariants, ensuring that message ordering remains inviolate even in the presence of contention among concurrent tasks. Such properties are essential in distributed environments where service components operate in a loosely coupled yet interdependent fashion. The deliberate focus on resilience and state consistency across asynchronous channels contributes to a robust messaging framework capable of sustaining high-performance internal communications in complex, multi-component systems.

Rust Code Snippet

```
use tokio::sync::mpsc;
use tokio::time::{sleep, Instant, Duration};
use std::sync::Arc;
use std::sync::atomic::{AtomicU64, Ordering};

// Define a message structure that carries a unique identifier and
↪   the timestamp when it was sent.
struct Message {
    id: u64,
    sent: Instant,
}

// Constants to configure the simulation.
const CHANNEL_CAPACITY: usize = 100; // Bounded channel capacity to
↪   implement back-pressure.
const N_MESSAGES: u64 = 1000;         // Total number of messages to
↪   be sent.
```

```rust
// Main asynchronous runtime entry point.
#[tokio::main]
async fn main() {
    // Create a bounded channel with the specified capacity.
    let (tx, mut rx) = mpsc::channel::<Message>(CHANNEL_CAPACITY);

    // Atomic counters used to track the number of processed
    // ↳ messages and accumulate total latency in microseconds.
    let msg_counter = Arc::new(AtomicU64::new(0));
    let total_latency = Arc::new(AtomicU64::new(0));

    // Spawn a consumer task to receive messages from the channel.
    // This simulates the message-consuming agent in the
    // ↳ intra-service architecture.
    let consumer_counter = msg_counter.clone();
    let consumer_latency = total_latency.clone();
    let consumer_handle = tokio::spawn(async move {
        // Continuously receive messages until the channel is
        // ↳ closed.
        while let Some(message) = rx.recv().await {
            // Simulate processing delay (e.g., computation or I/O
            // ↳ work).
            let processing_delay = Duration::from_micros(50);
            sleep(processing_delay).await;

            // Compute the latency delta, , for each message.
            let elapsed = message.sent.elapsed();
            // Accumulate latency in microseconds.
            consumer_latency.fetch_add(elapsed.as_micros() as u64,
            // ↳ Ordering::Relaxed);
            // Increment the processed message count.
            consumer_counter.fetch_add(1, Ordering::Relaxed);
        }
    });

    // Record the start time for performance measurement.
    let start = Instant::now();

    // Producer loop: send N_MESSAGES into the channel.
    // According to the performance formula, throughput T = N / t.
    for i in 0..N_MESSAGES {
        let msg = Message {
            id: i,
            sent: Instant::now(),
        };
        // The send call is asynchronous. If the channel is full, it
        // ↳ awaits until there is capacity (back-pressure).
        if let Err(e) = tx.send(msg).await {
            eprintln!("Failed to send message: {}", e);
            break;
        }
    }
```

```rust
    // Drop the sender to close the channel and signal the consumer
    ↪  task that no more messages will be sent.
    drop(tx);

    // Wait for the consumer task to finish processing all the
    ↪  messages.
    consumer_handle.await.unwrap();

    // Calculate the total elapsed time since the production began.
    let elapsed_time = start.elapsed().as_secs_f64();
    let processed = msg_counter.load(Ordering::Relaxed);

    // Throughput calculation: T = N / t,
    // where N is the number of messages processed and t is the
    ↪  elapsed time in seconds.
    let throughput = processed as f64 / elapsed_time;

    // Average processing delay  calculation (in microseconds) over
    ↪  all messages.
    let avg_latency = if processed > 0 {
        total_latency.load(Ordering::Relaxed) as f64 / processed as
        ↪  f64
    } else {
        0.0
    };

    // Display the performance metrics.
    println!("Processed {} messages in {:.4} seconds", processed,
    ↪  elapsed_time);
    println!("Throughput T = {:.2} messages/second", throughput);
    println!("Average processing delay  = {:.2} microseconds",
    ↪  avg_latency);
}
```

Chapter 28

Implementing Publish/Subscribe Patterns

Architectural Framework for a Publish/- Subscribe System

The publish/subscribe paradigm embodies an architectural model in which message emitters (publishers) and message receivers (subscribers) interact indirectly through decoupled communication channels. In such systems, the publisher generates events without explicit knowledge of the recipients, while subscribers register their interest in one or more topics. This decoupling is achieved through an intermediary component that orchestrates topic registration, message queuing, and distribution. The resulting architecture facilitates asynchronous interaction, where message propagation and task execution occur concurrently in a non-blocking manner. Such design patterns enable the construction of systems that exhibit high levels of scalability and fault containment, as the processing entities operate independently within an event-driven framework.

Asynchronous Topic Management

Topic management within a publish/subscribe system is a critical facet that underpins the entire communication protocol. Each topic is formally represented as an index associated with one or more subscribers, and an efficient mapping mechanism is employed to maintain the correspondence between topics and their registered consumers. In an asynchronous context, the topic registry must be updated concurrently by multiple operations such as subscription requests, topic creation, and unsubscription events. This necessitates the adoption of lock-free data structures and atomic operations to ensure that the mapping remains consistent under concurrent access patterns. For instance, when a new subscriber issues a registration request, an atomic compare-and-swap operation guarantees that the update to the registry occurs without disruption, thus preserving the consistency and integrity of the system's state. The emphasis on non-blocking behaviors further implies that synchronous lock acquisition is eschewed in favor of asynchronous primitives which allow for continuous propagation of events across dynamically created and destroyed topics.

Asynchronous Message Distribution Mechanisms

Message distribution in a publish/subscribe architecture is predicated on the decoupling of message production from consumption. When a publisher emits a message, the system performs a dual operation: it enqueues the message within the corresponding topic channel and asynchronously signals waiting subscribers. The mechanism ensures that message broadcast is performed in a non-blocking fashion such that each message is processed independently of other concurrent operations. Message distribution is commonly realized through asynchronous channels that guarantee first-in-first-out (FIFO) ordering. This ordering is essential to maintain the logical sequence of events across multiple subscribers. The operational behavior of the system can be empirically characterized by examining the relationship

$$\delta = \frac{\Delta T}{M},$$

where ΔT denotes the cumulative time taken for message dissemination, M represents the number of subscribers affected by the event, and δ corresponds to the average processing delay per subscriber. The adoption of asynchronous patterns minimizes blocking time by utilizing event-driven computations, whereby the propagation of message signals is scheduled alongside other computational tasks. Consequently, the message distribution mechanism achieves high throughput even under scenarios of intense publish activity.

Scalability and Performance Considerations

The overall performance of a publish/subscribe system is inherently linked to its ability to scale in response to ambient load and the frequency of asynchronous events. Scalability is enhanced through the integration of non-blocking operations and lock-free data structures in both topic management and message distribution modules. From a performance perspective, the interplay between channel capacity, scheduling overhead, and processing delays establishes a quantitative framework for system evaluation. Let C represent the concurrency factor, which is optimally aligned with the number of physical processing cores P, such that

$$C \approx P.$$

This relationship guarantees that the operational overhead incurred by context switching is minimized, and the system can sustain a high volume of messages without deleterious effects on latency. Furthermore, the rigorous application of atomic synchronization and error-resilient techniques ensures that transient inconsistencies or message loss do not propagate through the system. Such measures are critical in distributed environments where consistent state management across asynchronous channels is paramount. The design accommodates both bounded and unbounded queuing strategies; bounded channels inherently enforce back-pressure by limiting queue lengths, whereas unbounded channels favor throughput by allowing message accumulation. These design decisions are instrumental in achieving a scalable publish/subscribe infrastructure that can dynamically adapt to variations in workload and maintain a robust performance profile under high concurrency conditions.

Rust Code Snippet

```rust
use tokio::sync::mpsc;
use tokio::time::{sleep, Duration, Instant};
use tokio::task;
use futures::future::join_all;
use dashmap::DashMap;
use std::sync::Arc;

/// A message struct carrying the content and the timestamp when
↪   published.
///
/// The timestamp helps in computing the processing delay for each
↪   subscriber.
/// This delay is analogous to the equation:
///     = T / M,
/// where T is the cumulative time taken for message dissemination,
/// M is the number of subscribers and  is the average processing
↪   delay.
#[derive(Clone, Debug)]
struct Message {
    content: String,
    timestamp: Instant,
}

/// A simple publish/subscribe system that maps topics to subscriber
↪   channels.
///
/// For high-performance asynchronous messaging, we use a concurrent
↪   data structure
/// (DashMap) to manage topic registrations in a lock-free manner.
struct PubSub {
    topics: Arc<DashMap<String, Vec<mpsc::Sender<Message>>>>,
}

impl PubSub {
    /// Create a new PubSub instance.
    fn new() -> Self {
        Self {
            topics: Arc::new(DashMap::new()),
        }
    }

    /// Subscribe to a given topic.
    ///
    /// Returns a receiver end of an async channel that will get the
    ↪   published messages.
    async fn subscribe(&self, topic: &str) ->
    ↪   mpsc::Receiver<Message> {
        let (tx, rx) = mpsc::channel(100);
        // The update to the topic registry is lock-free via
        ↪   DashMap's internal mechanisms.
```

189

```rust
        self.topics.entry(topic.to_string()).or_default().push(tx);
        rx
    }

    /// Publish a message to a given topic.
    ///
    /// The message is broadcasted asynchronously to all
    ↪    subscribers.
    async fn publish(&self, topic: &str, msg: Message) {
        if let Some(subscribers) = self.topics.get(topic) {
            // For non-blocking behavior, messages are sent
            ↪    concurrently to each subscriber.
            let futures = subscribers.value().iter().map(|tx| {
                let m = msg.clone();
                async move {
                    // The send operation is asynchronous and
                    ↪    non-blocking.
                    let _ = tx.send(m).await;
                }
            });
            join_all(futures).await;
        }
    }
}

/// The main execution demonstrating the publish/subscribe system.
///
/// In this example, we simulate a topic ("news") with multiple
↪    subscribers.
/// Each subscriber computes the delay between message publication
↪    and reception,
/// showcasing the equation:
///      = T / M,
/// where for each message T is computed, and in this simulation
↪    each subscriber's delay
/// represents its share of the processing time.
///
/// The concurrency factor is implied as C  P, where the number of
↪    subscribers is chosen
/// to align with available processing cores (for demonstration, we
↪    use 4 subscribers).
#[tokio::main]
async fn main() {
    let pubsub = PubSub::new();
    let topic = "news";
    // For demonstration, we assume 4 subscribers.
    let num_subscribers = 4;
    let mut subscriber_handles = Vec::new();

    // Spawn subscriber tasks.
    for i in 0..num_subscribers {
        let mut rx = pubsub.subscribe(topic).await;
        let subscriber_id = i;
```

190

```rust
        let handle = task::spawn(async move {
            // Each subscriber continuously receives messages.
            while let Some(msg) = rx.recv().await {
                // Compute processing delay (T) for the received
                ↪   message.
                let delay = msg.timestamp.elapsed();
                // In a real system, averaging over multiple
                ↪   messages would yield = T / M.
                println!(
                    "Subscriber {} received '{}' with delay: {:?}",
                    subscriber_id,
                    msg.content,
                    delay
                );
            }
        });
        subscriber_handles.push(handle);
    }

    // Simulate a publisher emitting messages at regular intervals.
    let publish_interval = Duration::from_millis(500);
    for i in 0..10 {
        let msg = Message {
            content: format!("Message {}", i),
            timestamp: Instant::now(),
        };
        pubsub.publish(topic, msg).await;
        sleep(publish_interval).await;
    }

    // Give subscribers time to process pending messages.
    sleep(Duration::from_secs(2)).await;
    println!("Finished publishing messages.");

    // Abort subscriber tasks (in a real system, you might signal
    ↪   shutdown gracefully).
    for handle in subscriber_handles {
        handle.abort();
    }
}
```

Chapter 29

Custom TCP Protocol Design

Foundations of Protocol Customization

The Transmission Control Protocol (TCP) constitutes the canonical basis for reliable byte-stream communication in contemporary networks. Nevertheless, conventional TCP implementations impose fixed segmentation, predetermined flow control, and standard error recovery mechanisms that may constrain the performance of data streaming when application-specific requirements are at play. Custom TCP protocol designs emerge from the need to reconfigure these operational parameters. The underlying principle involves analyzing and extending the traditional protocol in order to accommodate variable data sizes, irregular inter-arrival times, and dynamic communication patterns. In scenarios where data streaming demands deviation from standard operational envelopes, the protocol must satisfy conditions such that the throughput T and latency L obey relationships of the form

$$T \geq \frac{D}{L_{\max}},$$

where D represents the aggregate data volume and $L_{\max}$ signifies the maximum permissible latency. This adaptation necessitates a rigorous reassessment of default settings and introduces adjustable parameters that reflect application-specific constraints.

Custom Data Streaming Framework

The architectural framework for a custom TCP protocol is predicated upon the redefinition of packet segmentation and data encapsulation mechanisms. In a tailored design, packets may be structured to include additional headers or control fields that provide enhanced semantic context regarding the streaming session. This information can be leveraged for purposes such as dynamic prioritization, adaptive retransmission strategies, and fine-grained congestion avoidance. A central element in this framework comprises the novel segmentation algorithm, which partitions an incoming data stream into fragments that are optimally sized for the specific network conditions and application requirements. Furthermore, this design paradigm embraces variable-length segments to underpin scenarios where the logical boundaries of the data stream do not correspond to fixed-size payloads. The resultant protocol is thus characterized by its capacity to modulate packet size and sequence in response to temporal variations within the transmission channel.

Adaptive Flow and Congestion Control Mechanisms

The standard TCP flow control and congestion avoidance algorithms are inherently reactive in nature, relying on aggregate indicators such as round-trip time and packet loss. In a custom protocol design, it is possible to incorporate adaptive mechanisms that react to instantaneous metrics. The selective adjustment of the congestion window W, for example, can be governed by a dynamic function

$$W = f(\mathrm{RTT}, \varepsilon, \Theta),$$

where RTT denotes the round-trip time, ε embodies the packet loss rate, and Θ symbolizes additional context derived from the application's operational parameters. This function permits the modulation of sending rates so as to closely match the fluctuating availability of network resources. By integrating continuous feedback loops and probabilistic estimation methods, the custom protocol is capable of preemptively adjusting its behavior to mitigate congestion rather than merely reacting after an incipient failure has been observed. Through the calibration of flow control parameters to the specific needs of high-volume or latency-sensitive applications, significant improvements in data streaming efficiency and network utilization can be achieved.

Enhanced Error Recovery and Session Consistency

Error detection and recovery in custom TCP protocols demand a sophisticated approach that transcends traditional checksum and timeout methods. The enhanced design incorporates supplementary mechanisms for verifying the integrity of data beyond the conventional cyclic redundancy check. In advanced configurations, the probability of erroneous transmission, expressed as P_{err}, is continuously estimated and used to adapt retransmission strategies in real-time. Alternative redundancy techniques, such as forward error correction strategies, can be integrated seamlessly into the protocol to minimize retransmission overhead. Moreover, session consistency is upheld through the implementation of stateful tracking of acknowledgments and sequence numbers. This ensures that the synchronization of data streams is maintained even under conditions of variable delay or packet reordering. The resulting protocol not only augments the reliability of the communication channel but also guarantees that application-specific data streams persist in an orderly fashion, thus preserving the overall coherence of the session.

Analytical Modeling and Performance Optimization

The custom protocol design is further underscored by analytical models that capture the relationship between system parameters and performance outcomes. The interplay between segment size, transmission rate, and delay can be formalized through mathematical models that express throughput as a function of design variables. For instance, when the achievable throughput is denoted by T, and the effective segment size by S, a relationship of the form

$$T = \frac{S}{\Delta t}$$

may be utilized to assess the system performance under varying loads. Optimization techniques focus on identifying the set of protocol parameters that maximize T while adhering to latency bounds and ensuring error resilience. The evaluation of these parameters is performed using both theoretical analyses and simulation-based experiments. The optimized model therefore provides concrete guidelines for fine-tuning the custom TCP protocol to meet the precise data streaming and communication requirements that are intrinsic to specialized applications.

Rust Code Snippet

```rust
use std::time::{Duration, Instant};

/// Calculate the minimum required throughput based on the total
↪   data (D) and maximum latency (L_max).
///
/// Equation: T >= D / L_max
fn required_throughput(total_data: f64, max_latency: f64) -> f64 {
    total_data / max_latency
}

/// Compute an adaptive congestion window using instantaneous
↪   metrics.
///
/// Equation: W = f(RTT, , )
/// Here we simulate the function f with a simple formula:
///    W = k * (1 / (RTT + loss_rate + context))
/// where k is an adjustment factor.
fn adaptive_congestion_window(rtt: f64, loss_rate: f64, context:
↪   f64) -> f64 {
    let k: f64 = 1.5; // Adjustment factor, may be tuned based on
    ↪   experiments.
    k * (1.0 / (rtt + loss_rate + context))
}

/// Calculate throughput based on segment size (S) and transmission
↪   duration (t).
///
/// Equation: T = S / t
fn throughput(segment_size: f64, duration: f64) -> f64 {
    segment_size / duration
}

/// Custom segmentation algorithm that splits the data into variable
↪   length segments.
/// For demonstration, the algorithm simply breaks the data into
↪   chunks of an ideal size.
/// In a real-world scenario, this algorithm may use network
↪   conditions to adjust the segment sizes.
```

195

```
fn segment_data(data: &[u8], ideal_segment_size: usize) ->
↪   Vec<Vec<u8>> {
    data.chunks(ideal_segment_size)
        .map(|chunk| chunk.to_vec())
        .collect()
}

fn main() {
    // Simulation parameters: sizes in bytes and time in seconds.
    let total_data: f64 = 1000.0;    // Total data volume (D)
    let max_latency: f64 = 0.2;       // Maximum permissible
    ↪   latency (L_max)
    let rtt: f64 = 0.05;             // Round-trip time (RTT)
    let loss_rate: f64 = 0.01;        // Packet loss probability ()
    let context: f64 = 0.1;           // Additional operational
    ↪   context ()

    // Compute the required throughput lower bound.
    let required_t = required_throughput(total_data, max_latency);
    println!("Required throughput (T >= D / L_max): {:.3}
    ↪   bytes/sec", required_t);

    // Simulate adaptive congestion control by computing the
    ↪   congestion window.
    let cwnd = adaptive_congestion_window(rtt, loss_rate, context);
    println!("Adaptive Congestion Window (W = f(RTT, , )): {:.3}
    ↪   (arbitrary units)", cwnd);

    // Create a sample data stream to simulate custom segmentation.
    let data: Vec<u8> = (0..total_data as usize).map(|x| (x % 256)
    ↪   as u8).collect();
    let ideal_segment_size: usize = 100; // Ideal segment size in
    ↪   bytes.
    let segments = segment_data(&data, ideal_segment_size);
    println!("Total segments created: {}", segments.len());

    // Simulate transmission of each segment.
    // Assume each segment takes a fixed duration to transmit.
    let segment_duration: f64 = 0.01; // Transmission time per
    ↪   segment (t)
    for (i, segment) in segments.iter().enumerate() {
        // Calculate throughput for the segment.
        let seg_throughput = throughput(segment.len() as f64,
        ↪   segment_duration);
        println!(
            "Segment {:>2}: Size = {:>3} bytes, Throughput = {:.3}
            ↪   bytes/sec",
            i + 1,
            segment.len(),
            seg_throughput
        );
    }
```

```
    // Example of analytical modeling:
    // Given a segment size S and transmission duration t, the
    ↪    throughput is:
    // T = S / t which is demonstrated above per segment.
}
```

Chapter 30

Subprotocol Negotiation in WebSocket Communication

Foundational Concepts in WebSocket Subprotocols

The WebSocket protocol, as formally standardized in RFC 6455, introduces a bidirectional communication channel over a single TCP connection. Embedded within the initial handshake is the provision to negotiate a subprotocol, an optional mechanism whereby both client and server may agree on a mutually supported set of messaging semantics. In this context, the subprotocol field functions as an essential indicator for delineating the expected structure and semantics of exchanged messages. The negotiation process is inherently designed to reconcile the diverse specifications that may govern distinct messaging schemes, thereby ensuring that protocol-level interpretations remain coherent even when multiple syntactic or semantic conventions are available. In theoretical terms, the subprotocol negotiation process may be understood as establishing an implicit contract wherein the intersection of a client's proposal and the server's advertised capabilities defines the operational parameters for subsequent communication.

Subprotocol Negotiation Architecture

The architectural model for subprotocol negotiation is constructed around the interplay between the client's request header and the server's response header, wherein the Sec-WebSocket-Protocol field is pivotal. An intricate sequence of message exchanges occurs during the upgrade process from HTTP to a persistent WebSocket connection. This phase is marked by the evaluation of candidate subprotocols as communicated by the client, followed by the invocation of a selection algorithm on the server side. The architecture mandates that the server maintains an internal registry of supported subprotocols, along with associated priorities or quality parameters that may be derived from both performance metrics and application-specific constraints. Upon receipt of a client request containing a set of proposed subprotocol values, the server engages in a decision process that involves matching, ranking, and ultimately selecting an appropriate subprotocol. This selection is then communicated back to the client as part of the handshake, thereby establishing the framework for all succeeding messaging exchanges. The entire mechanism is sensitive to variations in both network conditions and application requirements, ensuring that the negotiated subprotocol is robust in the face of heterogeneous message types and diverse operational demands.

Formal Criteria and Selection Algorithms

A rigorous formulation of the subprotocol negotiation process may be articulated using formal set-theoretic and algorithmic constructs. Define the client's proposed set of subprotocols as $\Sigma_c = \{\sigma_1, \sigma_2, \ldots, \sigma_n\}$ and the server's supported set as $\Sigma_s = \{\tau_1, \tau_2, \ldots, \tau_m\}$. The negotiation algorithm seeks to determine an element $\pi \in (\Sigma_c \cap \Sigma_s)$ that maximizes a utility function $U : (\Sigma_c \cap \Sigma_s) \to \mathbb{R}$. This utility function encapsulates quantitative measures such as latency sensitivity, throughput optimization, and protocol-specific overhead. The selected subprotocol π must satisfy the condition

$$\pi = \underset{\sigma \in (\Sigma_c \cap \Sigma_s)}{\arg\max} \ U(\sigma),$$

ensuring that the chosen protocol optimally aligns with both the client's proposals and the server's performance criteria. In scenarios where the intersection is empty, the algorithm may either default to a predefined fallback protocol or terminate the handshake, thereby precluding incompatible exchanges. The formal framework thus provides a structured methodology for evaluating candidate protocols on the basis of measurable criteria, thereby instilling rigor and consistency in the subprotocol selection process.

Dynamic Adaptation and Messaging Scheme Integration

Once a subprotocol is negotiated and agreed upon during the handshake phase, the established parameters assume a central role in orchestrating the subsequent messaging schemes. The negotiated subprotocol acts as a configuration parameter that informs the runtime behavior of both message parsing and handling mechanisms. In environments where multiple messaging schemes are supported—such as those accommodating mixed binary and text data—the system leverages dynamic dispatch and stateful processing strategies to adapt to the specific requirements of each message type. The subprotocol not only delineates the format of the payload but also influences ancillary properties such as error detection, framing conventions, and data compression techniques. This dynamic adaptation is achieved through a modular design in which the core communication layer interfaces with a collection of specialized components, each engineered to process messages in accordance with the negotiated subprotocol. The resulting integration ensures that the system maintains high levels of interoperability and flexibility, achieving consistent performance even as the nature of the transmitted data varies in real time.

Negotiation Process: Practical Considerations

The practical implementation of subprotocol negotiation involves a suite of considerations that extend beyond the theoretical framework. Paramount among these is the handling of edge cases, such as instances where the client's proposed subprotocols do not overlap with the server's supported set. In such cases, the protocol may invoke a fallback mechanism that either reverts to a minimal messaging scheme or aborts the connection outright to preserve integrity. Additionally, the negotiation process must account for potential security vulnerabilities, ensuring that the subprotocol selection cannot be exploited to induce protocol downgrade attacks or to circumvent data validation routines. Performance considerations also play a significant role; the negotiation algorithm must operate with minimal overhead, particularly in scenarios where rapid connection establishment is critical. These practical constraints necessitate the integration of robust error-handling routines and adaptive timeout strategies. The overall process is thus characterized by a balanced synthesis of formal criteria and pragmatic engineering, wherein each decision point is evaluated not only in terms of theoretical optimality but also in the context of operational efficiency and security compliance.

Rust Code Snippet

```
//! This Rust code implements the subprotocol negotiation algorithm
↪   described in the chapter.
//! It selects an optimal subprotocol from the intersection of
↪   client-proposed protocols
//! (_c) and server-supported protocols (_s) based on a calculated
↪   utility function U.
//! The selection follows the formula:
//!
//!      = argmax_{ (_c  _s)} U()
//!
//! If no common protocol is found, a fallback protocol is returned.

use std::cmp::Ordering;

/// Calculates a utility value for a given subprotocol.
/// Higher utility values indicate a stronger preference for that
↪   protocol.
fn calculate_utility(protocol: &str) -> f64 {
    // The utility values are defined based on protocol-specific
    ↪   criteria.
    // For illustration, we assign:
    // - "protocol_v2" a high utility,
    // - "protocol_v1" a moderate utility,
    // - "protocol_beta" a lower utility,
    // - All others a minimal default utility.
    match protocol {
        "protocol_v2" => 10.0,
        "protocol_v1" => 8.0,
        "protocol_beta" => 5.0,
        _ => 1.0,
    }
}
```

```rust
/// Negotiates and selects the best subprotocol from the client's
/// proposals and the
/// server's supported subprotocols using the argmax algorithm on
/// the utility function.
///
/// # Arguments
///
/// * `client_protocols` - Slice of subprotocols proposed by the
/// client (_c).
/// * `server_protocols` - Slice of subprotocols supported by the
/// server (_s).
/// * `fallback` - A fallback protocol to use if there is no
/// intersection.
///
/// # Returns
///
/// The selected subprotocol that maximizes the utility function, or
/// the fallback if no match occurs.
fn negotiate_subprotocol<'a>(
    client_protocols: &[&'a str],
    server_protocols: &[&'a str],
    fallback: &'a str,
) -> &'a str {
    // Determine the intersection of client and server protocols.
    let candidate_protocols: Vec<&'a str> = client_protocols
        .iter()
        .filter(|&&p| server_protocols.contains(&p))
        .cloned()
        .collect();

    // If intersection is empty, use the fallback protocol.
    if candidate_protocols.is_empty() {
        println!("No matching subprotocol found. Using fallback
        protocol.");
        return fallback;
    }

    // Select the protocol that maximizes the utility function.
    // This corresponds to:  = argmax_{  (_c   _s)} U()
    let mut best_protocol = candidate_protocols[0];
    let mut best_utility = calculate_utility(best_protocol);
    for &protocol in candidate_protocols.iter().skip(1) {
        let utility = calculate_utility(protocol);
        if utility > best_utility {
            best_protocol = protocol;
            best_utility = utility;
        }
    }
    best_protocol
}

fn main() {
```

```rust
    // Define the client-proposed subprotocols (_c) and
    //    server-supported subprotocols (_s).
    let client_protocols = ["protocol_alpha", "protocol_beta",
        "protocol_v1"];
    let server_protocols = ["protocol_v1", "protocol_v2",
        "protocol_gamma"];

    // Define a fallback protocol in case there is no common
    //    subprotocol.
    let fallback_protocol = "default_protocol";

    // Execute the negotiation algorithm.
    let selected_protocol = negotiate_subprotocol(&client_protocols,
        &server_protocols, fallback_protocol);

    println!("Negotiated subprotocol: {}", selected_protocol);
}

// Unit tests for the negotiation algorithm.
#[cfg(test)]
mod tests {
    use super::*;

    #[test]
    fn test_negotiate_with_common_protocol() {
        // In this scenario, the intersection contains "protocol_v1"
        //    and "protocol_beta".
        // Since "protocol_v1" has a higher utility (8.0) than
        //    "protocol_beta" (5.0),
        // "protocol_v1" should be selected.
        let client = ["protocol_v1", "protocol_beta"];
        let server = ["protocol_beta", "protocol_v1"];
        let fallback = "default_protocol";
        let selected = negotiate_subprotocol(&client, &server,
            fallback);
        assert_eq!(selected, "protocol_v1");
    }

    #[test]
    fn test_negotiate_use_fallback() {
        // Here, there is no intersection between client and server
        //    protocols,
        // so the fallback should be used.
        let client = ["protocol_unknown"];
        let server = ["protocol_v1", "protocol_v2"];
        let fallback = "default_protocol";
        let selected = negotiate_subprotocol(&client, &server,
            fallback);
        assert_eq!(selected, fallback);
    }
}
```

Chapter 31

Macro-Driven API Generation

Conceptual Foundations

Macro-driven generation constitutes an advanced metaprogramming paradigm that leverages compile-time code transformation to alleviate redundancy in API development. In this framework, macros function as formal mapping mechanisms, where the transformation

$$M : P \to C$$

is defined from a domain P of parameterized patterns to a codomain C of complete API constructs. The inherent regularity of API design is exploited by identifying recurring syntactic and semantic constructs and encoding the corresponding transformation rules into macros. This approach systematically suppresses boilerplate code, ensuring that endpoint definitions adhere to a consistent architectural template while enforcing type safety and structural invariance.

The abstraction provided by macros enables the encapsulation of complex API behaviors into succinct meta constructs. Building on principles drawn from formal language theory and rewriting systems, the macro expansion process is analogous to substitution operations as seen in the λ-calculus. The rigorous formalization inherent in this methodology establishes a reproducible foundation for automated API generation, thereby minimizing manual intervention and reducing the potential for inconsistencies across large codebases.

Architectural Constructs in Macro Systems

The architectural framework underlying macro-driven API generation operates at the intersection of syntactic pattern matching and semantic validation. Integrated with the compiler, the macro system performs early-stage analysis to detect and expand reusable patterns during compilation. This architecture can be viewed as comprising a dual-phase process: the first phase focuses on the identification of code segments that conform to predefined templates, while the second phase executes a transformation function that yields fully elaborated API components.

Consider a finite collection of abstract API specifications

$$E = \{e_1, e_2, \ldots, e_n\}.$$

Each element of E is transformed by a function T, such that

$$T(e_i)$$

represents a complete code construct incorporating functionalities such as routing, parameter validation, and error handling. The design of the macro system as an intermediary layer effectively abstracts the complexity of repetitive code into succinct, automated transformations. This layered structure not only enhances maintainability but also ensures that all generated endpoints conform to a unified set of design constraints.

Automated Synthesis of API Endpoints

The automated synthesis of API endpoints via macros is predicated on the extraction and formalization of invariant syntactic structures characteristic of standard API definitions. Abstract patterns identified in the source specifications serve as the basis for constructing macro rules that automatically expand into fully structured endpoints. The process is formally conceptualized as an expansion function

$$E : S \to O,$$

where S denotes the space of abstract API specifications and O is the set of synthesized code constructs.

This mechanism minimizes manual overhead by capitalizing on inherent properties of the language's syntax. The expansion function generates code that uniformly integrates error handling, parameter parsing, and response formatting. As a result, modifications made to macro definitions propagate automatically across all generated endpoints, thereby ensuring consistency and reducing the likelihood of discrepancies. The systematic nature of this approach operationalizes high-level abstraction and automation, which are central to effectively reducing boilerplate in API development.

Considerations in Macro-Driven API Generation

The deployment of macros for API generation requires careful consideration of both methodological and practical aspects that ensure the robustness and reliability of the generated code. A primary concern is the maintenance of type safety throughout the macro expansion process. Given the inherent complexity of macros, the output must undergo stringent compile-time checks to validate that both syntactic and semantic correctness are preserved. This necessity drives the formulation of macros to include invariant conditions that mirror the rigorous specifications dictated by the underlying language.

Scalability represents an additional critical factor, particularly in environments where API structures undergo frequent evolution. The abstraction layer provided by macros must accommodate a wide range of API patterns with minimal performance overhead. Ensuring that macro expansions conform to a predictable and verifiable transformation model allows for systematic propagation of design changes across the entire codebase. The incorporation of formal verification techniques, including invariant checks and substitution consistency, further reinforces the dependability of the macro-driven approach. These considerations underscore the effectiveness of macros in reducing redundancy and enforcing systematic architectural standards in the realm of API generation.

Rust Code Snippet

```rust
#[derive(Debug, PartialEq, Clone)]
enum HttpMethod {
    GET,
    POST,
    // Additional methods could be added here.
}

#[derive(Debug, Clone)]
struct Request {
    method: HttpMethod,
    path: String,
    body: String,
}

#[derive(Debug)]
struct Response {
    status: u16,
    body: String,
}

// ------------------------------------------------------
// The following struct and functions model the conceptual
//    equations:
// Transformation function M : P -> C, where P represents an
//    abstract API
// specification and C a complete API endpoint construct.
// ------------------------------------------------------
// Abstract API specification (pattern, P)
struct AbstractApiSpec {
    method: HttpMethod,
    path: &'static str,
    handler: fn(Request) -> Response,
}

// Transformation function M : P -> C
// This function converts an AbstractApiSpec into a complete
//    endpoint closure.
fn transform_spec(spec: AbstractApiSpec) -> Box<dyn Fn(Request) ->
    Response> {
    Box::new(move |req: Request| {
        if req.method == spec.method && req.path == spec.path {
            (spec.handler)(req)
        } else {
            Response {
                status: 404,
                body: "Not Found".into(),
            }
        }
    })
}
```

```
// ---------------------------------------------------------
// Expansion function E : S -> O, where S is a collection of
↪    abstract API
// specifications and O is a set of synthesized complete endpoint
↪    closures.
// ---------------------------------------------------------
fn expand_api_spec(specs: Vec<AbstractApiSpec>) -> Vec<Box<dyn
↪    Fn(Request) -> Response>> {
    specs.into_iter().map(transform_spec).collect()
}


// ---------------------------------------------------------
// Macro-driven transformation T(e_i):
// The following macro encapsulates the mapping from an abstract API
↪    design to a
// complete API endpoint function. This mirrors the transformation
↪    T(e_i) in the
// chapter, automatically generating code for routing, parameter
↪    validation,
// and error handling.
// ---------------------------------------------------------
macro_rules! api_endpoint {
    (
        $name:ident,
        method: $method:ident,
        path: $path:expr,
        handler: $handler:ident
    ) => {
        fn $name(req: Request) -> Response {
            // Check if the incoming request matches the predefined
            ↪    method and path.
            if req.method == HttpMethod::$method && req.path ==
            ↪    $path {
                // Delegate to the specified handler.
                $handler(req)
            } else {
                // Default response for unmatched requests.
                Response {
                    status: 404,
                    body: "Not Found".to_string(),
                }
            }
        }
    };
}

// Example handler functions for API endpoints.
fn get_users_handler(req: Request) -> Response {
    // Emulate parameter validation and error handling.
    if req.body.is_empty() {
        Response {
            status: 200,
```

```
                body: "User list: Alice, Bob, Charlie".into(),
            }
        } else {
            Response {
                status: 400,
                body: "Unexpected body content".into(),
            }
        }
    }
}

fn create_user_handler(req: Request) -> Response {
    Response {
        status: 201,
        body: format!("User '{}' created", req.body),
    }
}

// Generate API endpoints using the macro.
// This expansion is an example of using macro-driven code
↪   generation to
// reduce boilerplate and enforce uniform architectural standards.
api_endpoint!(get_users, method: GET, path: "/users", handler:
↪   get_users_handler);
api_endpoint!(create_user, method: POST, path: "/users", handler:
↪   create_user_handler);

fn main() {
    // --------------------------------------------------
    // Example usage of manually transformed API specifications via
↪   the
    // expansion function E : S -> O.
    // --------------------------------------------------
    let spec_get = AbstractApiSpec {
        method: HttpMethod::GET,
        path: "/users",
        handler: get_users_handler,
    };

    let spec_create = AbstractApiSpec {
        method: HttpMethod::POST,
        path: "/users",
        handler: create_user_handler,
    };

    // Expand the abstract specifications into runnable endpoints.
    let endpoints = expand_api_spec(vec![spec_get, spec_create]);

    // Create test requests.
    let req_get = Request {
        method: HttpMethod::GET,
        path: "/users".to_string(),
        body: "".to_string(),
    };
```

```rust
    let req_post = Request {
        method: HttpMethod::POST,
        path: "/users".to_string(),
        body: "Dave".to_string(),
    };

    // Invoke endpoints generated by the expansion function.
    println!("--- Invoking endpoints from expanded API specs ---");
    for endpoint in endpoints {
        // Each endpoint is a Boxed closure implementing the
        // ↪  complete API construct.
        let res = endpoint(req_get.clone());
        println!("Response: {:?}\n", res);
    }

    // ----------------------------------------------------
    // Invoke the macro-generated API endpoints.
    // These functions are generated according to the transformation
    // ↪  T(e_i).
    // ----------------------------------------------------
    println!("--- Invoking macro-generated endpoints ---");
    let res_macro_get = get_users(req_get);
    let res_macro_post = create_user(req_post);
    println!("Macro Generated GET Response: {:?}", res_macro_get);
    println!("Macro Generated POST Response: {:?}", res_macro_post);
}
```

Chapter 32

Enhancing REST APIs with Attribute Macros

Declarative Specification of RESTful Endpoints

Attribute macros serve as a formal mechanism for declaratively annotating function definitions such that the intrinsic properties of RESTful endpoints are captured at the syntactic level. In this paradigm, the annotated function is viewed as a high-level specification, and the attribute macro acts as a transformation that maps this specification into an endpoint construct with well-defined behavior. The correspondence between the specification and the generated endpoint may be represented by a mapping

$$A : F \to E,$$

where F denotes the space of functions with embedded endpoint semantics and E denotes the space of fully elaborated REST API endpoints with explicit routing, parameter validation, and error handling capabilities. This mapping leverages the consistency of declarative annotations to eliminate redundancies and enforce uniformity across API definitions.

1 Annotative Syntax and Semantic Enrichment

The formalism underlying attribute macros encapsulates essential metadata—such as HTTP method type, routing information, and descriptive semantics—directly within the function header. This embedded metadata bridges the gap between abstract API contracts and their concrete realization through compile-time transformation. The inherent regularity in REST API design is thus exploited by encoding recurring patterns into attribute annotations. The macro system rigorously enforces that each annotated function adheres to design invariants corresponding to RESTful architecture, thereby ensuring that the generated endpoints are semantically enriched and structurally consistent.

Macro-Based Transformation Mechanism

The core functionality of attribute macros lies in their ability to transform annotated constructs into fully specified API endpoints during the compilation process. This transformation is governed by a semantic function

$$T : F \to E,$$

which is defined over the syntactic space of annotated functions. The transformation function T conducts a series of compile-time analyses, including pattern matching against predetermined annotations and the application of rewrite rules that generate endpoint implementations with built-in routing logic and error handling. Through the rigorous application of such rules, the macro expansion process embeds a layer of formal verification, ensuring that the semantics of the REST API contract are preserved precisely in the generated code.

1 Formal Modeling of Macro Expansion

The transformation induced by attribute macros can be formally modeled using concepts borrowed from term rewriting systems and λ-calculus. Given an annotated function equipped with a set of declarative attributes, the macro expansion applies a sequence of deterministic substitution rules, resulting in a low-level representation that is both type-safe and conformant to the RESTful specification. In particular, the process guarantees that the mapping

$$T(\varphi) = \psi,$$

for any annotated function φ, yields a function ψ which retains the original type signature while incorporating additional routing and validation logic. The correctness of this transformation relies on the invariant preservation of both syntactic structure and semantic meaning during macro expansion.

Type-Safe Endpoint Synthesis

A salient feature of attribute macros is their integration with the host language's type system, an aspect that decisively influences the reliability of the generated endpoints. The macro expansion process is designed to perform early-stage type checking, ensuring that the augmented endpoints not only satisfy the prescribed syntactic patterns but also adhere to the stringent type constraints imposed by the underlying framework. This synthesis can be considered as an injection

$$I : E \hookrightarrow R,$$

which embeds the elaborated endpoint into a runtime environment where R denotes the set of executable responses conforming to REST protocols.

1   Integration with the Static Type System

The compilation pipeline leverages the static type system to validate that the expanded endpoints maintain type consistency. During macro expansion, each attribute annotation is verified for compatibility with the expected function signature. This results in an automated assurance that any deviations from the declared API contract are detected at compile time, thereby preventing a class of runtime errors. The attribute macro mechanism thus enforces a strict correlation between the endpoint specification and the actual implementation, ensuring that the transformation process is both sound and complete.

2   Structural Invariance and Consistency Checks

The design of attribute macros mandates that the structural properties of the original function are preserved after transformation. In this context, the macro system implements a series of consistency checks that ensure the invariance of endpoint behavior. These checks are integrated into the compile-time analysis such that any modification to the attribute annotations propagates uniformly across all instances of the API endpoint definitions. This level of control over the expansion process not only minimizes code duplication but also establishes a robust framework within which large-scale REST API architectures can be maintained with high reliability.

Rust Code Snippet

```
// rest_api_macros/src/lib.rs
//
// This crate implements a procedural macro attribute called
↪   `rest_endpoint` that
// transforms a declaratively annotated function (F) into a fully
↪   elaborated REST API
// endpoint (E), following the mapping A: F → E. The transformation
↪   T: F → E is applied
// at compile time, and the resulting endpoint is injected into the
↪   runtime environment
// via I: E   R.
//
// To use this macro, add this crate as a dependency in your
↪   Cargo.toml and annotate your
// endpoint functions with #[rest_endpoint(...)].

extern crate proc_macro;
use proc_macro::TokenStream;
use quote::quote;
use syn::{parse_macro_input, AttributeArgs, ItemFn, NestedMeta,
↪   Meta, Lit};

#[proc_macro_attribute]
pub fn rest_endpoint(attr: TokenStream, item: TokenStream) ->
↪   TokenStream {
    // Parse attribute arguments from the macro invocation.
    let args = parse_macro_input!(attr as AttributeArgs);
    let input_fn = parse_macro_input!(item as ItemFn);

    // Default HTTP method and route path.
    let mut method = String::from("GET");
    let mut path = String::from("/");

    // Process provided attribute arguments to override defaults.
    for arg in args {
        if let NestedMeta::Meta(Meta::NameValue(nv)) = arg {
            let ident = nv.path.get_ident().unwrap().to_string();
            if ident == "method" {
                if let Lit::Str(lit_str) = nv.lit {
                    method = lit_str.value();
                }
            } else if ident == "path" {
                if let Lit::Str(lit_str) = nv.lit {
                    path = lit_str.value();
```

```rust
                }
            }
        }
    }

    // Capture details of the annotated function.
    let fn_name = &input_fn.sig.ident;
    let fn_attrs = &input_fn.attrs;
    let fn_sig = &input_fn.sig;
    let fn_block = &input_fn.block;

    // The following code simulates the transformation:
    // T: F → E, where the annotated function (F) is wrapped with
    // ↪   routines to
    // log routing, validate parameters, and handle errors, turning
    // ↪   it into
    // a concrete API endpoint (E). The endpoint is later injected
    // ↪   into the
    // runtime (I: E  R).
    let expanded = quote! {
        #(#fn_attrs)*
        #fn_sig {
            println!(
                "Mapping function '{}' to endpoint with method '{}'
                ↪   at path '{}'",
                stringify!(#fn_name), #method, #path
            );
            // Execute the original function logic.
            let response = (|| #fn_block )();
            println!(
                "Injecting endpoint '{}' into runtime response
                ↪   handler",
                stringify!(#fn_name)
            );
            response
        }
    };

    TokenStream::from(expanded)
}


// app/src/main.rs
//
// This is an example application that demonstrates how to use the
// ↪   `rest_endpoint`
// attribute macro. The annotated function `create_user` expresses a
// ↪   high-level,
// declarative specification of a RESTful endpoint. Under the hood,
// ↪   the macro applies
// the mapping A: F → E, transforms it (T: F → E), and injects it
// ↪   into the runtime (I: E  R).
```

215

```rust
use rest_api_macros::rest_endpoint;

#[rest_endpoint(method = "POST", path = "/api/create_user")]
fn create_user(username: &str) -> String {
    // Declarative specifications, captured by attribute macros,
    //   serve as high-level
    // endpoint contracts. Here, we simulate validation and
    //   processing logic.
    if username.trim().is_empty() {
        "Error: Username cannot be empty.".to_string()
    } else {
        format!("User '{}' created successfully.", username)
    }
}

fn main() {
    let user = "Alice";
    println!("Invoking REST endpoint 'create_user' for user: {}",
      user);
    let result = create_user(user);
    println!("API Response: {}", result);
}
```

Chapter 33

Generics and Trait-based Reusability in Service Layers

Parametric Abstraction in Service Component Design

A central tenet in the construction of flexible service components is the introduction of parametric polymorphism to abstract over varying data types and operational behaviors. In this context, generics are employed to express components in a manner that is independent of any particular concrete type. Let T, U, and similar symbols denote type parameters over which service functions or structures are defined. The use of generics allows the specification of interfaces without committing to an implementation detail, and the derived components exhibit a high degree of reusability. This abstraction is particularly advantageous in settings where the same core logic is applied to diverse data representations or where the service component must accommodate multiple forms of input. The careful application of trait constraints within these generic interfaces ensures that only types fulfilling predetermined contracts can be substituted, thereby enforcing both semantic consistency and compile-time safety.

Trait-based Interface Abstraction and Enforcement

Traits serve as the formal mechanism to delineate expected behavior and interfaces within a type system. In the design of service layers, traits provide the blueprint for what constitutes a valid implementation of a service component, encapsulating method signatures, expected outputs, and error handling semantics. For instance, a trait may be defined to capture a set of operations required for API logic, and any type parameter S used in the construction of a service component is constrained via a bound such as S : `ServiceInterface`. This constraint mandates that the substituting type implements all the methods specified by the trait and adheres to any side-effect or performance requirements implicit in the API contract. The imposition of such constraints not only enforces consistency across various components but also leverages the compiler as a tool for formal verification, ensuring that the abstract design directly maps onto concrete implementations.

Integration and Synergy between Generics and Trait Constraints

The interplay between generics and trait constraints forms the cornerstone of reusable service layer design. When a service component is parameterized by a type variable that is bounded by a trait, the framework automatically gains the ability to handle multiple implementations that share common behavior. Consider a situation where a service layer is defined in terms of a generic parameter X subject to a constraint X : `ApiLogic`; such a construction supports the injection of any component that conforms to the abstract behavior codified by the trait. This synthesis encourages modularity by allowing components to be composed, recombined, and substituted without altering the foundational architecture. The inherent rigidity of static type checking, when allied with generic programming, results in a system that not only is free from a large class of runtime errors but also exhibits an elegance in how abstract interfaces are respected across diverse modules.

Semantic Refinement through Compile-time Type Safety

The robust enforcement of API logic is achieved through the meticulous application of compile-time checks inherent in systems that combine generics and trait constraints. The static type system performs a dual role: it verifies that each service component adheres to its declared interface and it ensures that the transformations between abstract specifications and concrete implementations preserve semantic properties. In such systems, each generic component subject to trait constraints is treated as a contract, whereby the compiler validates that all type parameters and associated behaviors align with the service's formal specification. This level of verification provides an assurance that the service layer, as a whole, is internally consistent and resistant to inadvertent implementation errors. The static analysis of these constructs yields a form of semantic refinement where the correctness of API logic is not merely assumed but is substantiated by rigorous type checking at compile time.

Rust Code Snippet

```rust
use std::ops::{Add, Mul};

/// Evaluate a polynomial given its coefficients and an input value
/// x.
/// The polynomial is defined as:
///     P(x) = a + a·x + a·x² + ... + a·x
///
/// Generic type T must implement Copy, addition, multiplication,
/// and conversion from u8.
/// This function demonstrates parametric abstraction over numeric
/// types.
fn evaluate_polynomial<T>(coeffs: &[T], x: T) -> T
where
    T: Copy + Add<Output = T> + Mul<Output = T> + From<u8>,
{
    let mut result = T::from(0);
    let mut power_of_x = T::from(1); // Represents x^0 initially.
    for &coeff in coeffs {
        result = result + coeff * power_of_x;
        power_of_x = power_of_x * x;
    }
    result
}
```

```rust
/// Trait defining the interface for a service component.
/// Any concrete service must implement the execute method,
/// which processes an input and returns an output.
trait ServiceInterface {
    fn execute(&self, input: i32) -> i32;
}

/// A concrete implementation of ServiceInterface performing
↪   arithmetic operations.
/// In this example, the service evaluates a polynomial with
↪   provided coefficients.
struct ArithmeticService {
    coeffs: Vec<i32>, // Polynomial coefficients: [a, a, a, ...]
}

impl ArithmeticService {
    /// Constructs a new ArithmeticService with given polynomial
    ↪   coefficients.
    fn new(coeffs: Vec<i32>) -> Self {
        Self { coeffs }
    }
}

impl ServiceInterface for ArithmeticService {
    fn execute(&self, input: i32) -> i32 {
        // Evaluates the polynomial: a + a·x + a·x² + ... using the
        ↪   generic function.
        evaluate_polynomial(&self.coeffs, input)
    }
}

/// A generic service layer that is parameterized by any type
↪   implementing ServiceInterface.
/// This layer abstracts over the concrete service implementation,
↪   ensuring reusability.
struct ServiceLayer<T: ServiceInterface> {
    service: T,
}

impl<T: ServiceInterface> ServiceLayer<T> {
    /// Constructs a new ServiceLayer wrapping the specified
    ↪   service.
    fn new(service: T) -> Self {
        Self { service }
    }

    /// Handles an incoming request by delegating execution to the
    ↪   underlying service component.
    fn handle_request(&self, request: i32) -> i32 {
        self.service.execute(request)
    }
}
```

```rust
/// Additional trait demonstrating further abstraction in API logic.
/// This trait defines a behavior for processing string data.
trait ApiLogic {
    fn process(&self, data: &str) -> String;
}

/// An example implementation of ApiLogic representing an echo
↪    service.
struct EchoService;

impl ApiLogic for EchoService {
    fn process(&self, data: &str) -> String {
        format!("Echo: {}", data)
    }
}

/// A generic function that leverages trait constraints to work with
↪    any type implementing ApiLogic.
/// This function encapsulates the processing behavior and returns
↪    the result.
fn run_api_logic<T>(logic: T, data: &str) -> String
where
    T: ApiLogic,
{
    logic.process(data)
}

fn main() {
    // Create an instance of ArithmeticService with polynomial
    ↪    coefficients.
    // For example, [1, 2, 3] represents the polynomial: 1 + 2·x +
    ↪    3·x².
    let arithmetic_service = ArithmeticService::new(vec![1, 2, 3]);

    // Construct the ServiceLayer with the arithmetic service.
    let service_layer = ServiceLayer::new(arithmetic_service);

    // Handle a request where x = 5.
    let input_value = 5;
    let result = service_layer.handle_request(input_value);
    println!("Result of polynomial evaluation for x = {}: {}",
    ↪    input_value, result);

    // Demonstrate the use of trait-based abstraction with
    ↪    EchoService.
    let echo_service = EchoService;
    let echoed = run_api_logic(echo_service, "Hello, Rust!");
    println!("{}", echoed);
}
```

Chapter 34

Trait-Based Abstractions for Async Services

Theoretical Foundations of Trait-Based Interfaces

The construction of robust service frameworks in modern systems relies upon the formalization of interfaces that encapsulate both synchronous and asynchronous semantics. In this paradigm, traits act as contracts that specify the required operations and behavioral guarantees for service components. The abstraction provided by traits ensures that any type T satisfying a given trait is obligated to adhere to a well-defined interface, thereby establishing a consistent framework for interaction. This formal guarantee is instrumental in deploying both synchronous and asynchronous strategies under a unified interface while preserving the core semantics expected from each service. The use of trait-based interfaces leverages the inherent strengths of static typing systems that enforce compile-time correctness, reducing the potential for discrepancies between intended and realized behavior.

Unification of Synchronous and Asynchronous Paradigms

The explicit separation between synchronous and asynchronous code often leads to divergent design patterns and error-prone conversion layers. By developing interfaces that are agnostic to the execution model, it becomes feasible to abstract over the underlying method of invocation. A critical design decision involves the specification of trait contracts that inherently support operations in both blocking and non-blocking contexts. In this unified model, a trait defines a set of operations where the implementation may either perform a direct computation or defer execution via an asynchronous mechanism. Such an abstraction allows the interchangeable use of components that execute immediately with those that rely on scheduling and deferred execution. The uniform interface thus achieved enables a seamless blend of synchronous semantics with asynchronous processing, ensuring that service behavior remains consistent regardless of the execution context.

Enforcing Consistency and Compile-Time Guarantees

A central objective in service layer design is to maintain semantic uniformity across various implementations. Trait-based abstractions enforce this uniformity through strict compile-time checks that validate the adherence to the predefined contracts. By constraining implementations with trait bounds, it is ensured that any component S, whether operating synchronously or asynchronously, satisfies critical properties such as determinism, type safety, and operational consistency. The compiler, serving as an arbiter of correctness, verifies that each concrete realization meets the obligations specified by the trait, thereby mitigating anomalies that could arise from partially implemented or inconsistent behaviors. This rigorous approach to interface validation permits the development of sophisticated and modular service layers, in which the integration of asynchronous primitives does not compromise the overall reliability and predictable behavior of the system.

Rust Code Snippet

```rust
use std::future::Future;
use std::pin::Pin;
use std::time::Duration;
use std::future;
use tokio::time::sleep;

/// A unified trait for service components that encapsulate both
/// synchronous and asynchronous behaviors. The trait abstracts the
/// operation "call" in such a way that the caller always receives a
↳   Future,
/// regardless of whether the underlying implementation performs its
↳   task
/// synchronously or asynchronously.
pub trait Service<Request> {
    type Response;
    type Error;
    // The Future returned must be Send and 'static so that it can
    ↳   be
    // executed in asynchronous runtimes safely.
    type Future: Future<Output = Result<Self::Response,
    ↳   Self::Error>> + Send;

    fn call(&self, req: Request) -> Self::Future;
}

/// A simple request structure carrying two integer operands.
/// This request model is used by both synchronous and asynchronous
↳   services.
#[derive(Debug)]
pub struct ComputeRequest {
    pub a: i32,
    pub b: i32,
}

/// Synchronous service implementation that performs addition.
/// It returns a "ready" future wrapping an immediate result.
pub struct SyncAdder;

impl Service<ComputeRequest> for SyncAdder {
    type Response = i32;
    type Error = ();
    type Future = future::Ready<Result<Self::Response,
    ↳   Self::Error>>;

    fn call(&self, req: ComputeRequest) -> Self::Future {
        // Direct computation returning immediately as a completed
        ↳   Future.
        future::ready(Ok(req.a + req.b))
    }
}
```

224

```rust
/// Asynchronous service implementation that performs
↪    multiplication.
/// It simulates an asynchronous operation by introducing a delay.
pub struct AsyncMultiplier;

impl Service<ComputeRequest> for AsyncMultiplier {
    type Response = i32;
    type Error = ();
    // Boxed future allows for dynamic dispatch of the asynchronous
    ↪    block.
    type Future = Pin<Box<dyn Future<Output = Result<Self::Response,
    ↪    Self::Error>> + Send>>;

    fn call(&self, req: ComputeRequest) -> Self::Future {
        Box::pin(async move {
            // Simulate asynchronous delay to emulate non-blocking
            ↪    processing.
            sleep(Duration::from_millis(100)).await;
            Ok(req.a * req.b)
        })
    }
}

/// The main function demonstrates the unification of synchronous
↪    and asynchronous
/// paradigms using the common Service trait. Both implementations
↪    are invoked
/// uniformly by awaiting their returned futures.
#[tokio::main]
async fn main() {
    // Construct a request with two numbers.
    let req_add = ComputeRequest { a: 3, b: 4 };
    let req_mul = ComputeRequest { a: 3, b: 4 };

    // Instantiate the synchronous service (SyncAdder).
    let sync_adder = SyncAdder;
    let add_result = sync_adder.call(req_add).await;
    match add_result {
        Ok(sum) => println!("SyncAdder Result (3 + 4): {}", sum),
        Err(_) => println!("SyncAdder encountered an error"),
    }

    // Instantiate the asynchronous service (AsyncMultiplier).
    let async_multiplier = AsyncMultiplier;
    let mul_result = async_multiplier.call(req_mul).await;
    match mul_result {
        Ok(product) => println!("AsyncMultiplier Result (3 * 4):
        ↪    {}", product),
        Err(_) => println!("AsyncMultiplier encountered an error"),
    }
}
```

Chapter 35

Stateful Request Handling with Async State Machines

Formal Framework of Asynchronous State Machines

In asynchronous programming paradigms, state machines provide a rigorous formal mechanism for managing non-linear control flows and encapsulating the progression of intricate request lifecycles. A state machine is rigorously defined as a tuple $M = (Q, \Sigma, \delta, q_0, F)$, where Q represents a finite set of states, Σ is the input alphabet, $\delta : Q \times \Sigma \to Q$ is the transition function that governs state changes, $q_0 \in Q$ is the initial state, and $F \subseteq Q$ comprises the set of terminal states. This abstraction facilitates the precise delineation of allowed state transitions and provides a mathematical foundation for reasoning about asynchronous operations. The formal framework not only enables the systematic mapping of both instantaneous and deferred actions to defined state transitions but also underpins the verification of behavioral correctness within complex asynchronous systems.

Modeling Request Lifecycles

The lifecycle of a request in asynchronous environments is naturally complex, often encompassing multiple phases such as initialization, active processing, awaiting external stimuli, and final resolution, either successful or erroneous. Each phase is modeled as a distinct state within the state machine, and the evolution of a request is captured through a sequence of state transitions dictated by the transition function δ. This approach formalizes the dynamic progression of a request by mapping events and temporal conditions to transitions between states, thereby capturing both deterministic and probabilistic behaviors. The state machine model elucidates the interactions among concurrent operations and offers a structured means to monitor progression, thus ensuring that the multifaceted lifecycle of a request is managed with methodological precision.

Integration with Asynchronous Execution Models

The integration of state machine patterns with asynchronous execution models builds a bridge between abstract control flow and concrete processing mechanisms. In modern asynchronous frameworks, constructs such as futures and promises encapsulate deferred computations, and the use of state machines allows for their orchestration in a controlled manner. The abstraction partitions the orchestration logic from the underlying execution context, thereby enabling the scheduler to handle state transitions based on the current status of a request. This decoupling contributes to enhanced modularity and scalability, as the state machine governs high-level behavior while the asynchronous runtime manages scheduling and execution details. The resulting framework allows complex sequences of operations to be represented, analyzed, and executed in a manner that is both robust and amenable to refinement through formal analysis.

Ensuring Consistency through Static Guarantees and Controlled Transitions

The adoption of state machines in the asynchronous domain yields significant benefits in enforcing consistency and correctness. By encoding the state transitions as part of the system's formal specification, compile-time mechanisms can verify that every state change adheres strictly to the predefined contract. This static assurance is augmented by strong type systems and explicit trait bounds that collectively ensure determinism and operational safety. Each permissible state transition is scrutinized at compile time, thereby mitigating the risk of unforeseen runtime behaviors. Additionally, the controlled nature of state transitions permits systematic handling of exceptional or transient conditions, ensuring that the system responds coherently in the face of irregular inputs. The synthesis of mathematical abstraction with robust compile-time checks underlines a disciplined approach to managing the multifarious aspects of asynchronous request lifecycles.

Rust Code Snippet

```
//! This code snippet implements a simple asynchronous state machine
//! that models the lifecycle of a request. It closely follows the
↪   formal
//! framework presented in the chapter where a state machine is
//! defined as a tuple M = (Q, , , q, F):
//!
//!   • Q: The set of states (represented by the enum `State`)
//!   • : The input alphabet/events (represented by the enum
↪   `Event`)
//!   • : The transition function : Q ×  -> Q (implemented in the
↪   `transition` method)
//!   • q: The initial state (set as `State::Initial` when creating
↪   `AsyncStateMachine`)
//!   • F: The set of final/terminal states (here,
↪   `State::Completed` and `State::Failed`)
//!
//! The asynchronous execution model is integrated using the Tokio
↪   runtime,
//! and state transitions are executed in response to asynchronous
↪   events.
//!
use tokio::time::{sleep, Duration};

/// Represents the states in our asynchronous state machine.
```

```rust
#[derive(Debug, Clone, PartialEq)]
enum State {
    /// Initial state (q)
    Initial,
    /// State representing active processing
    Processing,
    /// State when waiting for an external event
    Waiting,
    /// Final state indicating successful completion (member of F)
    Completed,
    /// Final state indicating failure (member of F)
    Failed,
}

/// Events represent the input alphabet () of our state machine.
#[derive(Debug)]
enum Event {
    /// Event to start processing
    Start,
    /// Event indicating data receipt with a payload
    DataReceived(String),
    /// Event representing a timeout
    Timeout,
    /// Represents an error event with message
    Error(String),
    /// Event indicating the completion of an asynchronous wait
    Complete,
}

/// The AsyncStateMachine struct encapsulates our state machine.
/// It maintains the current state (an element of Q) and provides a
↪  transition function.
struct AsyncStateMachine {
    state: State,
}

impl AsyncStateMachine {
    /// Creates a new state machine in the initial state (q =
    ↪  State::Initial)
    fn new() -> Self {
        Self {
            state: State::Initial,
        }
    }

    /// Asynchronous transition function: : Q ×  -> Q.
    /// This function takes an event and transitions the state
    ↪  machine to a new state.
    async fn transition(&mut self, event: Event) -> Result<(),
    ↪  String> {
        // Using pattern matching to define deterministic state
        ↪  transitions.
        self.state = match (self.state.clone(), event) {
```

```rust
            (State::Initial, Event::Start) => State::Processing,
            (State::Processing, Event::DataReceived(data)) => {
                println!("Processing received data: {}", data);
                // Transition to waiting; simulating deferred/async
                ↪   action.
                State::Waiting
            }
            (State::Waiting, Event::Complete) => State::Completed,
            (State::Processing, Event::Error(err)) => {
                println!("Error encountered: {}", err);
                State::Failed
            }
            // If a timeout occurs in any state, transition to
            ↪   Failed.
            (_, Event::Timeout) => State::Failed,
            // Default: for unhandled events, retain the current
            ↪   state.
            (current_state, _) => current_state,
        };
        Ok(())
    }

    /// Checks whether the state machine has reached a terminal
    ↪   state.
    fn is_final(&self) -> bool {
        matches!(self.state, State::Completed | State::Failed)
    }
}

/// Simulates processing a request using the asynchronous state
↪   machine.
/// Uses Tokio timers to mimic asynchronous operations between
↪   transitions.
async fn process_request(mut fsm: AsyncStateMachine) ->
↪   Result<State, String> {
    // Trigger the start of processing.
    fsm.transition(Event::Start).await?;
    println!("State after Start: {:?}", fsm.state);

    // Simulate an asynchronous operation for receiving data.
    sleep(Duration::from_millis(100)).await;
    fsm.transition(Event::DataReceived("Example
    ↪   payload".to_string())).await?;
    println!("State after DataReceived: {:?}", fsm.state);

    // If the state machine is in the Waiting state, simulate
    ↪   further async wait.
    if let State::Waiting = fsm.state {
        sleep(Duration::from_millis(100)).await;
        // Completing the waiting period, transitioning to
        ↪   Completed.
        fsm.transition(Event::Complete).await?;
    }
```

230

```rust
    Ok(fsm.state)
}

/// Entry point using the Tokio runtime.
#[tokio::main]
async fn main() -> Result<(), Box<dyn std::error::Error>> {
    let fsm = AsyncStateMachine::new();
    let final_state = process_request(fsm).await?;
    println!("Final state of the request: {:?}", final_state);
    Ok(())
}
```

Chapter 36

Lifetime Management in Asynchronous Contexts

Fundamentals of Lifetime Annotations in Rust

Lifetime annotations in Rust serve as formal instruments to guarantee that references remain valid for the duration of their intended use. Central to this mechanism is the concept that every reference is associated with a lifetime parameter, typically denoted as α, which expresses the temporal scope in which the reference is active. This annotation system ensures that data is accessed only within valid regions, thereby precluding the possibility of dangling pointers or undefined behaviors. The lifetime of a reference is often mathematically modeled as an interval on the time axis, and relationships between lifetimes (for example, $\alpha_1 \subseteq \alpha_2$) are established to certify that an inner scope cannot outlive an outer scope. In asynchronous contexts, such detailed annotations are indispensable owing to the fact that control may suspend and resume across discrete time slices, making it imperative to statically analyze and verify that all references are confined to their proper regions.

Challenges in Concurrent Environments

Concurrent environments impose additional complexity on lifetime management due to the interleaving of task executions and non-deterministic scheduling. In such settings, asynchronous tasks may traverse multiple suspension points, during which the state of the system is preserved and subsequently resumed. The challenge arises when references that originate in one execution context need to persist across asynchronous boundaries, potentially interacting with data in concurrently executing tasks. This situation necessitates a nuanced understanding of the borrow rules and lifetime propagation. The lifetime of any given reference must be meticulously tracked to ensure that, despite concurrent access from multiple threads or tasks, no reference outlives the data to which it refers. The asynchronous execution model thereby transforms lifetime verification into a constraint satisfaction problem, where invariants must hold in the presence of unpredictable scheduling and concurrent modifications. A rigorous mathematical treatment of these issues ensures that lifetime constraints are maintained, preserving memory safety without compromising on efficiency.

Advanced Lifetime Strategies in Asynchronous Systems

The complexity of asynchronous systems often demands advanced strategies for managing lifetimes that extend beyond the basic annotation mechanisms. In these systems, stateful asynchronous operations may encapsulate references within futures or generators, whose execution is deferred and resumed at non-deterministic times. To address these challenges, explicit lifetime annotations must be introduced into function signatures and intermediate abstractions to capture the extended scope over which a reference remains valid. Additionally, the use of region-based analysis provides a systematic framework for subdividing the lifetime of data into well-defined segments, each with its own set of constraints. This decomposition enables a refined control over resource management in concurrent settings, ensuring that references are safely shared between asynchronous operations while maintaining the integrity of the borrowing rules. In scenarios where mutable state is shared across tasks, the combination of strict lifetime annotations with synchronization primitives helps in delineating clear boundaries for data access, thus harmonizing safety with high-performance concurrent processing.

Static Analysis and Verification of Lifetimes

The verification of lifetime correctness in asynchronous contexts is achieved through static analysis techniques that are integral to Rust's compilation process. The borrow checker rigorously examines the code to construct a graph of lifetime dependencies, where nodes represent allocated resources and directed edges denote borrowing relationships. This graph-theoretic representation allows for the application of fixed-point iterations and constraint solving methods, ensuring that every lifetime constraint is satisfied even in the presence of multiple asynchronous suspensions. The analysis involves verifying that for any two lifetimes, the necessary inclusion relationships—such as $\alpha_1 \subseteq \alpha_2$—are maintained throughout the execution, regardless of how tasks are scheduled. By reducing lifetime verification to a problem in linear inequality solving over partially ordered sets, the static analysis framework provides strong compile-time guarantees. These guarantees are essential in high-performance network services, where the correctness of memory access patterns directly impacts both safety and efficiency. The discipline enforced by these static checks leads to robust systems where asynchronous operations and concurrent executions are orchestrated without incurring memory safety penalties.

Rust Code Snippet

```
use std::future::Future;
use std::pin::Pin;
use std::task::{Context, Poll};
use std::time::Duration;
use tokio::time::{sleep, Sleep};

/// Struct representing an asynchronous task that holds a reference
↪   with lifetime 'a.
/// This demonstrates advanced lifetime management in an
↪   asynchronous context.
///
/// Mathematical invariant (expressed in comments):
///   Let  be the lifetime of `data`. We require that:
```

```
///         (valid scope)
/// which guarantees that the reference remains valid across all
↪    asynchronous suspension points.
struct AsyncTask<'a> {
    data: &'a str,
    delay: Pin<Box<Sleep>>,
}

impl<'a> AsyncTask<'a> {
    /// Constructs a new AsyncTask with the provided data and a
    ↪    delay duration.
    fn new(data: &'a str, delay_duration: Duration) -> Self {
        AsyncTask {
            data,
            delay: Box::pin(sleep(delay_duration)),
        }
    }
}

impl<'a> Future for AsyncTask<'a> {
    type Output = (&'a str, usize);

    fn poll(self: Pin<&mut Self>, cx: &mut Context<'_>) ->
    ↪    Poll<Self::Output> {
        // Obtain a mutable reference to the underlying AsyncTask.
        let this = self.get_mut();

        // Poll the internal delay future.
        // When the delay completes, we yield the data along with
        ↪    its length.
        if let Poll::Ready(_) = this.delay.as_mut().poll(cx) {
            // Static lifetime check (conceptual):
            // The lifetime 'a associated with `data` must encompass
            ↪    the asynchronous operation.
            // This ensures the condition:    (current context
            ↪    lifetime).
            Poll::Ready((this.data, this.data.len()))
        } else {
            Poll::Pending
        }
    }
}

/// An asynchronous function that processes input data using
↪    AsyncTask.
/// It demonstrates lifetime propagation where the lifetime 'a of
↪    the input is maintained
/// throughout the asynchronous execution, ensuring that no
↪    reference outlives its data.
///
/// It mirrors the algorithmic requirement that for any two
↪    lifetimes,
```

235

```rust
/// if we need to guarantee    , then all references derived from
//   `input` must live within 'a.
async fn process_data<'a>(input: &'a str) -> (&'a str, usize) {
    // Create an asynchronous task with a simulated delay (1
    //   second).
    let task = AsyncTask::new(input, Duration::from_secs(1));
    task.await
}

#[tokio::main]
async fn main() {
    // Define a string slice (with an effectively static lifetime in
    //   this instance).
    let message = "Asynchronous Lifetime Management in Rust";

    // Process the message using the asynchronous
    //   lifetime-controlled function.
    let (result, length) = process_data(message).await;

    println!("Processed message: \"{}\" with length: {}", result,
      length);
}
```

Chapter 37

Dynamic Dispatch with Trait Objects in Web Services

Foundations of Trait Objects as a Mechanism for Polymorphism

Dynamic dispatch mediated by trait objects in Rust establishes a rigorous framework for runtime polymorphism within network systems. Trait objects, typically represented as $\&dynTrait$ or $\text{Box} < dynTrait >$, encapsulate both a pointer to the underlying concrete type and an associated virtual method table (vtable). The vtable is a structured data construct that maps method identifiers to their corresponding function pointers. This mapping, denoted mathematically as V : Method Identifier $\rightarrow$ Function Pointer, is established during compilation and utilized at runtime to resolve method calls. The separation of interface from implementation inherent in trait objects fosters an environment wherein heterogeneous types can be manipulated through a uniform interface, thereby decoupling service components and enhancing the modularity of web-based network systems.

Runtime Resolution and Vtable-Based Dispatch Mechanisms

At the core of dynamic dispatch lies the mechanism of vtable-based resolution. Every trait object is associated with a vtable that stores the concrete implementations of the trait's methods, enabling method invocations to be deferred until runtime. When a method is invoked on a trait object, the call is redirected to the appropriate function pointer by referencing the vtable structure. Formally, consider two distinct types, each implementing a shared trait; their respective vtables, V_1 and V_2, provide a systematic mapping of method identifiers to function implementations. This indirection, though incurring a modest computational overhead, ensures that the correct behavior is executed regardless of the actual type of the object. The mathematical rigor embedded in this mechanism guarantees that the invariant of type safety is maintained even when the precise implementation is determined dynamically.

Implications for Modular and Extensible Network Components

The utilization of trait objects for dynamic dispatch is particularly advantageous in the construction of modular and extensible network services. Modern network architectures frequently rely on a composition of independently developed modules, each responsible for discrete functionalities such as request routing, protocol handling, and security enforcement. Employing trait objects allows these modules to expose a common interface, facilitating the interchangeable use of components and the integration of new implementations without the necessity for systemic rewrites. The inherent abstraction provided by trait objects supports decoupling at both design and implementation levels, thereby enabling flexible reconfiguration of service pipelines. This architectural paradigm, rooted in object-oriented principles yet refined through Rust's stringent type system, permits the seamless amalgamation of diverse network components while preserving the efficiency and reliability demanded by high-performance web services.

Quantitative Considerations and Performance Trade-Offs

The shift to dynamic dispatch via trait objects must be carefully balanced against performance considerations inherent in high-volume network operations. Each method invocation through a trait object introduces an additional level of indirection, which can be quantified by an overhead term C_{dyn} such that the effective method call cost is given by $C_{eff} = C_{stat} + C_{dyn}$. Although the incremental cost C_{dyn}—attributable to vtable lookups and potential cache inefficiencies—is typically minor relative to the baseline static dispatch cost C_{stat}, the impact must be rigorously assessed in latency-sensitive environments. Performance metrics relevant to dynamic dispatch are often derived from detailed benchmarking and profiling within realistic service deployments. These quantitative analyses ensure that the flexibility afforded by runtime polymorphism does not undermine the throughput and responsiveness required in contemporary web services, thus affirming a balanced approach between architectural elegance and computational efficiency.

Rust Code Snippet

```rust
use std::time::{Duration, Instant};

// Define a trait to simulate a web service handler interface.
// This trait represents the abstraction that allows dynamic
↪    dispatch via trait objects.
trait WebService {
    // The process_request method simulates handling a network
↪    request.
    // It returns a processed response as a String.
    fn process_request(&self, request: &str) -> String;
}

// Implementation using static dispatch (concrete type known at
↪    compile time).
struct StaticService;

impl WebService for StaticService {
    fn process_request(&self, request: &str) -> String {
        // Simulate processing logic with static dispatch.
        // Here, no indirect lookup is needed, so C_dyn is
↪        effectively zero.
        format!("StaticService processed: {}", request)
```

```
    }
}

// Implementation using dynamic dispatch (via trait object).
struct DynamicService;

impl WebService for DynamicService {
    fn process_request(&self, request: &str) -> String {
        // Simulate processing logic under dynamic dispatch.
        // The method call is routed via a vtable at runtime.
        format!("DynamicService processed: {}", request)
    }
}

// Function to compute the effective cost of method invocation.
// It implements the equation: C_eff = C_stat + C_dyn,
// where C_stat is the static cost and C_dyn is the additional
↪    overhead
// from dynamic (vtable) dispatch.
fn calculate_effective_cost(c_stat: u32, c_dyn: u32) -> u32 {
    c_stat + c_dyn
}

// Function to emulate processing using static dispatch.
// This function explicitly receives a StaticService reference.
fn process_with_static(service: &StaticService, request: &str) ->
↪    String {
    let c_stat = 50; // Baseline cost for static dispatch
    let c_dyn = 0;    // No vtable overhead in static dispatch
    let c_eff = calculate_effective_cost(c_stat, c_dyn);
    let response = service.process_request(request);
    format!("Response: {}\nEffective Cost: {}", response, c_eff)
}

// Function to emulate processing using dynamic dispatch.
// The service is accepted as a trait object, triggering runtime
↪    resolution.
fn process_with_dynamic(service: &dyn WebService, request: &str) ->
↪    String {
    let c_stat = 50; // Baseline cost remains the same
    let c_dyn = 10;  // Additional overhead from vtable lookup
    ↪    (dynamic dispatch)
    let c_eff = calculate_effective_cost(c_stat, c_dyn);
    let response = service.process_request(request);
    format!("Response: {}\nEffective Cost: {}", response, c_eff)
}

fn main() {
    let request = "GET /api/data";

    // Demonstrate static dispatch with a concrete type.
    let static_service = StaticService;
```

240

```rust
    let result_static = process_with_static(&static_service,
↪   request);
    println!("Static Dispatch:\n{}\n", result_static);

    // Demonstrate dynamic dispatch using a trait object.
    let dynamic_service = DynamicService;
    let result_dynamic = process_with_dynamic(&dynamic_service,
↪   request);
    println!("Dynamic Dispatch:\n{}\n", result_dynamic);

    // Demonstrate polymorphism:
    // Create a vector of Boxed trait objects to hold heterogeneous
↪   service types.
    let services: Vec<Box<dyn WebService>> = vec![
        Box::new(StaticService),
        Box::new(DynamicService),
    ];

    // Loop over the services and execute the request, showing
↪   runtime resolution.
    for service in services.iter() {
        let output = service.process_request(request);
        println!("Polymorphic Processing => {}", output);
    }

    // Benchmark dynamic dispatch performance:
    // This loop mimics high-volume network operations where
↪   multiple dynamic calls are invoked.
    let iterations = 1000;
    let start = Instant::now();
    for service in services.iter() {
        for _ in 0..iterations {
            let _ = service.process_request(request);
        }
    }
    let duration = start.elapsed();
    println!("\nTotal time for {} iterations over dynamic dispatch
↪   services: {:?}", iterations * services.len(), duration);

    // Explanation of vtable-based dispatch:
    // In Rust, every trait object (e.g., &dyn WebService or Box<dyn
↪   WebService>)
    // is composed of two pointers:
    // 1. A pointer to the concrete data.
    // 2. A pointer to a vtable, which can be viewed as a mapping:
    //    V: Method Identifier -> Function Pointer.
    //
    // When a method (e.g., process_request) is invoked on the trait
↪   object,
    // the runtime performs the following operation:
    //    response = (vtable.process_request)(data_pointer, request)
    //
```

```
    // The additional cost, defined as C_dyn in the effective cost
    ↪   equation,
    // represents the overhead due to this extra level of
    ↪   indirection.
}
```

Chapter 38

Custom Middleware for Security Validations

Theoretical Foundations of Middleware Security Validations

Within the paradigm of network service architectures, middleware serves as the intermediary layer that intercepts and processes incoming requests prior to their delegation to the core application logic. Security validations embedded within these middleware layers assume the role of preliminary checkpoints that assess both authentication credentials and data integrity. Formally, the validation process may be abstracted as a function $S : \mathcal{R} \rightarrow \{0, 1\}$, where $\mathcal{R}$ is the set of incoming requests and an output of 1 signifies that a request satisfies designated security requirements. The construction of such a function is underpinned by rigorous mathematical and algorithmic principles, ensuring that only requests conforming to established authentication and data integrity parameters are permitted further processing.

Architectural Decomposition of Security Middleware

The systematic integration of security validations within middleware necessitates an architectural decomposition that emphasizes modularity and functional separation. Middleware components are frequently organized into discrete submodules, each tasked with specific responsibilities such as parsing, transformation, and security evaluation. In scenarios where security validations are embedded, the middleware architecture can be envisioned as a composition of functions $\{f_1, f_2, \ldots, f_n\}$, where the composite mapping $F = f_n \circ \cdots \circ f_1$ governs the progression of an incoming request. Each function f_i encapsulates a distinct security check—ranging from credential verification to integrity confirmation—thereby contributing to a layered defense mechanism. This decomposition not only facilitates the isolation and testing of individual security aspects but also enhances the overall maintainability of the system by enabling parallel development and verification of each security submodule.

Mechanisms for Authentication Enforcement

Authentication enforcement within the middleware layer is achieved through a confluence of cryptographic and protocol-based mechanisms. The middleware performs an initial examination of request headers and tokens, applying a secure transformation function $H : \mathcal{I} \to \mathcal{H}$, where $\mathcal{I}$ represents the space of authentication inputs and $\mathcal{H}$ denotes the resulting hash space. The transformation acts as a cryptographic fingerprint, ensuring that any modification to the input data is readily identifiable. By comparing the computed hash against a trusted value, the middleware validates the authenticity of the request. This methodology provides a mathematically robust framework for authentication, wherein the probability of an undetected alteration in the authentication token is minimized by the security parameterization inherent to the hash function. The in situ evaluation of authentication not only bolsters the security posture but also isolates authentication logic from the business logic executed downstream.

Data Integrity Monitoring and Validation

Data integrity within network communications is safeguarded by embedding validation mechanisms directly into the middleware. This approach involves the deployment of cryptographic checks such as digital signatures and secure checksums. Given a message

$m \in \mathcal{M}$, a secure digest function $D : \mathcal{M} \rightarrow \Sigma$ computes a signature $\sigma \in \Sigma$, which is subsequently compared against an expected value. The middleware utilizes this comparison, expressed through the relation $\sigma_{\text{computed}} = \sigma_{\text{expected}}$, to ascertain that the message has remained unaltered during transit. By executing these integrity checks as an intrinsic part of the middleware pipeline, the system ensures that only messages that have passed rigorous validation are propagated. This verification process is essential for upholding data consistency across distributed architectures, particularly in environments where data tampering or transmission errors may compromise service reliability.

Analytical Perspectives on Performance Trade-Offs

The incorporation of security validations into middleware layers, while essential for robust network defenses, introduces additional computational overhead that warrants analytical scrutiny. The overall cost of processing a request within the middleware environment can be expressed as $C_{\text{total}} = C_0 + C_{\text{sec}}$, where C_0 represents the baseline execution cost absent security operations, and C_{sec} embodies the incremental overhead attributable to authentication and integrity validations. The design objective is to optimize C_{sec} such that the enhanced security does not impose prohibitive latency or resource consumption. To that end, quantitative models and performance profiling are employed, balancing computational efficiency against the requisite rigor of security validations. This analytical perspective provides a formal basis for evaluating trade-offs and advancing the design of middleware that is not only secure but also scalable and performant in high-throughput network environments.

Rust Code Snippet

```
use std::collections::HashMap;
use std::time::Instant;

// External crates needed: sha2 and hex. Add in Cargo.toml:
// sha2 = "0.10"
// hex = "0.4"
use sha2::{Digest, Sha256};
```

```rust
/// Represents an incoming network request.
#[derive(Debug)]
struct Request {
    headers: HashMap<String, String>,
    body: Vec<u8>,
    auth_token: String,
    expected_digest: String,
}

/// Compute a cryptographic hash of the input string.
/// This function corresponds to H :  → .
fn compute_hash(input: &str) -> String {
    let mut hasher = Sha256::new();
    hasher.update(input.as_bytes());
    let result = hasher.finalize();
    hex::encode(result)
}

/// Compute a secure digest of the message.
/// This function models D :  →  for data integrity checks.
fn compute_digest(message: &[u8]) -> String {
    let mut hasher = Sha256::new();
    hasher.update(message);
    let result = hasher.finalize();
    hex::encode(result)
}

/// Type alias for a middleware function that processes a request.
/// Each middleware function corresponds to a function f from the
/// ↪ composite F = f  ...  f.
type MiddlewareFn = fn(&mut Request) -> Result<(), &'static str>;

/// Middleware function to parse headers.
/// Ensures that required headers such as "Content-Type" are
/// ↪ present.
fn parse_headers(req: &mut Request) -> Result<(), &'static str> {
    if req.headers.contains_key("Content-Type") {
        Ok(())
    } else {
        Err("Missing required header: Content-Type")
    }
}

/// Middleware function for authentication enforcement.
/// Represents the security validation S :  → {0,1} by verifying the
/// ↪ auth token.
fn auth_validator(req: &mut Request) -> Result<(), &'static str> {
    // Compute the cryptographic hash of the auth token.
    // This simulates the transformation H :  → .
    let computed_hash = compute_hash(&req.auth_token);
```

```rust
    // In a real scenario, the trusted hash would be securely stored
    ↪  and managed.
    let trusted_hash = "trusted_hash_value";

    if computed_hash == trusted_hash {
        Ok(())
    } else {
        Err("Authentication failed: invalid auth token.")
    }
}


/// Middleware function for data integrity validation.
/// Computes the digest of the request body and compares it against
↪  the expected digest.
fn integrity_validator(req: &mut Request) -> Result<(), &'static
↪  str> {
    let computed_digest = compute_digest(&req.body);
    if computed_digest == req.expected_digest {
        Ok(())
    } else {
        Err("Data integrity check failed: digest mismatch.")
    }
}

/// Processes the request through a chain of middleware functions.
/// The composite function F = f ... f is executed sequentially.
/// Additionally, this function evaluates the performance cost:
/// C_total = C + C_sec, where C is the baseline cost and C_sec is
↪  the accumulative security cost.
fn process_request(req: &mut Request, middleware_chain:
↪  &[MiddlewareFn]) -> Result<(), &'static str> {
    // Baseline execution cost (C) is defined arbitrarily.
    let baseline_cost: u128 = 100;
    // Security cost accumulator (C_sec), measured in nanoseconds.
    let mut security_cost: u128 = 0;

    for function in middleware_chain {
        let start = Instant::now();
        // Execute current middleware function.
        function(req)?;
        let elapsed = start.elapsed().as_nanos();
        security_cost += elapsed;
    }

    let total_cost = baseline_cost + security_cost;
    println!(
        "Request processed with total cost: {} (Baseline: {} ns,
        ↪  Security: {} ns)",
        total_cost, baseline_cost, security_cost
    );
    Ok(())
}
```

```rust
fn main() {
    // Construct a sample request with headers, body, and
    // ↪ authentication token.
    let mut headers = HashMap::new();
    headers.insert("Content-Type".to_string(),
    ↪ "application/json".to_string());
    let body = b"{ \"data\": \"example\" }".to_vec();

    // Pre-compute expected digest to simulate secure transmission.
    let expected_digest = compute_digest(&body);
    let auth_token = "secret_token".to_string();

    let mut request = Request {
        headers,
        body,
        auth_token,
        expected_digest,
    };

    // Create the middleware chain:
    // F = integrity_validator  auth_validator  parse_headers.
    let middleware_chain: [MiddlewareFn; 3] = [parse_headers,
    ↪ auth_validator, integrity_validator];

    // Process the request through the middleware chain.
    match process_request(&mut request, &middleware_chain) {
        Ok(()) => println!("Request successfully passed all security
        ↪ validations."),
        Err(e) => println!("Request processing failed: {}", e),
    }
}
```

Chapter 39

Implementing Token-Based Authentication

Token Structure and Cryptographic Foundations

The authentication mechanism under consideration is predicated on the construction of a digital token, formally defined as an element t belonging to the token space $\mathcal{T}$. A token is typically composed of multiple segments, each of which conveys specific metadata and claims regarding the authenticated entity. The structural framework of a token often comprises a header, a payload, and a signature. The header contains information about the cryptographic algorithm and token type, while the payload encodes claims such as the identity of an entity, issued timestamps, and expiration details. The signature, computed using a secret key K and a predetermined signing algorithm, guarantees the integrity and authenticity of the token. Mathematically, the signature function may be denoted as

$$S(t) = \text{Sign}(P, K),$$

where P represents the concatenation of header and payload data. The robustness of this approach relies on the collision-resistance and pre-image resistance properties of the underlying cryptographic hash functions employed within the signing algorithm.

Mechanisms for Token Creation

Token creation involves a series of precisely engineered operations designed to ensure both randomness and verifiability. In this context, a set of claims $\mathcal{C}$ is first assembled, representing the necessary assertions about the identity and privileges of the client entity. The generation process incorporates secure random number generators to produce nonces or unique identifiers, thus preventing token replay and ensuring temporal uniqueness. The collective information, along with temporal data such as issuance timestamp τ_{iss} and expiration timestamp τ_{exp}, is encoded into the payload P. Subsequently, the digital signature is generated by applying a secure transformation to the payload, resulting in a signature S that is intrinsically bound to the token's content. The complete token t can be notionally represented as a tuple

$$t = \langle H, P, S \rangle,$$

where H denotes the header. The deliberate incorporation of cryptographic operations during the token creation phase serves to mitigate vulnerabilities and enhances the overall security posture of the authentication process.

Token Validation and Integrity Verification

Validation of a token is a critical operation that ensures only legitimate tokens grant access to secure API endpoints. The token validation process is executed through an algorithm $V : \mathcal{T} \to \{0, 1\}$, where a return value of 1 signifies successful authentication. The procedure commences with the decomposition of the token t into its constituent components and proceeds with a re-computation of the signature using the same cryptographic algorithm and secret key K. Let P be the payload extracted from the token; then, validation requires that the computed signature $\text{Sign}(P, K)$ matches the signature S embedded in the token. Furthermore, it is necessary to inspect the temporal claims by verifying that the current timestamp τ_{curr} satisfies the condition

$$\tau_{iss} \leq \tau_{curr} \leq \tau_{exp},$$

thus ensuring that the token is neither prematurely used nor expired. The integrity verification, therefore, is a dual process encompassing both signature authentication and temporal validation, ensuring that any alterations to the token's data are detected with high probability.

Token Renewal and Lifecycle Management

The controlled renewal of tokens forms an integral part of sustaining secure API access over extended periods. Lifecycle management of tokens involves the periodic reassessment of the validity of each token, followed by reissuance when certain conditions are met. Renewal is generally initiated prior to the token's expiration, allowing the system to furnish a new token that upholds the same assertions as its predecessor while incorporating fresh temporal credentials. This process may involve a refresh mechanism in which a secondary token, often referred to as a refresh token, is exchanged for a new access token. Formally, let $R : \mathcal{T} \times \mathcal{C} \to \mathcal{T}$ denote the renewal function, where $\mathcal{C}$ encapsulates any additional credential checks performed during the renewal process. The implementation of such a function critically depends on strict adherence to security policies that regulate token lifetime and revalidation intervals. A thorough lifecycle management strategy also entails the revocation of tokens that have been compromised or are otherwise deemed insecure, thereby preserving the integrity of the authentication framework.

Security Challenges and Cryptographic Considerations

The deployment of token-based authentication is accompanied by a variety of security challenges that necessitate rigorous cryptographic safeguards. Among these challenges is the threat of token forgery, which is mitigated by employing robust cryptographic primitives that assure the uniqueness and integrity of each token. Replay attacks are countered through the inclusion of nonces and timestamp-based validation, ensuring that tokens cannot be reused outside their intended lifespans. Key rotation strategies serve to periodically update the secret key K, thereby reducing the window of opportunity for adversaries in the event of a key compromise. These cryptographic considerations are not only theoretical; they have direct implications on the practical security of API endpoints.

The careful design of the token generation, validation, and renewal procedures, combined with stringent key management practices, underpins a resilient authentication system that withstands a wide spectrum of attack vectors.

Rust Code Snippet

```rust
use chrono::Utc;
use rand::Rng;
use sha2::{Digest, Sha256};

// Define the token header structure, representing H in t = <H, P,
↪  S>
#[derive(Debug, Clone)]
struct Header {
    alg: String, // Algorithm used for signing (e.g., HS256)
    typ: String, // Token type (e.g., JWT)
}

// Define the token payload structure, representing P in t = <H, P,
↪  S>
#[derive(Debug, Clone)]
struct Payload {
    claims: Vec<(String, String)>, // Set of claims, e.g., user_id,
    ↪  role, etc.
    issued_at: i64,    // iss: Token issuance timestamp
    expires_at: i64,   // exp: Token expiration timestamp
    nonce: String,     // Unique identifier to prevent replay attacks
}

// Define the complete token structure as a tuple <H, P, S>
#[derive(Debug, Clone)]
struct Token {
    header: Header,
    payload: Payload,
    signature: String, // S = Sign(P, K)
}

// Function to compute the signature S(t) = Sign(P, K)
// It simulates a signing operation using SHA256 hash, incorporating
↪  a secret key.
fn sign(payload: &Payload, secret: &str) -> String {
    // Concatenate payload elements: the claims, timestamps, and
    ↪  nonce.
    let mut data = String::new();
    for (key, value) in &payload.claims {
        data.push_str(&format!("{}:{}", key, value));
    }
    data.push_str(&payload.issued_at.to_string());
    data.push_str(&payload.expires_at.to_string());
```

```rust
    data.push_str(&payload.nonce);

    // Compute the hash by combining the serialized payload and the
    ↪    secret key.
    let mut hasher = Sha256::new();
    hasher.update(data.as_bytes());
    hasher.update(secret.as_bytes());
    let result = hasher.finalize();

    // Return the resulting hash as a hexadecimal string.
    format!("{:x}", result)
}

// Function to create a token.
// Implements token creation: t = <H, P, S> where the signature S is
↪    computed as Sign(P, K)
fn create_token(secret: &str, claims: Vec<(String, String)>,
↪    valid_duration: i64) -> Token {
    let now = Utc::now().timestamp();
    let header = Header {
        alg: "HS256".to_string(),
        typ: "JWT".to_string(),
    };

    // Generate a random nonce to ensure uniqueness of the token
    let nonce = rand::thread_rng().gen::<u64>().to_string();
    let payload = Payload {
        claims,
        issued_at: now,
        expires_at: now + valid_duration,
        nonce,
    };

    // Compute the signature S = Sign(P, K)
    let signature = sign(&payload, secret);

    Token {
        header,
        payload,
        signature,
    }
}

// Function to validate a token.
// Implements the validation algorithm V: (T) → {0, 1} by verifying
↪    the signature and temporal constraints.
fn validate_token(token: &Token, secret: &str) -> bool {
    let now = Utc::now().timestamp();

    // Check if the current timestamp falls within the valid period:
    ↪    iss   curr   exp
    if now < token.payload.issued_at || now >
    ↪    token.payload.expires_at {
```

```rust
        return false;
    }

    // Re-compute the signature using the payload and secret key.
    let computed_signature = sign(&token.payload, secret);

    // Validate that the computed signature matches the token's
    //     embedded signature.
    computed_signature == token.signature
}

// Function to renew an existing token.
// Implements renewal R: T × C → T, creating a new token with
//     updated temporal credentials while preserving claims.
fn renew_token(token: &Token, secret: &str, extension: i64) ->
    Option<Token> {
    let now = Utc::now().timestamp();

    // Renew only if the token is still valid (i.e., not expired).
    if now > token.payload.expires_at {
        return None;
    }

    // Maintain the original claims and generate a new token with
    //     updated issuance and expiration times.
    let claims = token.payload.claims.clone();
    let remaining_time = token.payload.expires_at - now;
    let new_duration = remaining_time + extension;
    Some(create_token(secret, claims, new_duration))
}

fn main() {
    // Secret key K used for signing tokens.
    let secret = "my_super_secret_key";

    // Define a set of claims () that include identity and privilege
    //     data.
    let claims = vec![
        ("user_id".to_string(), "42".to_string()),
        ("role".to_string(), "admin".to_string()),
    ];

    // Create a new token valid for 3600 seconds (1 hour)
    // This corresponds to assembling the token with header H,
    //     payload P, and signature S.
    let token = create_token(secret, claims, 3600);
    println!("Generated Token: {:?}", token);

    // Validate the token using the algorithm V :   → {0, 1}.
    let is_valid = validate_token(&token, secret);
    println!("Token valid: {}", is_valid);
```

```rust
    // Attempt to renew the token with an extension of 1800 seconds
    ↪  (30 minutes)
    match renew_token(&token, secret, 1800) {
        Some(new_token) => println!("Renewed Token: {:?}",
        ↪  new_token),
        None => println!("Token renewal failed; token expired."),
    }
}
```

Chapter 40

Asynchronous OAuth2 Flows

Protocol Architecture and Flow Semantics

The OAuth2 authorization framework defines a structured process for delegated access to protected resources. Within this framework, distinct roles such as the client, resource server, and authorization server are formally delineated. At its core, the protocol enables a client to obtain an access token after a successful validation of an authorization grant that evidences the resource owner's consent. In an asynchronous context, the non-blocking nature of network communications and the variable latencies inherent in distributed systems necessitate adaptations in the protocol's execution model. This adaptation involves decoupling I/O-bound operations from the core protocol logic and introducing concurrency abstractions that manage state transitions with rigorous temporal coordination.

Non-Blocking Token Exchange Mechanisms

The exchange of an authorization grant for an access token is the principal operation in the OAuth2 protocol. In an asynchronous implementation, this exchange is managed as a non-blocking task, thereby allowing a high degree of concurrency without incurring the overhead of thread blocking. The token generation process can be abstractly modeled as a transformation function

$$\mathcal{E} : \mathcal{G} \to \mathcal{T},$$

where $\mathcal{G}$ denotes the set of valid authorization grants and $\mathcal{T}$ represents the token space. The asynchronous execution of this function necessitates the utilization of efficient scheduling mechanisms that permit the deferment of network responses without compromising the deterministic progression of protocol state. Advanced asynchronous primitives facilitate the seamless orchestration of multiple concurrent token exchanges while integrating robust error handling, thus preserving the integrity of the operation even under conditions of intermittent network failures.

Concurrent State Management and Synchronization

The asynchronous execution of OAuth2 flows imposes stringent requirements for managing the protocol state. Each request undergoes a series of state transitions from grant validation to token issuance, transitions that are often modeled by a finite state automaton. Let Σ denote the set of protocol states and $\delta : \Sigma \times E \to \Sigma$ the state transition function in response to an event E. In an asynchronous paradigm, it is critical to implement synchronization mechanisms that prevent race conditions while avoiding deadlocks. These mechanisms ensure that concurrent operations accessing shared state—such as token generation and revocation—are executed in a controlled manner. The design of these concurrency controls is fundamental to maintaining consistency in the presence of overlapping asynchronous procedures.

Asynchronous Metrics and Security Implications

Incorporating asynchronous processing within OAuth2 flows affects both performance metrics and security guarantees. Non-blocking operations contribute to higher throughput, which may be quantified by the ratio

$$\rho = \frac{N_c}{T_r},$$

where N_c is the number of concurrent client requests and T_r represents the mean response time per request. While improved throughput is a notable benefit, the asynchronous model also introduces potential security challenges that must be rigorously addressed. Issues such as token leakage, replay attacks, and transient state inconsistencies demand enhanced cryptographic measures and strict validation routines. In the asynchronous context, operations like key rotation, nonce management, and token revocation are integrated into the workflow, reinforcing the overall security posture and ensuring that token exchanges remain robust against adversarial exploits.

Temporal Dynamics and Refresh Mechanisms

The management of temporal constraints is integral to the OAuth2 protocol, particularly with respect to token expiration and the subsequent refresh processes. Each access token is associated with a validity interval denoted by $[\tau_{\mathrm{iss}}, \tau_{\mathrm{exp}}]$, during which it maintains its authorization properties. In an asynchronous setting, the renewal of tokens is orchestrated through non-blocking procedures that automatically revalidate credentials and extend token lifetimes. This process can be conceptualized as a mapping

$$R : \mathcal{T} \times \tau \to \mathcal{T},$$

where τ represents the additional time granted prior to token expiration. The refresh mechanism leverages concurrent scheduling to reinitiate the issuance process without interrupting ongoing operations or degrading system throughput. Such careful temporal management ensures the continuity of secure API access even amidst high-load asynchronous environments.

Rust Code Snippet

```rust
use std::time::{Duration, Instant};
use tokio::time::sleep;

// Define an error type for OAuth2 operations.
#[derive(Debug)]
enum OAuth2Error {
    InvalidGrant,
```

```rust
    NetworkError,
    Other(String),
}

// Represents an authorization grant.
#[derive(Debug)]
struct Grant {
    id: String,
}

impl Grant {
    fn new(id: &str) -> Self {
        Self { id: id.to_string() }
    }
}

// Represents an access token with an expiration time.
#[derive(Debug)]
struct Token {
    value: String,
    expiry: Instant,
}

// Asynchronously exchanges a valid authorization grant for an
↪   access token.
// This simulates the transformation function E:  →  .
async fn exchange_token(grant: Grant) -> Result<Token, OAuth2Error>
↪   {
    // Simulate non-blocking network delay.
    sleep(Duration::from_millis(100)).await;
    if grant.id.is_empty() {
        return Err(OAuth2Error::InvalidGrant);
    }
    // Create a token with a fixed lifetime (e.g., 3600 seconds).
    Ok(Token {
        value: format!("token_for_{}", grant.id),
        expiry: Instant::now() + Duration::from_secs(3600),
    })
}

// Enumerates the possible states in the OAuth2 finite state
↪   machine.
#[derive(Debug, Clone, Copy)]
enum State {
    Start,
    Validated,
    TokenIssued,
    Refreshed,
    Failed,
}

// Enumerates events that trigger state transitions.
#[derive(Debug, Clone, Copy)]
```

```rust
enum Event {
    GrantValidated,
    TokenIssued,
    RefreshRequested,
    ErrorOccurred,
}

// A simple state machine to model protocol state transitions.
// The state transition function :   × E →   is embedded in
↪   process_event.
#[derive(Debug)]
struct StateMachine {
    current: State,
}

impl StateMachine {
    fn new(initial: State) -> Self {
        Self { current: initial }
    }

    // Processes an event asynchronously and updates the current
    ↪   state.
    async fn process_event(&mut self, event: Event) {
        // Simulate asynchronous operation delay.
        sleep(Duration::from_millis(50)).await;
        self.current = match (self.current, event) {
            (State::Start, Event::GrantValidated) =>
            ↪   State::Validated,
            (State::Validated, Event::TokenIssued) =>
            ↪   State::TokenIssued,
            (State::TokenIssued, Event::RefreshRequested) =>
            ↪   State::Refreshed,
            (_, Event::ErrorOccurred) => State::Failed,
            (s, _) => s,
        };
        println!("State updated to: {:?}", self.current);
    }
}

// Asynchronously refreshes a token by extending its expiration
↪   time.
// This models the mapping R:   ×   →   .
async fn refresh_token(token: Token, extension: Duration) -> Token {
    // Simulate delay in processing the token refresh.
    sleep(Duration::from_millis(75)).await;
    Token {
        value: token.value + "_refreshed",
        expiry: Instant::now() + extension,
    }
}

// Computes throughput as the ratio   = Nc / Tr,
```

```rust
// where nc is the number of concurrent client requests and tr is
↪    the mean response time.
fn compute_throughput(nc: f64, tr: f64) -> f64 {
    nc / tr
}

// The main asynchronous function demonstrating the OAuth2 flow.
#[tokio::main]
async fn main() {
    // Simulate receiving an authorization grant.
    let grant = Grant::new("example_grant");
    println!("Received grant: {:?}", grant);

    // Asynchronously exchange the grant for a token.
    match exchange_token(grant).await {
        Ok(token) => {
            println!("Issued Token: {:?}", token);

            // Initialize and process state transitions.
            let mut state_machine = StateMachine::new(State::Start);

            ↪    state_machine.process_event(Event::GrantValidated).await;
            state_machine.process_event(Event::TokenIssued).await;

            // Asynchronously refresh the token (simulate token
            ↪    renewal).
            let refreshed_token = refresh_token(token,
            ↪    Duration::from_secs(3600)).await;
            println!("Refreshed Token: {:?}", refreshed_token);
        }
        Err(e) => {
            eprintln!("Error exchanging token: {:?}", e);
        }
    }

    // Compute and display throughput metrics.
    let throughput = compute_throughput(1000.0, 0.05);
    println!("Computed Throughput: {:.2}", throughput);
}
```

Chapter 41

Building JSON Web Token (JWT) Systems

JWT Structural Composition and Architectural Paradigm

A JSON Web Token (JWT) is defined by a tripartite structure that serves as a compact, URL-safe means of representing claims to be transferred between two parties. The token consists of three components: a header, a payload, and a signature. The header is a JSON object that specifies both the type of the token and the cryptographic algorithm used for signing (e.g., HS256 or RS256). The payload contains a set of claims, which are assertions about an entity and other metadata. These claims, once defined, are Base64 URL encoded to ensure safe transmission in HTTP environments. The signature is produced by applying a cryptographic algorithm to the concatenated, encoded header and payload, and then combining the result with a secret or key. This structure enables a stateless authentication mechanism whereby the token itself encapsulates all requisite authentication information, eliminating the need for persistent session storage.

Cryptographic Construction and Signing Process

The construction of a JWT necessitates rigorous cryptographic procedures that guarantee both integrity and authenticity. The signing process begins with the generation of a cryptographic digest from the concatenated token components. For symmetric key algorithms, consider a hash function H and a secret key K; the resulting signature is defined as

$$S = H(K,\ B_H \parallel B_P)\,,$$

where B_H and B_P denote the Base64 URL encoded representations of the header and payload, respectively, and $\parallel$ denotes concatenation with a period delimiter. In the case of asymmetric signing methods, the private key is used to generate the signature, while its corresponding public key is later employed during verification. The cryptographic foundation of the token ensures that any alteration of the header or payload results in a mismatch when the signature is recalculated on the receiver side, thereby providing a robust mechanism to prevent tampering.

Token Generation and Claims Encoding

The generation of a JWT involves carefully encoding a set of claims that assert authenticated information about a subject. These claims may include standard fields such as *iss* (issuer), *sub* (subject), *aud* (audience), *exp* (expiration time), and *nbf* (not before), as well as any application-specific data required by the service. The payload is serialized into a JSON object, then transformed into a Base64 URL encoded string to ensure compatibility with internet transport protocols. This encoding process is non-reversible and guarantees that special characters are replaced in a manner that precludes misinterpretation in transit. The deterministic nature of this encoding supports a secure mapping from the claim set to the token body, providing a basis for stateless authentication where the bearer of the token can be authenticated solely on the merits of the contained claims.

Verification Processes and Security Enforcement

Verification is an indispensable phase in the JWT lifecycle, one that is responsible for confirming both the integrity of the token and the validity of its claims. On receipt, the encoded header and payload are decoded to retrieve their original JSON structures, and the signature is recomputed using the identical cryptographic process that was applied during token issuance. A successful match between the recomputed signature and the provided signature verifies the token's integrity. In addition, temporal claims, such as exp (expiration) and nbf (not before), are examined to ensure that the token is being used within its defined validity window. Further scrutiny of claims like aud (audience) prevents tokens from being exploited outside of their intended context. This sequence of validation steps forms the cornerstone of a secure, stateless authentication process, ensuring that each token is both genuine and contextually appropriate for access to protected resources.

Stateless Authentication and System Integration

JWTs offer a framework for stateless authentication that seamlessly integrates with distributed system architectures. The self-contained nature of the token allows each server instance to independently validate authentication without recourse to a centralized session store. This property is of particular importance in environments that demand horizontal scaling and load balancing, as it reduces inter-server dependencies and minimizes the need for shared state across network boundaries. The use of JWTs facilitates a decoupled authentication process in which the verification of signatures and claims is executed in a deterministic and reproducible manner. To maintain security in this stateless paradigm, careful attention must be given to key management practices, including secure key distribution, rotation, and revocation. The inherent design of JWT systems thus supports the creation of resilient, high-performance services that are capable of handling the demands of modern, distributed authentication scenarios.

Rust Code Snippet

```rust
use serde::{Serialize, Deserialize};
use serde_json;
use base64::{engine::general_purpose, Engine as _};
use hmac::{Hmac, Mac};
use sha2::Sha256;
use std::time::{SystemTime, UNIX_EPOCH};

/// Define the JWT header structure.
#[derive(Serialize, Deserialize, Debug)]
struct Header {
    alg: String,
    typ: String,
}

/// Define the JWT claims payload.
#[derive(Serialize, Deserialize, Debug)]
struct Claims {
    iss: String, // Issuer
    sub: String, // Subject
    aud: String, // Audience
    exp: u64,    // Expiration time (as UNIX timestamp)
    nbf: u64,    // Not before time (as UNIX timestamp)
}

/// Type alias for HMAC-SHA256.
type HmacSha256 = Hmac<Sha256>;

/// Helper function to perform Base64 URL-safe encoding (without
↪  padding).
fn base64_url_encode(input: &[u8]) -> String {
    general_purpose::URL_SAFE_NO_PAD.encode(input)
}

/// Create a JSON Web Token (JWT) using a symmetric key (HS256).
///
/// The function performs the following steps:
/// 1. Serialize the header and claims into JSON strings.
/// 2. Base64 URL encode both the header and the payload.
/// 3. Concatenate the encoded header and payload with a period
↪  delimiter.
/// 4. Compute the signature using HMAC-SHA256, following the
↪  equation:
///     S = H(K, B_H || B_P),
///     where B_H and B_P are the Base64 URL encoded header and
↪  payload.
/// 5. Append the Base64 URL encoded signature to the token.
fn create_jwt(header: &Header, claims: &Claims, secret: &[u8]) ->
↪  String {
    // Serialize header and claims to JSON.
```

265

```rust
    let header_json = serde_json::to_string(header).expect("Header
    ↪   serialization failed");
    let claims_json = serde_json::to_string(claims).expect("Claims
    ↪   serialization failed");

    // Encode both parts with a Base64 URL safe encoder.
    let header_encoded = base64_url_encode(header_json.as_bytes());
    let claims_encoded = base64_url_encode(claims_json.as_bytes());

    // Concatenate header and payload using a dot.
    let data = format!("{}.{}", header_encoded, claims_encoded);

    // Initialize HMAC-SHA256 with the provided secret key.
    let mut mac = HmacSha256::new_from_slice(secret)
        .expect("HMAC initialization failed with provided key");
    mac.update(data.as_bytes());
    let signature = mac.finalize().into_bytes();
    let signature_encoded = base64_url_encode(&signature);

    // Combine all parts to form the final JWT.
    format!("{}.{}", data, signature_encoded)
}

/// Verify a JWT using the provided secret.
///
/// This function splits the token into its constituent parts,
/// re-computes the signature, and then compares it with the
↪   provided signature.
/// Additionally, it could be extended to validate claim times such
↪   as `exp` and `nbf`.
fn verify_jwt(token: &str, secret: &[u8]) -> bool {
    let parts: Vec<&str> = token.split('.').collect();
    if parts.len() != 3 {
        return false;
    }

    // Reconstruct the data (header and payload).
    let data = format!("{}.{}", parts[0], parts[1]);
    let signature_provided = parts[2];

    let mut mac = HmacSha256::new_from_slice(secret)
        .expect("HMAC initialization failed with provided key");
    mac.update(data.as_bytes());
    let result = mac.finalize();
    let signature_calculated = result.into_bytes();
    let signature_calculated_encoded =
    ↪   base64_url_encode(&signature_calculated);

    // Check if the provided signature matches the computed
    ↪   signature.
    signature_calculated_encoded == signature_provided
}
```

```rust
fn main() {
    // Define the header specifying the algorithm and type.
    let header = Header {
        alg: "HS256".to_string(),
        typ: "JWT".to_string(),
    };

    // Establish current time and set token validity.
    let current_time = SystemTime::now()
        .duration_since(UNIX_EPOCH)
        .expect("Time went backwards")
        .as_secs();

    // Define the claims with standard JWT fields.
    let claims = Claims {
        iss: "example_issuer".to_string(),
        sub: "example_subject".to_string(),
        aud: "example_audience".to_string(),
        exp: current_time + 3600, // Expires in one hour.
        nbf: current_time,        // Token is valid immediately.
    };

    // Secret key used for signing the JWT.
    let secret = b"my_secret_key";

    // Generate the JWT.
    let token = create_jwt(&header, &claims, secret);
    println!("Generated JWT: {}", token);

    // Verify the generated token.
    if verify_jwt(&token, secret) {
        println!("JWT verification successful.");
    } else {
        println!("JWT verification failed.");
    }
}
```

Chapter 42

Asynchronous Logging in Network Services

Fundamentals of Asynchronous Logging

Asynchronous logging constitutes a paradigm in which logging operations are decoupled from the principal execution flow of network services. In contrast to traditional synchronous approaches, asynchronous techniques employ buffering and concurrent processing to defer potentially blocking input/output activities. Operational data is captured and enqueued without immediate disk or network writes, thereby reducing the effective logging latency. The fundamental tenet involves a separation of concerns where the computational thread responsible for processing network requests delegates logging tasks to an auxiliary subsystem. This delegation permits the primary execution thread to continue operation with minimal interruption. Quantitatively, if T_{sync} represents the processing delay introduced by synchronous logging and T_{async} denotes the overhead of enqueuing data for deferred handling, then the desired relationship is $T_{async} \ll T_{sync}$, ensuring that the overall service performance remains unimpeded.

Non-Blocking Logging Mechanisms

Non-blocking logging mechanisms are engineered to annihilate the potential for I/O operations to become a bottleneck. At the core of these mechanisms lies the utilization of lock-free data structures and bounded queues, which permit concurrent access without resorting to expensive synchronization primitives. When logging calls are issued, the corresponding data is formatted as event messages and stored in an intermediate buffer. This process is further optimized by adopting deferred flush strategies; the buffered events are periodically consolidated and persisted to external storage or transmitted over the network. The overall system employs a model wherein the logging operations progress independently from the main computational tasks. In such architectures, the throughput of logging operations can be characterized by the rate R, which is maintained even under extreme load, provided that the queue depth and flushing frequency are judiciously calibrated.

Techniques for Capturing Operational Data

Capturing operational data in network services entails precise attention to the nature and volume of events generated during high-speed processing. Each log entry typically encapsulates metadata, diagnostic information, and timestamps that collectively describe the system state at a given instant. The asynchronous design mandates that these elements be serialized and enqueued in a format that minimizes memory overhead yet retains sufficient fidelity for later analysis. Techniques such as structured logging and batched event aggregation are employed to ensure that the transient buffering of log entries does not compromise the integrity of the recorded data. The conversion of in-memory log records to a persistent form is managed apart from the core service loop, so that the cost associated with format conversion and I/O latency is not incurred during critical path execution. Such methodologies ensure that the system achieves a balance between comprehensive diagnostic capabilities and the imperative for high-throughput performance.

Integration of Asynchronous Logging Libraries

The integration of asynchronous logging libraries into network service architectures necessitates a deep understanding of both the systems' operational requirements and the intrinsic properties of non-blocking I/O. Libraries implementing these techniques typically rely on event-driven designs along with a robust use of concurrency primitives to ensure that logging tasks are executed in parallel with primary service operations. The architectural integration involves embedding lightweight logging calls into the code base, which perform non-intrusive data capture and offload the persistence tasks to dedicated background processes. The overall design is predicated on guaranteeing that logging operations abide by strict non-blocking constraints; that is, any logging invocation must return control to the caller without waiting for disk synchronization or remote transmission. This integration strategy is critical in scenarios where even minor interruptions can cascade into significant performance degradations. The meticulous decoupling provided by asynchronous logging libraries enables a seamless capture of operational data while preserving the deterministic performance of the network service.

Performance Implications and Mitigation of Overhead

In environments characterized by high-volume network traffic, the impact of logging overhead on overall system performance cannot be understated. Asynchronous logging techniques are specifically designed to mitigate these effects by confining the majority of logging-related processing to non-critical execution paths. The performance benefit is realized through the minimization of blocking time on the main service threads, thereby allowing them to operate at peak efficiency. The effectiveness of this approach is quantifiable by the reduction in effective latency per logging event, with the relationship expressed as $\Delta L = L_{sync} - L_{async}$, where the target is to maximize ΔL. Additionally, throughput stability is maintained by ensuring that the buffering mechanism adapts to fluctuations in log volume, preserving system responsiveness even during transient load spikes. The trade-off between immediate data persistence and deferred logging is rigorously managed by tuning parameters such as buffer size, flush interval, and batching thresholds. Such careful calibration is essential to ensure that the logging system does not inadvertently introduce new performance bottlenecks while striving to achieve comprehensive operational monitoring in network services.

Rust Code Snippet

```rust
use tokio::sync::mpsc::{self, Sender, Receiver};
use tokio::time::{interval, sleep, Duration, Instant};
use std::error::Error;

/// A log entry capturing the time and message.
#[derive(Debug)]
struct LogEntry {
    timestamp: Instant,
    message: String,
}

/// Asynchronous logger that buffers log entries and flushes them
↪   periodically.
struct AsyncLogger {
    sender: Sender<LogEntry>,
    flush_interval: Duration,
}

impl AsyncLogger {
    /// Create a new AsyncLogger with a bounded channel and defined
    ↪   flush interval.
    fn new(buffer_size: usize, flush_interval: Duration) -> Self {
        let (sender, receiver) = mpsc::channel(buffer_size);
        let logger = Self { sender, flush_interval };
        logger.start_flusher(receiver);
        logger
    }

    /// Launches a background task that flushes the buffered log
    ↪   entries either when the
    /// buffer reaches a threshold or after a specified flush
    ↪   interval.
    fn start_flusher(&self, mut receiver: Receiver<LogEntry>) {
        let flush_interval = self.flush_interval;
        // Spawn an asynchronous task to process flushing of log
        ↪   entries.
        tokio::spawn(async move {
            let mut flush_timer = interval(flush_interval);
            let mut buffer: Vec<LogEntry> = Vec::new();
            loop {
                tokio::select! {
                    // Collect incoming log entries.
                    maybe_log = receiver.recv() => {
                        if let Some(log) = maybe_log {
                            buffer.push(log);
                            // Flush immediately if buffer exceeds a
                            ↪   threshold.
                            if buffer.len() >= 10 {
                                flush_logs(&mut buffer).await;
                            }
```

```
                    } else {
                        // Channel closed - flush any remaining
                        ↪  logs.
                        if !buffer.is_empty() {
                            flush_logs(&mut buffer).await;
                        }
                        break;
                    }
                }
                // Flush periodic timer tick.
                _ = flush_timer.tick() => {
                    if !buffer.is_empty() {
                        flush_logs(&mut buffer).await;
                    }
                }
            }
        }
    });
}

/// Enqueues a log message asynchronously.
async fn log(&self, message: String) {
    let entry = LogEntry {
        timestamp: Instant::now(),
        message,
    };
    // Sending to the channel represents our asynchronous
    ↪  logging overhead (T_async).
    if let Err(e) = self.sender.send(entry).await {
        eprintln!("Failed to send log entry: {}", e);
    }
}
}

/// Simulates the flush operation which writes the buffered log
↪  entries
/// to persistent storage (here, we simply print them).
async fn flush_logs(buffer: &mut Vec<LogEntry>) {
    println!("Flushing {} log(s)...", buffer.len());
    // Here we simulate an I/O flush (representative of T_sync delay
    ↪  in a real system).
    for log in buffer.iter() {
        // Print elapsed time since log generation and the log
        ↪  message.
        println!("[+{} ms] {}", log.timestamp.elapsed().as_millis(),
        ↪  log.message);
    }
    buffer.clear();
}

/// Simulates a synchronous logging operation that incurs a blocking
↪  delay.
async fn simulate_sync_logging(message: &str) {
```

272

```
    // Introduce an artificial delay to mimic blocking I/O (T_sync).
    sleep(Duration::from_millis(50)).await;
    println!("(sync) {}", message);
}

#[tokio::main]
async fn main() -> Result<(), Box<dyn Error>> {
    // Define flush interval for background logging and buffer size.
    let flush_interval = Duration::from_secs(2);
    let logger = AsyncLogger::new(100, flush_interval);

    // Variables to accumulate total latencies.
    let mut total_sync_latency: u128 = 0;
    let mut total_async_latency: u128 = 0;
    let num_logs = 50;

    for i in 0..num_logs {
        let message = format!("Log message number {}", i);

        // Simulate synchronous logging delay (T_sync).
        let start_sync = Instant::now();
        simulate_sync_logging(&message).await;
        let elapsed_sync = start_sync.elapsed().as_micros();
        total_sync_latency += elapsed_sync;

        // Asynchronous logging (T_async, which should be much lower
        ↪   than T_sync).
        let start_async = Instant::now();
        logger.log(message).await;
        let elapsed_async = start_async.elapsed().as_micros();
        total_async_latency += elapsed_async;

        // Pause between log events to simulate processing load.
        sleep(Duration::from_millis(100)).await;
    }

    // Allow time for background flushes to complete.
    sleep(Duration::from_secs(3)).await;

    // Compute the improvement: Delta L = L_sync - L_async
    println!("\n--- Performance Metrics ---");
    println!("Total synchronous logging latency: {} µs",
    ↪   total_sync_latency);
    println!("Total asynchronous logging overhead: {} µs",
    ↪   total_async_latency);
    println!("Improvement (L): {} µs", total_sync_latency as i128 -
    ↪   total_async_latency as i128);

    Ok(())
}
```

Chapter 43

Custom Iterator Implementations for Streaming Data

Fundamental Principles of Iterator Design

Custom iterator constructs constitute an essential abstraction in the management of sequential data flow, especially when the processing frame involves streaming large data sets in network responses. The core philosophy of such iterators is rooted in the concept of lazy evaluation, whereby values are produced on demand rather than computed in bulk. This paradigm is of particular interest in environments where resource constraints necessitate careful control over memory consumption and processing latency. In these iterative patterns, an iterator is conceptualized as a state machine; at each invocation, the underlying state transitions from an initial state S to a subsequent state S', emitting a value that contributes to the processing pipeline. Moreover, this architectural style permits the deferral of heavy computations and buffer allocations until they become strictly necessary within the flow of a network service.

Structural Abstractions and Internal Mechanisms

The internal structure of bespoke iterators is characterized by a dual-layer model that encompasses both a public interface and a private state management system. The public interface adheres to the predictable semantics of element retrieval, while the private state encapsulates control variables, intermediate buffers, and pointers to structural components. This segregation facilitates a systematic approach to state transition, whereby each iteration adjusts internal counters or pointer positions in a deterministic manner. Formally, if the internal state is denoted as I, then the transformation function f operates such that for every iteration i, the state evolution $I_{i+1} = f(I_i)$ holds. Adherence to these invariants ensures that the iterator maintains consistency and reliability, even under the pressure of concurrent access patterns commonly observed in network data streams.

Streaming Architectures Employing Custom Iterators

Large datasets, often encountered in high-throughput network environments, impose a distinct set of challenges that are effectively managed by custom iterator patterns. These iterators are specifically engineered to consume and produce data in a pipelined fashion, thereby eradicating the need to materialize the entire data set in memory. By employing a lazy evaluation strategy, each element is fetched, processed, and transmitted sequentially, which naturally aligns with streaming methodologies. The iterative machinery integrates seamlessly with non-blocking I/O operations typical of network responses, ensuring that delays in data availability do not stall the overall service. In such an architecture, the iterator operates as a proxy, managing the flow of data elements while accommodating fluctuations in bandwidth and computational load through dynamic buffering and on-the-fly processing.

Modularity and Composability in Iterative Patterns

A defining strength of custom iterator implementations lies in their intrinsic modularity and composability. Each iterator, designed as a self-contained unit, can be composed with additional iterators to form sophisticated pipelines capable of performing multiple transformations and filtering operations. This compositional design leverages higher-order functions and abstraction principles to allow chaining of operations such as mapping, filtering, and folding. The composability is mathematically represented by the associative law of function composition; given iterators I_1, I_2, and I_3, the composition $(I_1 \circ I_2) \circ I_3$ is equivalent to $I_1 \circ (I_2 \circ I_3)$, guaranteeing that the end-to-end processing remains consistent and predictable. The design methodology underscores minimal overhead and efficient memory usage, where each unit in the compositional chain contributes to the overall functionality without necessitating redundant data copying or extensive synchronization.

Optimizations and Performance Considerations in Data Streaming

Optimizing iterative processes for streaming large volumes of data demands a careful balance between computational efficiency and memory safety. Custom iterators designed for this purpose are expected to deliver performance metrics that are competitive with hand-optimized implementations. Several strategies are employed to minimize overhead, including zero-copy data access, in-place transformation of elements, and judicious use of buffering to accommodate bursty network traffic. Under a performance model characterized by latency L and throughput T, the design aims to minimize the incremental latency ΔL, thereby ensuring that the cost of iteration remains marginal compared to network transmission delays. Furthermore, the iterator mechanism is integrated with a non-blocking execution framework that precludes stalling the main processing thread, thus maintaining a high throughput T even under adverse load conditions. The resulting architecture benefits from predictable bounds on resource utilization and a deterministic computational profile, making it well-suited for the rigorous demands of modern network services.

Rust Code Snippet

```rust
/// This code demonstrates a custom iterator for streaming data
↪    which embodies
/// the core idea of lazy evaluation and state transition. In our
↪    design, the
/// iterator represents a state machine where each invocation
↪    follows:
///     I_{i+1} = f(I_{i})
/// In this example, the state is encapsulated as the index into a
↪    data slice,
/// and the function f increments the index by a fixed chunk size.
↪    This lazy
/// evaluation ensures that data is processed on demand without
↪    requiring the
/// entire dataset to be held in memory. Additionally, the iterator
↪    is designed
/// to be composable with higher-order functions such as map and
↪    filter, thereby
/// enabling modular and efficient streaming pipelines.

/// A custom iterator that yields slices (chunks) of data from a
↪    byte slice.
struct ChunkedStream<'a> {
    data: &'a [u8],
    chunk_size: usize,
    index: usize,
}

impl<'a> ChunkedStream<'a> {
    /// Constructs a new ChunkedStream from a given data slice and
    ↪    chunk size.
    fn new(data: &'a [u8], chunk_size: usize) -> Self {
        ChunkedStream { data, chunk_size, index: 0 }
    }
}

impl<'a> Iterator for ChunkedStream<'a> {
    type Item = &'a [u8];

    /// On each call to next(), the iterator returns a slice of
    ↪    length up to chunk_size.
    /// The state transition follows the equation:
    ///     index_{i+1} = index_{i} + chunk_size
    /// which aligns with the mathematical formulation I_{i+1} =
    ↪    f(I_{i}).
    fn next(&mut self) -> Option<Self::Item> {
        if self.index >= self.data.len() {
            None
        } else {
            let end = (self.index +
            ↪    self.chunk_size).min(self.data.len());
```

```rust
        let chunk = &self.data[self.index..end];
        self.index += self.chunk_size;
        Some(chunk)
    }
  }
}

/// A processing function that transforms a data chunk. In this
↪   example, it
/// calculates the sum of the bytes in the chunk. This function
↪   serves as the
/// transformation f applied in our iterator chain.
fn process_chunk(chunk: &[u8]) -> u32 {
    chunk.iter().map(|&b| b as u32).sum()
}

fn main() {
    // Example data simulating a large sequential buffer.
    let data: Vec<u8> = (1..=100).collect();
    let chunk_size = 10;

    // Instantiate the custom iterator for streaming chunks of data.
    let stream = ChunkedStream::new(&data, chunk_size);

    // Compose the custom iterator with functional transformations.
    // The chaining of map and filter adheres to the associative law
    ↪   of function
    // composition: (map   filter)   (filter   map). Here, for each
    ↪   chunk:
    // 1. process_chunk() computes a transformation (sum of bytes).
    // 2. filter() retains only chunks whose sum is even.
    let processed_chunks: Vec<u32> = stream
        .map(|chunk| process_chunk(chunk))
        .filter(|&sum| sum % 2 == 0)
        .collect();

    // Output the results of the streaming pipeline.
    println!("Processed chunk sums (even only): {:?}",
    ↪   processed_chunks);
}
```

Chapter 44

Zero-Cost Abstractions for High-Throughput Byte Handling

Theoretical Underpinnings of Zero-Cost Abstractions

Zero-cost abstractions epitomize the synthesis of high-level programmability with the performance characteristics typically reserved for low-level, hand-optimized routines. The central tenet of these abstractions is that the layered structure of generic programming constructs and high-level interfaces introduces no additional runtime cost compared to their equivalent low-level implementations. In formal terms, when a high-level function is parameterized over a type T, the process of monomorphization instantiates a concrete version for each type, such that the cost model satisfies

$$cost(f^*(T)) \approx cost(g),$$

where g denotes an equivalent low-level implementation. This equivalence is a consequence of rigorous compile-time analysis, aggressive inlining, and loop optimization strategies which collectively eliminate redundant abstractions, thereby preserving the efficiency of core byte-level operations.

Leveraging Generics for Byte Stream Manipulation

Generics furnish a mechanism to write code that is both abstract and type-safe, allowing functions and data structures to be defined without sacrificing specificity. In the realm of byte stream processing, generics promote the construction of unified interfaces that can operate over diverse data representations while catering to the literal demands of memory and processing efficiency. The statically resolved dispatch ensures that operations such as filtering, mapping, and folding over byte arrays are resolved at compile time. As a result, the monomorphization process yields specialized code for each instantiation, thereby obviating the overhead typically associated with dynamic polymorphism. This design paradigm enables the abstraction of byte manipulation routines into concise, reusable components without incurring any performance penalty at runtime.

Compile-Time Optimizations and Inlining Strategies

Compiler-driven optimizations constitute the backbone of zero-cost abstractions in high-throughput environments. Through techniques such as inlining, constant propagation, and loop unrolling, the compiler can effectively convert high-level abstractions into streamlined sequences of machine instructions. By mandating that function calls in critical paths be inlined, the overhead of abstraction boundaries is eliminated, resulting in performance characteristics that closely mirror those of bespoke low-level implementations. Consider an operation where a transformation f is applied iteratively over a byte stream; the compiler's optimization passes ensure that the transformation is unrolled and solidified into an efficient loop, thereby reducing the incremental latency ΔL per iteration. This rigorous treatment of compile-time evaluation not only mitigates the performance penalty but also facilitates aggressive dead code elimination and resource allocation minimization, which are essential for sustaining high throughput in byte manipulation.

Architectural Implications for Byte-Level Operations

The deployment of zero-cost abstractions in byte handling necessitates meticulous architectural considerations that reconcile abstract design with hardware realities. Operations on byte streams are frequently subject to constraints imposed by memory alignment, cache locality, and processor pipelines. To address these challenges, the abstraction layers are judiciously designed to ensure that memory access patterns are optimized and unnecessary data copying is eliminated. The reliance on static dispatch and compile-time resolution guarantees that every call to a generic function operating on bytes is resolved into tight loops with predictable execution patterns. In this paradigm, when a composite function is defined as an operation over a byte stream, the invariance

$$I_{i+1} = f(I_i)$$

holds rigorously at every stage of processing, where I denotes the internal state of the iterator over the byte stream. The resulting specialization of each function instance, facilitated by the compiler's type analysis and inlining mechanisms, ensures that the final machine code is devoid of overhead typically associated with abstraction, thereby achieving optimal performance in high-throughput environments.

Rust Code Snippet

```
/*
    This code demonstrates zero-cost abstractions for high-throughput
    ↪   byte handling in Rust.
    It implements a generic byte processing pipeline that applies a
    ↪   transformation function
    to each byte in the stream. This transformation embodies the
    ↪   recurrence:

        I_{i+1} = f(I_{i})

    where f is the inlined transformation function defined below. At
    ↪   compile-time, generics
    and monomorphization ensure that the cost model satisfies:

        cost(f*(T))  cost(g)
```

```rust
        thus yielding performance comparable to low-level, hand-optimized
    ↪   implementations.
*/

#![allow(dead_code)]
#![allow(unused_imports)]

use std::fmt::Debug;

/// Trait defining a generic byte processor.
pub trait ByteProcessor {
    /// Process an input byte slice starting from an initial state.
    fn process(&self, input: &[u8], init: u32) -> u32;
}

/// Default processor implementing a simple, inlined transformation.
/// The transformation function follows the relation:
///     I_{i+1} = f(I_{i}) = I_{i} * 31 + byte
pub struct DefaultProcessor;

impl DefaultProcessor {
    /// Inline transformation function that embodies the equation
    ↪   I_{i+1} = f(I_{i}).
    #[inline(always)]
    fn transform(state: u32, byte: u8) -> u32 {
        state.wrapping_mul(31).wrapping_add(byte as u32)
    }
}

impl ByteProcessor for DefaultProcessor {
    #[inline(always)]
    fn process(&self, input: &[u8], init: u32) -> u32 {
        // Iteratively apply the transformation using fold.
        input.iter().fold(init, |state, &byte|
        ↪   Self::transform(state, byte))
    }
}

/// Generic function to process a byte stream with a provided
↪   transformation function.
/// The function is generic over the slice type T and the
↪   transformation function F,
/// ensuring inlined, compile-time resolution (zero-cost
↪   abstraction).
#[inline(always)]
fn process_stream<T, F>(data: T, transform_fn: F, init: u32) -> u32
where
    T: AsRef<[u8]>,
    F: Fn(u32, u8) -> u32,
{
    let mut state = init;
    for &byte in data.as_ref() {
        state = transform_fn(state, byte);
```

282

```rust
    }
    state
}

fn main() {
    // Example byte stream.
    let data = b"High-Throughput Byte Handling in Rust";
    let initial_state = 0u32;

    // Process using DefaultProcessor which uses the inlined
    ↪   transform function.
    let processor = DefaultProcessor;
    let result1 = processor.process(data, initial_state);

    // Process using the generic function, achieving the same
    ↪   zero-cost abstraction.
    let result2 = process_stream(data, DefaultProcessor::transform,
    ↪   initial_state);

    println!("Result from DefaultProcessor: {}", result1);
    println!("Result from process_stream: {}", result2);

    // Assert that both methods yield identical results.
    assert_eq!(result1, result2);
}
```

Chapter 45

Non-blocking File Streaming Over HTTP

Asynchronous File Reading Mechanisms

Non-blocking file streaming represents an advanced methodology in the realm of efficient network data transfer, particularly when the objective is to serve large files without incurring the performance penalties associated with synchronous I/O. Asynchronous file reading is predicated on the configuration of file descriptors to operate in a non-blocking mode, thereby enabling the operating system to signal the readiness of data without forcing computational threads to idle. The paradigm employs system-level constructs—such as epoll on Linux, kqueue on BSD-derived systems, or IOCP on Windows—which facilitate the monitoring of I/O events through an event loop that precludes blocking calls. Let the file size be denoted by F and the designated chunk size by Δ, so that the entire file is segmented into approximately $\lceil \frac{F}{\Delta} \rceil$ discrete read operations. This segmentation permits the asynchronous initiation of successive read requests prior to the completion of preceding operations, effectively overlapping disk I/O with network transmission. Such a design not only mitigates latency but also optimally utilizes system resources by eliminating idle waiting periods during file access.

Chunked Transfer Encoding in HTTP Protocol

Within the HTTP/1.1 specification, chunked transfer encoding is established as a mechanism to facilitate the transmission of data streams whose total size is either unknown at the commencement of transfer or impractically large for monolithic dispatch. In this approach, the output is partitioned into a series of variable-length segments. Each segment, or chunk, is preceded by its size—expressed in hexadecimal notation—and concluded by a carriage return-line feed sequence. The protocol mandates that each chunk size, denoted by S_i, satisfies the condition $S_i > 0$ until the terminal chunk is reached; termination is signified by a chunk where $S_n = 0$. This method allows for the progressive delivery of file contents concurrently with asynchronous read operations, thereby enabling the initiation of data transmission as soon as portions of the file are available. The architecture inherent to chunked transfer encoding eliminates the necessity for precomputing the total content length and minimizes buffering overhead, thus aligning with the performance imperatives of high-throughput systems.

Integration and Performance Considerations

The integration of asynchronous file reading with chunked transfer encoding engenders a highly efficient pipeline for serving large files over HTTP. This architectural fusion necessitates the seamless coordination between asynchronous I/O events and the assembly of HTTP responses. Within an event-driven framework, file descriptors set to non-blocking mode are continuously polled for readiness, and as data becomes available in segments, it is immediately encapsulated into discrete HTTP chunks. The effective transmission throughput, denoted by B_{eff}, can be characterized by the relation

$$B_{eff} = \frac{N \cdot \Delta}{T},$$

where N represents the number of chunks, Δ the size of each chunk, and T the total duration of the file streaming operation. The architecture permits the concurrent execution of reading and transmission routines, thereby reducing computational overhead associated with task context switching and minimizing memory copying through optimized buffer management. In addition, certain operating systems provide support for zero-copy techniques, wherein direct memory transfers between file and network buffers are achieved without routing data through user space. This capability further diminishes latency and sustains high throughput, which is critical in environments wherein concurrent connections and large file sizes are prevalent. The precise scheduling and resource allocation, governed by the asynchronous model, ensure that the coordinated processing of file I/O and HTTP response assembly adheres to stringent performance criteria while maintaining scalability and robustness in high-demand scenarios.

Rust Code Snippet

```rust
use tokio::fs::File;
use tokio::io::{self, AsyncReadExt, AsyncWriteExt};
use std::time::Instant;
use std::error::Error;

// This function demonstrates asynchronous file reading and HTTP
↪   chunked transfer encoding.
// It reads a file in configurable chunk sizes (), writes out each
↪   chunk with its hexadecimal size
// (to simulate HTTP/1.1 chunked encoding), and counts the number of
↪   chunks (N) processed.
async fn stream_file_chunks(file_path: &str, chunk_size: usize) ->
↪   Result<usize, Box<dyn Error>> {
    // Open the file in asynchronous (non-blocking) mode.
    let mut file = File::open(file_path).await?;
    let mut buffer = vec![0u8; chunk_size];
    let mut total_chunks = 0;

    // Simulate writing to an HTTP response stream using stdout.
    let mut stdout = io::stdout();

    loop {
        // Asynchronously read a chunk of data from the file.
        let bytes_read = file.read(&mut buffer).await?;
        // If no bytes are read, we've reached the end of the file.
        if bytes_read == 0 {
            break;
        }
        total_chunks += 1;

        // Create the chunk header: the size of the chunk (in
        ↪   hexadecimal) followed by CRLF.
        let header = format!("{:X}\r\n", bytes_read);
```

```rust
        stdout.write_all(header.as_bytes()).await?;

        // Write the actual chunk data.
        stdout.write_all(&buffer[..bytes_read]).await?;

        // Write the trailing CRLF after the chunk data.
        stdout.write_all(b"\r\n").await?;
    }

    // Write the final zero-length chunk to indicate the end of the
    ↪  chunked message.
    stdout.write_all(b"0\r\n\r\n").await?;
    stdout.flush().await?;
    Ok(total_chunks)
}

#[tokio::main]
async fn main() -> Result<(), Box<dyn Error>> {
    // Define the file path and chunk size ().
    // In the mathematical model, F is the total file size and the
    ↪  file is segmented into roughly F/ chunks.
    let file_path = "large_file.bin";
    let chunk_size: usize = 8192; // 8 KB per chunk.

    // Start time measurement to calculate total streaming duration
    ↪  (T).
    let start_time = Instant::now();

    // Asynchronously stream the file in chunks.
    let total_chunks = stream_file_chunks(file_path,
    ↪  chunk_size).await?;

    // Record the total elapsed time in seconds.
    let elapsed_time = start_time.elapsed().as_secs_f64();

    // Calculate the effective throughput (B_eff) using the formula:
    // B_eff = (N * ) / T, where N is the number of chunks,  is the
    ↪  chunk size, and T is the elapsed time.
    let effective_throughput = (total_chunks as f64 * chunk_size as
    ↪  f64) / elapsed_time;

    println!("Total chunks streamed: {}", total_chunks);
    println!("Total time taken: {:.4} seconds", elapsed_time);
    println!("Effective throughput (B_eff): {:.2} bytes/sec",
    ↪  effective_throughput);

    Ok(())
}
```

Chapter 46

Integrating Asynchronous Database Operations

Asynchronous Database Driver Architecture

The fundamental challenge of incorporating asynchronous database operations lies in reconciling the traditionally synchronous nature of relational and NoSQL systems with the non-blocking paradigm inherent in modern asynchronous programming. At the core of these solutions are asynchronous database drivers that exploit Rust's concurrency model by implementing the Future trait and integrating with event-driven runtimes. These drivers establish connections that, rather than blocking the executing thread during latency-bound operations, issue non-blocking system calls and register interest in the subsequent arrival of data via operating system notifications such as epoll on Linux, kqueue on BSD derivatives, or IOCP on Windows. This strategy ensures that the database connectivity layer is architected to allow the continuation of other computational tasks while waiting for responses from the remote database server. In this context, the inherent scalability of asynchronous drivers is underscored by their ability to handle a multitude of concurrent operations, each represented by an independent future that resolves when the corresponding I/O event is triggered.

Non-Blocking Query Execution Semantics

A cornerstone of effective asynchronous database interactions is the coding paradigm that transforms traditionally blocking query operations into non-blocking request paradigms. In this ecosystem, query operations are dispatched as independent futures that encapsulate the lifecycle of a database request. Upon issuance, a query is submitted over an established asynchronous channel, and the underlying driver defers the processing of the result until an external signal—often derived from a polling mechanism—indicates the availability of data. This approach leverages the event loop to schedule deferred computations, thereby eliminating idle waiting periods and introducing a level of concurrency that robustly supports high-throughput scenarios. Conceptually, the mechanism can be interpreted as a transient transformation of a blocking I/O operation into a series of asynchronous state transitions, wherein each transition addresses a specific phase of database communication, from connection initiation to data retrieval and result parsing. The state machine thus created ensures that each query operation is processed independently, and outcomes are eventually merged into the final application logic without necessitating a synchronous wait for complete execution.

Concurrency Control and Resource Management

The orchestration of asynchronous database operations requires an intricate balance between maximizing concurrency and managing the limited resources intrinsic to database systems. As multiple queries are dispatched concurrently over a shared connection pool, the asynchronous model must reconcile conflicting demands for connections, memory buffers, and transactional state. To this end, asynchronous drivers typically implement lightweight connection pooling strategies that enable dynamic allocation and reclamation of database connections. These pools are governed by non-blocking algorithms that judiciously schedule query submissions while preventing resource starvation or contention. Moreover, fine-grained concurrency control is achieved through the careful handling of locks and synchronization primitives, which are designed to minimize the overhead associated with shared state management. The architecture ensures that the latency inherent in network or disk I/O is effectively masked by overlapping query execution with the processing of complete transactions. In highly concurrent settings, the resource management framework is formalized by analyzing performance metrics such as throughput and latency, often modeled by equations of the form

$$R = \frac{Q \cdot C}{\tau},$$

where Q denotes the number of concurrent queries, C signifies the average cost per query, and τ represents the aggregate time required for transaction processing. Though this equation is abstract, it encapsulates the essence of balancing load and resource utilization in high-performance asynchronous database operations.

Fault Tolerance and Error Propagation Mechanisms

The integration of asynchronous database operations necessitates an equally robust framework for handling transient failures and propagating errors throughout the system. As the non-blocking architecture defers the resolution of query results until asynchronous events occur, error detection and handling must be designed to integrate seamlessly with the asynchronous execution model. In instances where network disruptions, query timeouts, or transactional conflicts arise, the asynchronous driver is responsible for capturing the error state and propagating it via the future returning mechanism. This propagation is engineered to ensure that errors in individual operations do not induce a cascading failure across the entire system. Instead, each asynchronous operation is encapsulated within a well-defined error boundary that can be logged, retried, or escalated based on the severity of the encountered fault. The subtle interplay between error handling routines and asynchronous control flow mandates the use of pattern matching and state-based recovery protocols, which collectively enhance the resilience of the database interaction layer. This design promotes a distributed sense of fault tolerance where the resolution of each query is decoupled from others, thereby maintaining overall system integrity even in the presence of intermittent faults.

Rust Code Snippet

```rust
use std::sync::Arc;
use std::time::{Duration, Instant};
use tokio::sync::{Semaphore, SemaphorePermit};

const MAX_CONNECTIONS: usize = 5;
const NUM_QUERIES: usize = 10;

// A simulated connection pool that controls concurrent access using
↪ a semaphore.
struct ConnectionPool {
    semaphore: Arc<Semaphore>,
}

impl ConnectionPool {
    // Create a new ConnectionPool with a maximum number of
    ↪ connections.
    fn new(limit: usize) -> Self {
        Self {
            semaphore: Arc::new(Semaphore::new(limit)),
        }
    }

    // Asynchronously acquire a connection (a permit) from the pool.
    async fn acquire(&self) -> SemaphorePermit<'_> {
        self.semaphore.acquire().await.expect("Failed to acquire a
        ↪ connection")
    }
}

// Simulate an asynchronous database query.
//
// Each query imitates non-blocking database I/O by awaiting a fixed
↪ delay. The "cost"
// of a query is also simulated as an arbitrary floating point
↪ value. In a real-world
// scenario, the cost might reflect processing time, computation, or
↪ resource usage.
//
// The function prints its progress to illustrate the asynchronous
↪ workflow.
async fn perform_query(id: usize, pool: Arc<ConnectionPool>) ->
↪ Result<f64, &'static str> {
    println!("Query {}: Waiting for connection...", id);
    let _permit = pool.acquire().await;
    println!("Query {}: Acquired connection.", id);

    // Simulate asynchronous delay (representing non-blocking I/O
    ↪ latency)
    tokio::time::sleep(Duration::from_millis(50)).await;
    println!("Query {}: Completed execution.", id);
```

291

```rust
    // Return a simulated cost for the query (for example, 50 units)
    Ok(50.0)
}

#[tokio::main]
async fn main() -> Result<(), Box<dyn std::error::Error>> {
    // Initialize the connection pool.
    let pool = Arc::new(ConnectionPool::new(MAX_CONNECTIONS));

    let start_time = Instant::now();
    let mut query_costs = Vec::new();
    let mut handles = Vec::new();

    // Launch multiple asynchronous query tasks concurrently.
    for id in 0..NUM_QUERIES {
        let pool_clone = Arc::clone(&pool);
        let handle = tokio::spawn(async move {
            // Each query is executed asynchronously within a task.
            perform_query(id, pool_clone).await
        });
        handles.push(handle);
    }

    // Wait for all queries to complete and collect their costs.
    for handle in handles {
        let result = handle.await??;
        query_costs.push(result);
    }

    // Calculate the elapsed time () in seconds.
    let elapsed = start_time.elapsed();
    let tau = elapsed.as_secs_f64();

    // Compute total and average cost per query (C).
    let total_cost: f64 = query_costs.iter().sum();
    let avg_cost = total_cost / (query_costs.len() as f64);

    // Q represents the number of queries processed.
    let q = NUM_QUERIES as f64;

    // Calculate throughput using the equation:
    //    R = (Q * C) /
    let throughput = (q * avg_cost) / tau;

    println!("\n--- Summary ---");
    println!("Total queries (Q): {}", NUM_QUERIES);
    println!("Average query cost (C): {:.2}", avg_cost);
    println!("Total processing time (): {:.2} seconds", tau);
    println!("Computed throughput (R = Q * C / ): {:.2}",
    ↪  throughput);

    Ok(())
```

}

Chapter 47

Optimizing SQL Query Builders in Rust

Compile-Time Guarantees Through Type-Driven Abstractions

The design of SQL query builders in Rust leverages a robust type system to enforce correctness at compile time. This approach relies on advanced type-driven abstractions, wherein every component of a query—from table selection and column projection to filtering and aggregation—is represented by dedicated types. These types encapsulate the constraints and structural properties of SQL syntax, thereby precluding the possibility of constructing semantically invalid queries. By encoding compositional rules directly into the type system using generics, trait bounds, and phantom types, the query builder transforms the SQL construction process into a form of static analysis. In such a system, erroneous query formulations are detected during compilation rather than at runtime, thus obviating an entire class of potential bugs. Each query operator produces a new type that represents an intermediate state, and the final query is a well-typed object that is guaranteed to adhere to a prescribed schema and syntactic structure.

Integration with Asynchronous Execution Semantics

The evolution of asynchronous programming in Rust has introduced the necessity for query builders to integrate seamlessly with non-blocking execution models. In an asynchronous environment, SQL queries are often represented as future-like entities that encapsulate deferred computation. Rather than issuing immediate blocking calls, these entities schedule database interactions in conjunction with the event loop. This design allows for the concurrent execution of multiple queries without incurring the overhead associated with traditional synchronous operations. The decoupling of query construction from query execution is achieved by representing the execution phase as an asynchronous task whose lifecycle is managed by a runtime. The query builder's interface is thus responsible for returning an object that, when awaited, will eventually provide the query result. In this manner, the statically guaranteed correctness of the query structure is maintained while ensuring that execution can be interleaved with other asynchronous tasks without resource contention.

Type-Driven Query Composition and Safety Enforcement

Central to the paradigm of compiling safe SQL query builders is the principle of type-driven query composition. The method involves constructing queries as compositions of type-level operations where every transformation or filter enforces domain-specific constraints. For example, a selection operator may narrow down the set of valid columns based on the originating table's schema, and a join operator may allow only compatible key types to form a relationship. These restrictions are encoded statically by employing a rigorous system of trait implementations that validate the composition steps. The use of such type-driven mechanisms enables the early detection of mismatches and permits the compiler to verify invariants that are critical to maintaining database integrity and preventing runtime anomalies. The overall result is an articulation of query construction where every component, and its subsequent combination with others, adheres to specifications that are verified through compile-time checks, ensuring that only semantically valid queries are constructed.

Optimization Strategies and Performance Considerations

Beyond correctness, performance optimization becomes a significant focus when designing compile-time safe query builder systems. The architectural design must minimize runtime overhead while maximizing the throughput of query execution. One approach to achieving this is by decoupling the query construction phase from the execution phase, whereby query components are synthesized and then optimized as a whole before being dispatched asynchronously. Advanced static analysis techniques can be applied during compilation to infer constant expressions, simplify predicates, and restructure query fragments into an optimally executable form. The system can be modeled by considering the aggregate impact of each query operation as a function of the number of operations Q, the average computational cost per operation C, and the total asynchronous execution time τ, such that performance metrics can be abstractly defined by the expression

$$R = \frac{Q \cdot C}{\tau}.$$

This model, while theoretical, provides a framework for understanding how compile-time optimizations contribute to reduced latency and enhanced throughput. In practice, the query builder employs a series of optimization passes which eliminate redundant computations and perform lazy evaluation of query sub-expressions, ensuring that only necessary operations are executed asynchronously.

Ensuring Composability and Extensibility in Asynchronous Contexts

A key aspect of optimizing SQL query builders is the assurance of composability within an asynchronous environment. The architectural design must allow disparate query fragments to be combined in a manner that preserves both syntactic integrity and execution efficiency. This is achieved by adopting a modular design where each query component is treated as an independent unit that abides by a common interface. The introduction of trait objects and generic abstractions permits the dynamic composition of query plans while still benefiting from compile-time type checks. Furthermore, the asynchronous execution model demands that this composability extends to the management of non-blocking operations, where each component is responsible for signaling its readiness via future resolution. Such a design ensures that the query builder can be extended incrementally, with new operators and transformation mechanisms being introduced without compromising the overall system's correctness or performance. The resultant system is one which satisfies the dual objectives of high-level expressiveness and low-level efficiency, making it particularly well-suited for high-throughput database applications in an asynchronous runtime.

Rust Code Snippet

```rust
use std::marker::PhantomData;
use tokio::time::{sleep, Duration};

/// Computes the performance metric R as defined by the formula:
///     R = (Q * C) /
/// where:
///    - Q is the total number of operations,
///    - C is the average computational cost per operation,
///    -  is the total asynchronous execution time (in seconds).
fn compute_performance_metric(q: usize, c: f64, tau: f64) -> f64 {
    (q as f64 * c) / tau
}

mod sql_builder {
    use std::marker::PhantomData;
    use tokio::time::{sleep, Duration};

    // State markers for compile-time enforcement in the query
    ↪  builder.
    pub struct NoTable;
    pub struct WithTable;

    /// A type-safe SQL query builder where the construction process
    ↪  is
    /// statically validated using phantom types to represent the
    ↪  state.
    pub struct QueryBuilder<State> {
        query: String,
        _state: PhantomData<State>,
    }

    impl QueryBuilder<NoTable> {
        /// Initialize a new query builder with no table selected.
```

297

```rust
    pub fn new() -> Self {
        QueryBuilder {
            query: String::new(),
            _state: PhantomData,
        }
    }

    /// Specify the table for the query.
    /// This method transitions the builder from the "NoTable"
    ↪  to "WithTable" state.
    pub fn table(self, table: &str) -> QueryBuilder<WithTable> {
        let query_part = format!("FROM {}", table);
        QueryBuilder {
            query: query_part,
            _state: PhantomData,
        }
    }
}

impl QueryBuilder<WithTable> {
    /// Add a SELECT clause to the query with the provided
    ↪  column names.
    pub fn select(mut self, columns: &[&str]) -> Self {
        let cols = columns.join(", ");
        self.query = format!("SELECT {} {}", cols, self.query);
        self
    }

    /// Append a WHERE clause with the given condition to the
    ↪  query.
    pub fn filter(mut self, condition: &str) -> Self {
        self.query = format!("{} WHERE {}", self.query,
        ↪  condition);
        self
    }

    /// Execute the constructed query asynchronously.
    /// In a real system, this method would interface with a
    ↪  database driver.
    pub async fn execute(self) -> QueryResult {
        println!("Executing Query: {}", self.query);
        // Simulate asynchronous execution delay.
        sleep(Duration::from_millis(500)).await;
        // Return a simulated result.
        QueryResult { rows_affected: 42 }
    }
}

/// Represents the result of a query execution.
pub struct QueryResult {
    pub rows_affected: usize,
}
}
```

```rust
#[tokio::main]
async fn main() {
    // Example usage of performance metric calculation.
    // Suppose:
    //   Q (number of operations) = 10,
    //   C (average cost per operation) = 2.5,
    //     (execution time in seconds) = 1.0.
    let q: usize = 10;
    let c: f64 = 2.5;
    let tau: f64 = 1.0;

    let performance = compute_performance_metric(q, c, tau);
    println!(
        "Performance metric R = (Q * C) /  => R = {}",
        performance
    );

    // Demonstrating the compile-time safe SQL query builder.
    // The builder enforces proper construction order:
    //   1. Start with a new query builder (no table selected).
    //   2. Specify the table, transitioning to a state where a
    //      table is set.
    //   3. Add SELECT and WHERE clauses.
    //   4. Execute the query asynchronously.
    let result = sql_builder::QueryBuilder::new()
        .table("users")
        .select(&["id", "username", "email"])
        .filter("age > 18")
        .execute()
        .await;

    println!("Query executed, rows affected: {}",
        result.rows_affected);
}
```

Chapter 48

Type-Safe Stored Procedure Execution

Foundations in Rust's Type System for Stored Procedures

Stored procedure execution within an asynchronous framework demands not only rigorous runtime performance guarantees but also uncompromising static assurances regarding invocation correctness. Rust's type system serves as the principal mechanism to encode the invariants governing stored procedure calls. By representing stored procedure parameters, expected return types, and the permissible sequencing of procedure invocations as distinct type entities, the framework transforms potentially error-prone runtime operations into statically verifiable constructs. Fundamental to this approach is the use of advanced type features such as generics, trait bounds, and phantom types—which, when combined, create a model where each stored procedure call corresponds to a unique type narrative. In this model, the entire procedure call is encapsulated in a series of type transitions that together form a compile-time verified trajectory, ensuring that any deviation from the prescribed semantics is caught before execution.

Encapsulation of Stored Procedure Semantics in Type Contracts

A central concept in type-safe stored procedure execution is the translation of stored procedure semantics into explicit type contracts. Each stored procedure is associated with a type that encapsulates its signature, including both parameter types and return type specifications. These type contracts extend beyond traditional function signatures by incorporating constraints that capture domain-specific invariants. For instance, an invocation may be annotated with constraints that ensure proper parameter ordering and compatibility, akin to a function of type

$$f : T_1 \times T_2 \times \cdots \times T_n \to R,$$

where T_i represents a validated type for the ith parameter and R symbolizes a predetermined response type. This mathematical abstraction enforces that stored procedure calls adhere strictly to their intended contracts, mitigating possibilities for erroneous or unintended interactions at runtime.

Integration with the Asynchronous Execution Model

Embedding stored procedure execution within an asynchronous framework necessitates a careful interplay between static type assurances and dynamic execution paradigms. In this design, stored procedures are modeled as future-like entities, with their initiation and resolution phases governed by asynchronous task management systems. The type framework ensures that every stored procedure's state is faithfully represented throughout the asynchronous lifecycle. Each asynchronous stored procedure call is characterized by a state transition that is formalized within the type system, thereby ensuring that the initiation, waiting period, and eventual resolution of a call are all consistent with the expected type invariants. This result is the achievement of a system where asynchronous execution does not compromise the rigor of compile-time verifications and where concurrent stored procedure calls can be interleaved without risking state inconsistencies or resource contention.

Static Verification Through Compile-Time Analysis

The use of Rust's type system for stored procedure execution extends beyond simple type annotations and into the realm of full-fledged static analysis. Compile-time verification leverages the strength of Rust's compiler to conduct an exhaustive analysis of type transitions corresponding to stored procedure calls. Each transformation—whether it is the conversion of input parameters into a callable form, the scheduling of an asynchronous task, or the mapping of a procedure's result into an application domain—must satisfy a set of rigorous type constraints. The design is such that every intermediate state, represented by a distinct type, serves as a checkpoint where invariant properties are verified. This rigorous approach ensures that any deviation from the expected protocol of stored procedure execution results in a compile-time error, thereby eliminating a wide class of potential runtime failures. The static analysis mechanism works seamlessly with the asynchronous runtime, shifting many error checks from runtime overhead to compile time, which in turn optimizes system performance.

Implications for System Safety and Performance Optimizations

The adoption of type-safe stored procedure execution yields significant benefits in terms of overall system safety and performance efficiencies. By guaranteeing that stored procedure calls are statically verified, the approach minimizes runtime error handling and reduces the need for expensive dynamic checks. These assurances are particularly valuable in high-throughput database systems where even marginal improvements in error detection can lead to substantial performance gains. Furthermore, the integration of type contracts with asynchronous execution models facilitates parallelism without compromising on correctness. The system's error detection is deterministic, leading to consistent performance metrics and predictable resource allocation. The synergy between Rust's robust type system and the asynchronous paradigm ultimately results in a framework where secure, efficient, and scalable stored procedure execution is achieved through meticulously enforced compile-time invariants.

Rust Code Snippet

```rust
use std::marker::PhantomData;
use tokio::time::{sleep, Duration};

/// State markers representing the phases of stored procedure
↪   execution.
struct Init;
struct Running;
struct Completed;

/// A type-safe abstraction for a stored procedure call where:
/// - P represents the procedure parameters,
/// - R represents the result type,
/// - S represents the current state of the call.
#[derive(Debug)]
struct StoredProcedure<P, R, S> {
    params: P,
    result: Option<R>,
    _state: PhantomData<S>,
}

impl<P, R> StoredProcedure<P, R, Init> {
    /// Create a new stored procedure call with the given
    ↪   parameters.
    fn new(params: P) -> Self {
        StoredProcedure {
            params,
            result: None,
            _state: PhantomData,
        }
    }

    /// Schedule the stored procedure call, transitioning it from
    ↪   the Init
    /// state to the Running state. This enforces that only properly
    ↪   initialized
    /// calls may be scheduled for execution.
    fn schedule(self) -> StoredProcedure<P, R, Running> {
        StoredProcedure {
            params: self.params,
            result: None,
            _state: PhantomData,
        }
    }
}

impl StoredProcedure<(i32, i32), i32, Running> {
    /// Asynchronously execute the stored procedure. This
    ↪   implementation
    /// simulates the operation defined by the function:
    ///     f: T1 × T2 → R,
```

303

```rust
/// where here T1 and T2 are both i32 and R is i32 (calculating
↪   the sum).
async fn execute(self) -> StoredProcedure<(i32, i32), i32,
↪   Completed> {
    // Simulate an asynchronous delay to mimic a non-blocking
    ↪   I/O operation.
    sleep(Duration::from_millis(100)).await;
    let (a, b) = self.params;
    let sum = a + b;
    StoredProcedure {
        params: self.params,
        result: Some(sum),
        _state: PhantomData,
    }
}
}

impl<P, R> StoredProcedure<P, R, Completed> {
    /// Retrieve the result of the stored procedure execution.
    /// This method is only available once the execution has
    ↪   completed,
    /// ensuring that all compile-time invariants have been met.
    fn get_result(self) -> R {
        self.result.expect("Stored procedure execution did not
        ↪   produce a result.")
    }
}

#[tokio::main]
async fn main() {
    // Create a new stored procedure call in the Init state with
    ↪   specific parameters.
    let proc_call = StoredProcedure::<(i32, i32), i32,
    ↪   Init>::new((10, 20));

    // Transition the stored procedure to the Running state by
    ↪   scheduling it.
    let proc_call = proc_call.schedule();

    // Asynchronously execute the stored procedure, resulting in a
    ↪   state transition
    // from Running to Completed, with the result computed according
    ↪   to the function:
    //     f: (i32, i32) -> i32, where f(10, 20) = 30.
    let proc_call = proc_call.execute().await;

    // Retrieve and print the computed result. This call is only
    ↪   possible in the Completed state.
    let result = proc_call.get_result();
    println!("Result of stored procedure execution (10 + 20): {}",
    ↪   result);
}
```

Chapter 49

In-Memory Caching Strategies for API Performance

Conceptual Foundations of In-Memory Caching

In-memory caching constitutes a design paradigm that leverages volatile memory to transiently store frequently accessed data, thereby reducing reliance on persistent storage systems during API operations. The primary objective is to minimize latency by providing rapid access to data that would otherwise require repeated queries to slower, disk-based databases. The caching mechanism can be abstracted mathematically by considering the cache hit rate, defined as

$$h = \frac{H}{H + M},$$

where H denotes the number of cache hits and M represents the number of cache misses. This abstraction underscores the importance of designing caches that maximize h and reduce the aggregate access time in a high-throughput web service environment.

Data Structure Considerations and Storage Architectures

The selection of the underlying data structure is critical in achieving the desired performance characteristics of an in-memory cache. Data structures such as hash maps, balanced binary search trees, and arrays provide various trade-offs in terms of average and worst-case lookup times. In an ideal scenario, a hash map permits constant time complexity, expressed as $O(1)$, for insertion, deletion, and retrieval operations. Such performance guarantees are essential when cache latency must be minimized in the context of high-frequency API requests. Furthermore, the structural design should account for the temporal dimensions of data storage, ensuring that each cache entry is associated with metadata for verification of freshness and validity.

Eviction Policies and Consistency Mechanisms

Given the finite capacity of any physical memory, in-memory caching systems necessitate the implementation of eviction policies that intelligently remove obsolete or infrequently accessed entries. Among the most commonly utilized policies are Least Recently Used (LRU), Least Frequently Used (LFU), and First In First Out (FIFO). LRU algorithms maintain a temporal ordering of entries so that those unused for the longest duration are evicted first, while LFU approaches prioritize entries based on access frequency. The eviction process can be formalized by a function

$$E : S \to S',$$

where S represents the state of the cache prior to eviction and S' is the state after an eviction event, thereby ensuring that the system adheres to predetermined capacity constraints. In addition, consistency mechanisms are integrated to maintain synchronization between the cache and the underlying persistent storage, often by leveraging validation protocols that enforce freshness within a defined temporal window.

Concurrency Control and Synchronization in Caching Systems

In environments where concurrent access to the cache is prevalent, maintaining the integrity of shared data structures is paramount. Concurrency control is typically achieved through the use of synchronization primitives that protect against race conditions and ensure atomicity of cache operations. The design of such concurrent systems often involves the application of lock-free techniques and atomic operations to minimize the performance overhead associated with thread contention. Let C designate the set of cached entries and $S(C)$ denote the synchronization protocol governing concurrent modifications. The protocol is constructed such that

$$S(C) \subseteq \Gamma(C),$$

where $\Gamma(C)$ represents the set of all permissible state transitions under concurrent access. This formalization provides a framework for evaluating and proving the correctness of the cache's behavior under simultaneous access by multiple API requests.

Integration with API Request Handling Pipelines

The integration of in-memory caches within API request handling pipelines is instrumental in reducing system latency. In this architecture, the cache acts as an intermediary layer that intercepts incoming queries before they reach the primary datastore. Formally, consider an API request function

$$f : Q \to D,$$

where Q is the query space and D is the corresponding dataset. The caching function

$$C : Q \to D \cup \{\bot\},$$

is defined such that for a given query $q \in Q$, $C(q) = d$ if the cache contains a valid entry $d \in D$, and $C(q) = \bot$ (where $\bot$ denotes a cache miss) otherwise. This layered design rigorously ensures that cache hits facilitate near-instantaneous data retrieval, while cache misses trigger the fallback mechanism to retrieve data from the slower persistent storage. Furthermore, cache entries are commonly associated with Time-To-Live (TTL) values defined by a temporal expiry function

$$T : D \to \mathbb{R},$$

which enforces a maximum lifespan for each entry, thereby preserving the overall freshness and reliability of the cached data.

Performance Evaluation Metrics and System Optimization

Quantitative evaluation of in-memory caching strategies is predicated upon several performance metrics, including the cache hit ratio, latency reduction, and overall system throughput. The effectiveness of a caching strategy can be empirically measured by comparing the average response time experienced during cache hits, L_{cache}, against that during direct datastore access, $L_{\text{persistent}}$. The performance improvement is thereby captured as

$$\Delta L = L_{\text{persistent}} - L_{\text{cache}},$$

with the aim of maximizing ΔL. Additionally, the cache hit ratio, w, defined as

$$w = \frac{H}{N},$$

where H represents the total number of cache hits and N is the total number of API requests, serves as a direct measure of the caching system's operational efficacy. These metrics provide invaluable insight into the optimization of resource allocation and the overall impact on system performance, driving the development of increasingly efficient caching strategies that underpin robust and scalable web services.

Rust Code Snippet

```
use std::collections::HashMap;
use std::sync::{Arc, Mutex};
use std::thread;
use std::time::{Duration, Instant};

/// A cache entry storing the value, the time it was inserted, its
↪    last access time,
```

```rust
/// and the time-to-live (TTL) duration.
struct CacheEntry {
    value: String,
    inserted: Instant,
    last_accessed: Instant,
    ttl: Duration,
}

impl CacheEntry {
    /// Check if the entry is still valid based on its TTL.
    fn is_valid(&self) -> bool {
        Instant::now() <= self.inserted + self.ttl
    }
}

/// In-memory cache structure that keeps track of cache storage,
↪   capacity,
/// and performance metrics such as hit and miss counts.
struct Cache {
    store: HashMap<String, CacheEntry>,
    capacity: usize,
    hit_count: u64,
    miss_count: u64,
}

impl Cache {
    /// Create a new cache with the given capacity.
    fn new(capacity: usize) -> Self {
        Cache {
            store: HashMap::new(),
            capacity,
            hit_count: 0,
            miss_count: 0,
        }
    }

    /// Get a value from the cache. Returns `Some(&str)` if present
    ↪   and valid,
    /// otherwise returns `None`. Updates the last accessed time on
    ↪   hits.
    fn get(&mut self, key: &str) -> Option<&str> {
        if let Some(entry) = self.store.get_mut(key) {
            if entry.is_valid() {
                entry.last_accessed = Instant::now(); // Update for
                    ↪   LRU purposes.
                self.hit_count += 1;
                return Some(&entry.value);
            } else {
                // Entry expired, remove it.
                self.store.remove(key);
                self.miss_count += 1;
                return None;
            }
        }
```

```rust
        }
        self.miss_count += 1;
        None
    }

    /// Insert a key-value pair into the cache with a specified TTL.
    /// If the cache exceeds capacity, an eviction is performed.
    fn insert(&mut self, key: String, value: String, ttl: Duration)
    ↪  {
        let now = Instant::now();
        let entry = CacheEntry {
            value,
            inserted: now,
            last_accessed: now,
            ttl,
        };
        self.store.insert(key, entry);
        self.evict_if_needed();
    }

    /// Evict the least recently used (LRU) entry if the cache size
    ↪  exceeds capacity.
    fn evict_if_needed(&mut self) {
        if self.store.len() <= self.capacity {
            return;
        }
        // Find the key with the oldest last_accessed timestamp.
        if let Some((oldest_key, _)) = self.store.iter()
            .min_by_key(|(_, entry)| entry.last_accessed)
            .map(|(k, entry)| (k.clone(), entry.last_accessed)) {
            println!("Evicting key '{}' due to capacity
            ↪  constraints.", oldest_key);
            self.store.remove(&oldest_key);
        }
    }

    /// Compute the cache hit rate using the formula:
    ///
    ///     h = H / (H + M)
    ///
    /// where H is the number of hits and M is the number of misses.
    fn calculate_hit_rate(&self) -> f64 {
        let total = self.hit_count + self.miss_count;
        if total == 0 {
            0.0
        } else {
            self.hit_count as f64 / total as f64
        }
    }
}

/// Simulate fetching data from a persistent datastore for a given
↪  query.
```

```rust
/// Represents the function f: Q -> D and the fallback when cache
↪   misses occur.
fn persistent_fetch(key: &str) -> String {
    // In a real-world scenario, this would involve I/O or a
    ↪   database query.
    // Here, we simulate delay and data retrieval.
    println!("Fetching '{}' from persistent storage...", key);
    // Simulate delay (for demonstration purposes only)
    // std::thread::sleep(Duration::from_millis(50));
    format!("{}_from_db", key)
}

fn main() {
    // Wrap the cache in Arc<Mutex<...>> to ensure safe concurrent
    ↪   access.
    let cache = Arc::new(Mutex::new(Cache::new(3)));

    // Prepopulate the cache with some entries.
    {
        let mut c = cache.lock().unwrap();
        c.insert("a".to_owned(), "value_a".to_owned(),
        ↪   Duration::new(5, 0));
        c.insert("b".to_owned(), "value_b".to_owned(),
        ↪   Duration::new(5, 0));
        c.insert("c".to_owned(), "value_c".to_owned(),
        ↪   Duration::new(5, 0));
    }

    // Simulated API requests as keys. The caching function C: Q ->
    ↪   D   {} is used here.
    let request_keys = vec!["a", "b", "x", "c", "a", "x", "b", "c"];

    let mut handles = vec![];
    for key in request_keys {
        let cache_clone = Arc::clone(&cache);
        let key = key.to_string();
        // Spawn a thread for each API request to simulate
        ↪   concurrent access.
        let handle = thread::spawn(move || {
            let result = {
                let mut cache = cache_clone.lock().unwrap();
                match cache.get(&key) {
                    Some(val) => {
                        println!("Cache hit for key '{}': {}", key,
                        ↪   val);
                        val.to_owned()
                    }
                    None => {
                        println!("Cache miss for key '{}'.", key);
                        let fetched = persistent_fetch(&key);
                        // Insert the fetched value with a TTL,
                        ↪   simulating Time-To-Live (TTL)
                        ↪   expiration.
```

```rust
                    cache.insert(key.clone(), fetched.clone(),
                    ↪   Duration::new(5, 0));
                    fetched
                }
            }
        };
        result
    });
    handles.push(handle);
}

// Wait for all threads to complete.
for handle in handles {
    let _ = handle.join();
}

// Evaluate performance metrics.
let cache = cache.lock().unwrap();
println!("\nCache Performance Metrics:");
println!("Total Hits: {}", cache.hit_count);
println!("Total Misses: {}", cache.miss_count);
println!("Cache Hit Rate (h): {:.2}",
↪   cache.calculate_hit_rate());

// Performance improvement between persistent and cache access
↪   can hypothetically be computed as:
//   L = L_persistent - L_cache
// In this demonstration, we assume L_cache << L_persistent.
}
```

Chapter 50

Building a Custom Key-Value Store for Session Data

Architectural Design and System Objectives

A design that supports intensive session management requires an in-memory key–value store that meets stringent performance and consistency requirements. The system is architected to allocate volatile memory for session data such that rapid access, modification, and eviction can occur without reliance on external storage mechanisms. The focus is on optimizing concurrent access to ensure that simultaneous session queries and updates remain efficient under high-load conditions. The overall objective is to construct a system where the average session lookup and update operations approach an expected time complexity of $O(1)$, thereby supporting scalability in environments with thousands of active sessions.

Data Structures and Model Abstractions

At the core of the key–value store is the selection of an appropriate data structure that inherently supports fast lookup, insertion, and deletion. A hash map is employed as the principal data structure,

313

mapping a session identifier to its respective session state. Formally, let $\mathcal{K}$ denote the set of session keys and $\mathcal{V}$ the set of session values; the key–value store is then represented as a deterministic function $f : \mathcal{K} \to \mathcal{V}$, with the ideal performance characteristic that a lookup, $f(k)$ for any $k \in \mathcal{K}$, requires a constant number of operations on average. In this context, the session state encapsulates both the user information and temporal metadata essential for enforcing session validity. The data structures are designed with an emphasis on memory locality and minimal allocation overhead to further reduce the access latency inherent in session management operations.

Concurrency Control and Synchronization Techniques

The concurrent nature of session data accesses necessitates robust synchronization mechanisms. The key–value store must be structured to permit concurrent reads and writes while avoiding race conditions and ensuring consistency of session data. Techniques such as optimistic concurrency control and fine-grained locking are considered to mitigate the performance costs typically associated with global locks. To model these concurrent operations, let S represent the set of all session states, and let $\Gamma(S)$ denote the set of all permissible state transitions. A synchronization protocol, P, is then defined such that

$$P \subseteq \Gamma(S),$$

where P enforces atomicity and ordering constraints on each update. Moreover, the adoption of lock-free data structures and atomic compare-and-swap operations minimizes contention, particularly in scenarios where read operations predominate over writes. The rigorous application of these techniques ensures that session data remain consistent even when subjected to hundreds of simultaneous access requests.

Session Expiration Mechanisms and Consistency Protocols

Managing the temporal validity of session data is integral to the design of the key–value store. Each session entry is associated with a Time-To-Live (TTL) value that specifies its allowable lifespan in memory. Denote by $T : \mathcal{V} \to \mathbb{R}^+$ the function that assigns a TTL to each session value. A session entry is considered valid if, at time t, it satisfies

$$t < t_{\text{insert}} + T(v),$$

where t_{insert} is the timestamp corresponding to the insertion of the session and $v \in \mathcal{V}$. When this inequality fails, the session is deemed expired and must be synchronously removed or flagged for garbage collection. Consistency protocols within the key–value store incorporate mechanisms for the periodic validation or lazy cleanup of expired entries, ensuring that stale session data do not compromise system integrity. The integration of these protocols with concurrency controls further guarantees that the eviction policies execute atomically, preventing the appearance of transient inconsistencies during the cleanup process.

Scalability and Performance Considerations

The performance optimization of the in-memory key–value store is evaluated on two principal axes: throughput under concurrent access and minimal latency in session data retrieval. Scalability is achieved by distributing session access operations across multiple concurrent threads without introducing significant overhead. To quantify the operational efficiency, let L_{session} denote the latency incurred for a session read or write operation and let N represent the number of active sessions. The system is engineered such that

$$\lim_{N \to \infty} L_{\text{session}} \approx O(1),$$

indicating that the per-session latency remains statistically invariant as the number of sessions grows. In addition, the evaluation of performance metrics includes the analysis of synchronization costs, memory allocation overhead, and the rapid propagation of session state changes across multiple threads. By optimizing memory utilization and leveraging non-blocking algorithms, the design aims to diminish the cumulative impact of concurrent operations while ensuring a high degree of responsiveness in real-time session management.

Rust Code Snippet

```rust
//! A concurrent, high-performance, in-memory key-value store for
//!     session data.
//! This example implements the core design principles discussed:
//! 1. O(1) average time complexity for session lookup and update
//!     using a HashMap.
//! 2. Concurrency control via Arc and RwLock to allow simultaneous
//!     reads and updates.
//! 3. Session expiration based on TTL (Time-To-Live), following the
//!     condition:
//!     current time t < t_insert + T(v)
//! 4. A cleanup mechanism to remove expired sessions atomically.

use std::collections::HashMap;
use std::sync::{Arc, RwLock};
use std::time::{Duration, Instant};
use std::thread;

/// Represents a user session that stores user information along
///     with timing metadata.
#[derive(Clone, Debug)]
struct Session {
    user: String,
    /// The time at which this session was created.
    created_at: Instant,
    /// The session's time-to-live duration.
    ttl: Duration,
}

impl Session {
    /// Determines if the session is still valid.
    ///
    /// Implements the formula:
    ///     Valid if: current_time < created_at + ttl
    fn is_valid(&self) -> bool {
        Instant::now() < self.created_at + self.ttl
    }
}

/// A thread-safe store for managing sessions using a HashMap.
/// The key represents a session identifier and the value is the
///     session data.
/// Using RwLock ensures that many readers can access concurrently
///     while writes lock exclusively.
struct SessionStore {
    sessions: Arc<RwLock<HashMap<String, Session>>>,
}

impl SessionStore {
    /// Constructs a new, empty SessionStore.
    fn new() -> Self {
```

```rust
        SessionStore {
            sessions: Arc::new(RwLock::new(HashMap::new())),
        }
    }

    /// Inserts or updates a session corresponding to the given key.
    /// The operation has an average time complexity of O(1).
    fn insert_session(&self, key: String, session: Session) {
        let mut sessions = self.sessions.write().unwrap();
        sessions.insert(key, session);
    }

    /// Retrieves a clone of the session associated with the given
    ↪  key, if it exists.
    fn get_session(&self, key: &str) -> Option<Session> {
        let sessions = self.sessions.read().unwrap();
        sessions.get(key).cloned()
    }

    /// Performs a cleanup operation to remove expired sessions.
    ///
    /// The cleanup enforces that a session is kept only if it
    ↪  satisfies:
    ///    current_time < created_at + ttl
    fn cleanup_expired(&self) {
        let mut sessions = self.sessions.write().unwrap();
        sessions.retain(|_, session| session.is_valid());
    }
}

/// Demonstrates the use of SessionStore in a concurrent
↪  environment.
fn main() {
    let store = SessionStore::new();

    // Insert a session with a TTL of 10 seconds.
    store.insert_session(
        "session1".to_string(),
        Session {
            user: "user1".to_string(),
            created_at: Instant::now(),
            ttl: Duration::from_secs(10),
        }
    );

    // Spawn a thread to simulate concurrent session access.
    let store_clone = Arc::clone(&store.sessions);
    let handle = thread::spawn(move || {
        // Wait for 5 seconds before accessing the session.
        thread::sleep(Duration::from_secs(5));
        let sessions = store_clone.read().unwrap();
        if let Some(session) = sessions.get("session1") {
            if session.is_valid() {
```

```rust
                println!("(Thread) Session is valid for user: {}",
                ↪   session.user);
            } else {
                println!("(Thread) Session expired");
            }
        }
    });

    // Main thread waits 6 seconds before checking the session
    ↪   status.
    thread::sleep(Duration::from_secs(6));
    if let Some(session) = store.get_session("session1") {
        if session.is_valid() {
            println!("(Main) Session is valid for user: {}",
            ↪   session.user);
        } else {
            println!("(Main) Session expired");
        }
    }

    // Cleanup expired sessions while ensuring atomicity and
    ↪   consistency.
    store.cleanup_expired();

    // Verify if the session has been removed after its TTL expired.
    if store.get_session("session1").is_none() {
        println!("Session successfully expired and removed.");
    }

    // Wait for the concurrent thread to finish.
    handle.join().unwrap();

    // Note:
    // The design ensures O(1) average time complexity for lookup
    ↪   and update,
    // while the use of Arc and RwLock enforces robust concurrency
    ↪   control and memory safety.
}
```

Chapter 51

Implementing Rate Limiting with Token Bucket Algorithms

Fundamental Principles of the Token Bucket Model

The token bucket algorithm provides a systematic framework for controlling the frequency of API request processing. In this model, tokens are generated at a constant rate r and stored in a bucket with a finite capacity C. Each token represents the right to execute one API request. The bucket accumulates tokens when the incoming request rate is lower than r, thereby allowing short bursts of activity up to a maximum of C tokens. Conversely, when API requests occur in rapid succession, each request consumes a token; if no tokens remain, subsequent requests cannot be immediately serviced. This mechanism offers a dual advantage: it restricts the average processing rate while accommodating temporary surges in demand. The inherent flexibility of this model lies in the balance between the refill rate r and the bucket capacity C, which together determine both the steady state and the transient behavior of the rate-limiting system.

Mathematical Formulation and Analytical Modeling

Mathematically, the token bucket algorithm can be described by considering $T(t)$ as the number of tokens available at time t. Tokens are added over time according to the differential relation

$$\frac{dT}{dt} = r,$$

subject to the constraint

$$T(t) \leq C.$$

When an API request is received, a check is performed such that if $T(t) \geq 1$, the request is permitted and the token count is decremented:

$$T(t) \rightarrow T(t) - 1.$$

This formulation establishes that for any given time interval Δt, the maximum number of API requests that can be authorized does not exceed

$$r\Delta t + C.$$

The mathematical model effectively characterizes both the long-term average rate of operation and the short-term burst tolerance, ensuring that the system remains robust under varying traffic conditions.

Integration with API Request Management Systems

The practical implementation of the token bucket algorithm within an API management framework necessitates tight integration between token generation and request handling. Upon the arrival of an API call, the system inspects the current token count. If a token is available, the request is immediately processed and one token is deducted from the bucket. In the absence of available tokens, the system is configured either to defer the request until token replenishment occurs or to decline the request in order to maintain overall resource equilibrium. This integration is critical for enforcing a controlled rate of API consumption, as it synchronizes resource allocation with real-time demand. Atomic operations and concurrent processing primitives ensure that updates to the token bucket remain consistent even in high-load environments, thereby preventing race conditions and ensuring equitable distribution of processing capacity.

Performance Analysis and Resource Fairness Considerations

The performance characteristics of the token bucket algorithm are predominantly governed by the parameters r and C, which directly influence the allowable burst size and the steady-state throughput. Empirical analysis combined with formal modeling indicates that the effective limit on API requests over a measurement interval Δt is given by

$$r\Delta t + C,$$

which serves as a critical metric for assessing the fairness and efficiency of resource allocation. Under light load conditions, the algorithm permits rapid processing of incoming requests due to token accumulation. In contrast, during peak load periods, the gradual depletion of tokens enforces a controlled processing rate, thereby mitigating the risk of resource overutilization. The design of the token bucket model ensures that no client can monopolize the system, as the hard upper limit imposed by C and the consistent refill at rate r collectively enforce a balanced distribution of service capacity across all concurrent API consumers. Detailed analytical evaluations further account for factors such as refill latency and transient token starvation, providing a comprehensive framework for optimizing both throughput and response times in high-concurrency environments.

Rust Code Snippet

```
use std::sync::{Arc, Mutex};
use std::sync::atomic::{AtomicUsize, Ordering};
use std::time::{Duration, Instant};
use std::thread;

/// TokenBucket implements the token bucket algorithm for rate
↪    limiting.
///
/// Mathematical Model:
```

```rust
/// 1. Token refill is defined by the differential equation:
///     dT/dt = r
///     where r is the refill rate (tokens per second).
///
/// 2. The bucket has a finite capacity C, so T(t) <= C.
///
/// 3. When a request is processed, one token is consumed:
///     if T(t) >= 1 then T(t) -> T(t) - 1.
///
/// 4. Over a period t, the maximum number of allowed API requests
↪   is:
///     r * t + C,
///     which demonstrates both the steady-state rate limit and the
↪   burst tolerance.
pub struct TokenBucket {
    /// Maximum capacity of the bucket (C).
    capacity: usize,
    /// Refill rate in tokens per second (r).
    refill_rate: f64,
    /// Current token count T(t), stored atomically for concurrency.
    tokens: AtomicUsize,
    /// Timestamp of the last refill operation.
    last_refill: Mutex<Instant>,
}

impl TokenBucket {
    /// Constructs a new TokenBucket.
    ///
    /// # Arguments
    ///
    /// * `capacity` - Maximum tokens the bucket can hold.
    /// * `refill_rate` - Number of tokens added per second.
    pub fn new(capacity: usize, refill_rate: f64) -> Self {
        Self {
            capacity,
            refill_rate,
            tokens: AtomicUsize::new(capacity),
            last_refill: Mutex::new(Instant::now()),
        }
    }

    /// Refills the bucket based on the elapsed time since the last
    ↪   update.
    ///
    /// The equation used is:
    ///     tokens_to_add = floor((now - last_refill) * r)
    /// ensuring that the token count does not exceed C.
    fn refill(&self) {
        // Lock to access and update the last_refill time safely.
        let mut last = self.last_refill.lock().unwrap();
        let now = Instant::now();
        let elapsed = now.duration_since(*last);
        let elapsed_secs = elapsed.as_secs_f64();
```

```rust
        // Calculate the number of tokens to add based on the
        ↪   elapsed time.
        let tokens_to_add = (elapsed_secs *
        ↪   self.refill_rate).floor() as usize;
        if tokens_to_add > 0 {
            // Read current token count.
            let current_tokens =
            ↪   self.tokens.load(Ordering::Relaxed);
            // New token count is min(current + tokens_to_add,
            ↪   capacity)
            let new_token_count = std::cmp::min(current_tokens +
            ↪   tokens_to_add, self.capacity);
            self.tokens.store(new_token_count, Ordering::Relaxed);
            // Update the last refill time.
            *last = now;
        }
    }

    /// Attempts to consume a token.
    ///
    /// Returns true if a token was available and consumed,
    ↪   otherwise false.
    pub fn try_consume(&self) -> bool {
        // Refill tokens before checking.
        self.refill();

        // Atomically try to decrement the token count if available.
        loop {
            let current = self.tokens.load(Ordering::Relaxed);
            if current == 0 {
                // No tokens available, rate limit exceeded.
                return false;
            }
            // Attempt to decrement token count by 1.
            if self.tokens.compare_exchange(
                current,
                current - 1,
                Ordering::SeqCst,
                Ordering::SeqCst
            ).is_ok() {
                return true;
            }
            // If compare_exchange failed due to concurrent update,
            ↪   try again.
        }
    }
}

fn main() {
    // Set simulation parameters:
    // Bucket capacity C = 10 tokens, Refill rate r = 1 token per
    ↪   second.
```

```rust
    let capacity = 10;
    let refill_rate = 1.0;
    let bucket = Arc::new(TokenBucket::new(capacity, refill_rate));

    // Simulate multiple API requests using threads.
    // Each thread will attempt to consume a token representing an
    ↪ API request.
    let mut handles = Vec::new();
    for i in 0..20 {
        let bucket_clone = Arc::clone(&bucket);
        let handle = thread::spawn(move || {
            // Simulate staggered request arrivals.
            thread::sleep(Duration::from_millis((i * 100) as u64));
            if bucket_clone.try_consume() {
                println!("Request {} processed: token consumed.",
                    ↪ i);
            } else {
                println!("Request {} rejected: no tokens
                    ↪ available.", i);
            }
        });
        handles.push(handle);
    }

    // Wait for all threads to finish.
    for handle in handles {
        handle.join().unwrap();
    }
}
```

Chapter 52

Leaky Bucket Algorithms in Asynchronous Systems

Theoretical Foundations of the Leaky Bucket Model

The leaky bucket algorithm provides a robust mechanism for regulating the flow of requests by introducing a fixed-rate outflow, analogous to a physical bucket with a small aperture through which fluid steadily exits. In this model, incoming traffic is collected in a conceptual bucket that accumulates requests until they are processed at a constant rate r. The algorithm imposes a disciplined queueing structure that inherently smooths bursty arrivals by enforcing a regulated exit rate. A key property of the leaky bucket model is its ability to decouple the stochastic nature of request arrivals from the deterministic nature of service processing, thereby ensuring that sporadic surges in traffic do not overwhelm downstream components.

Fundamentally, the leaky bucket mechanism can be viewed as a low-pass filter for request flows. By constraining the departure rate to a constant r, the algorithm transforms erratic high-frequency bursts into a more consistent, lower-frequency output. This approach mitigates the adverse effects of transient overloads and aids in maintaining steady processing flows in environments where asynchronous events and variable latencies are the norm.

Mathematical Formulation of the Leaky Bucket Mechanism

Mathematical modeling of the leaky bucket algorithm provides a precise framework for analyzing its performance. Define $L(t)$ as the instantaneous load of the bucket at time t, where $L(t)$ represents the accumulated number of requests awaiting processing. The temporal evolution of $L(t)$ can be described by the differential relation

$$\frac{dL(t)}{dt} = \lambda(t) - r,$$

where $\lambda(t)$ denotes the instantaneous arrival rate of requests and r is the constant leak rate. This formulation implicitly assumes that $L(t)$ is bounded below by zero, ensuring that the bucket cannot contain a negative number of requests. Furthermore, in practical implementations, a maximum capacity C may be imposed such that any incoming requests beyond this capacity are either discarded or subjected to alternative handling mechanisms.

Over a discrete time interval Δt, the bucket's dynamics can be approximated by the recurrence relation

$$L(t + \Delta t) = \max\{0, L(t) + \Lambda(t) - r\Delta t\},$$

where $\Lambda(t)$ represents the total number of arrivals during the interval Δt. This equation encapsulates both the buffering capability of the bucket and the steady drainage imposed by the leak rate. When $\Lambda(t) \gg r\Delta t$, the bucket begins to accumulate load, potentially reaching capacity and triggering overflow policies as determined by system design.

Asynchronous Implementation Considerations

In asynchronous systems, the temporal decoupling between arrival events and service processing introduces additional layers of complexity into the implementation of the leaky bucket algorithm. The inherent unpredictability of asynchronous event scheduling necessitates precise synchronization mechanisms to maintain the integrity of the bucket's state. When request arrivals occur concurrently on multiple threads or event loops, the leaky bucket model must be integrated with non-blocking synchronization primitives and atomic updates to ensure that the leak rate r is faithfully enforced across the system.

The update of the bucket's level is performed at discrete time instances, often governed by a high-resolution system clock or an event-driven timer. The recurrence relation

$$L_{n+1} = \max\{0, L_n + \lambda_n - r\Delta t\}$$

captures the essence of this asynchronous behavior, where L_n is the load at the nth time step and λ_n is the number of arrivals during the interval Δt. The challenge lies in the precise measurement of Δt and the handling of intervals that may not be uniform due to scheduling delays or jitter. Asynchronous systems often employ fine-grained concurrency controls to mitigate race conditions and to ensure that the consistent leak rate is applied regardless of the inherent variability in scheduling.

Impact on Traffic Smoothing and Request Flow Regulation

The effectiveness of the leaky bucket algorithm in moderating request flows manifests in its ability to absorb transient traffic bursts while maintaining a steady output rate. During periods of high incoming traffic, the bucket temporarily buffers the surplus requests; however, the outflow is irrevocably constrained to the constant rate r. This regulated outflow not only prevents downstream components from being inundated with erratic workloads but also stabilizes response times by imposing uniform intervals between successive request processing events.

The performance of the leaky bucket mechanism can be quantified by examining the long-term balance between the cumulative arrival rate and the service rate. For sustained stability, the average arrival rate $\bar{\lambda}$ must satisfy

$$\bar{\lambda} \leq r,$$

ensuring that, over sufficiently long durations, the accumulated load does not perpetually increase. During short bursts of intensity, the algorithm permits temporary deviations from equilibrium, relying on the bucket's capacity C to accommodate transient surges. The interplay between C and r determines the maximum burst tolerance and the system's resilience to traffic variability.

Detailed analyses using both analytical models and simulation studies reveal that the leaky bucket model preserves a consistent service rhythm even under highly asynchronous conditions. By enforcing a fixed processing cadence, the algorithm minimizes the variance in service latency and contributes to a predictable and controlled system behavior. This property is of paramount importance in distributed environments where the synchronization of disparate processing elements is critical to the overall performance and fairness of resource allocation.

Rust Code Snippet

```rust
use tokio::sync::Mutex;
use tokio::time::{sleep, interval, Duration};
use std::sync::Arc;
use rand::Rng;

/// Represents the Leaky Bucket that accumulates request load and
↪   reduces it at a constant leak rate.
///
/// The update equation in discrete form is:
/// L_{n+1} = max{0, L_n + _n - r*t}
/// where L_n is the current load, _n is the number of arriving
↪   requests in the interval t,
/// and r is the leak rate.
#[derive(Debug)]
struct Bucket {
    /// Current number of requests in the bucket.
    load: u32,
    /// Maximum capacity of the bucket. Incoming requests beyond
    ↪   this are dropped.
    capacity: u32,
    /// Number of requests to leak (process) per tick.
    leak_rate: u32,
}

impl Bucket {
    /// Constructs a new Bucket with a given capacity and leak rate.
    fn new(capacity: u32, leak_rate: u32) -> Self {
        Bucket {
            load: 0,
            capacity,
            leak_rate,
```

```rust
        }
    }

    /// Adds arriving requests to the bucket.
    ///
    /// If the new load exceeds capacity, the excess requests are
    ↪   dropped.
    fn add_requests(&mut self, count: u32) {
        let new_load = self.load + count;
        if new_load > self.capacity {
            println!(
                "Bucket overflow! Dropping {} requests.",
                new_load - self.capacity
            );
            self.load = self.capacity;
        } else {
            self.load = new_load;
        }
    }

    /// Drains requests from the bucket based on the fixed leak
    ↪   rate.
    ///
    /// This simulates:
    /// L_{n+1} = max{0, L_n - leak_rate}
    fn leak(&mut self) {
        if self.leak_rate >= self.load {
            self.load = 0;
        } else {
            self.load -= self.leak_rate;
        }
    }
}

#[tokio::main]
async fn main() {
    // Create a shared Bucket object with capacity 100 and a leak
    ↪   rate of 5 requests per tick.
    let bucket = Arc::new(Mutex::new(Bucket::new(100, 5)));

    // Spawn an asynchronous task to simulate asynchronous arrival
    ↪   of requests.
    let bucket_clone = Arc::clone(&bucket);
    tokio::spawn(async move {
        loop {
            // Simulate random arrivals between 0 and 10 requests.
            let arrival = rand::thread_rng().gen_range(0..=10);
            {
                let mut bucket = bucket_clone.lock().await;
                bucket.add_requests(arrival);
                println!("Added {} requests, current load: {}",
                ↪   arrival, bucket.load);
            }
```

```rust
        // Sleep for a random duration between 100ms and 300ms
        ↪   to simulate irregular arrival intervals.
        let sleep_duration =
        ↪   Duration::from_millis(rand::thread_rng().gen_range(100..=300));
        sleep(sleep_duration).await;
    }
});

// Create a time interval for the leak operation (e.g., every 1
↪   second).
let mut tick = interval(Duration::from_secs(1));
loop {
    tick.tick().await;
    {
        let mut bucket = bucket.lock().await;
        bucket.leak();
        println!("After leaking, bucket load: {}", bucket.load);
    }
}
}
```

Chapter 53

Request Throttling Code Strategies

Architectural Overview of Dynamic Throttling

Dynamic throttling in high-load API services is concerned with the regulation of request flows through the design of adaptive mechanisms that modulate incoming traffic rates. In these architectures, the throttling component is embedded within the service pipeline and is tasked with monitoring instantaneous request rates, system capacity, and performance metrics to adjust the admittance of further requests dynamically. The conceptual model is built on the notion that a system under high load must be capable of modifying its operational parameters in real time, thereby ensuring that the processing units are not overwhelmed during transient spikes. A well-designed throttling strategy typically comprises continuous load measurement, threshold-based activation of throttling logic, and gradual recovery protocols that restore full service capacity as system metrics return to nominal levels.

Mathematical Modeling of Throttling Dynamics

The behavior of dynamic throttling systems can be rigorously analyzed using mathematical models that frame the system's adjustment of admission rates. Let $\lambda(t)$ denote the instantaneous arrival rate of requests at time t, and let μ represent the maximum processing capacity of the underlying API service. The throttling threshold $T(t)$ is then defined as a function of the discrepancy between $\lambda(t)$ and μ. A simple linear model may assume the form

$$T(t + \Delta t) = T(t) + \gamma \left[\lambda(t) - \mu \right] \Delta t,$$

where γ is a control parameter (or learning rate) that determines the sensitivity of the throttling mechanism to deviations in load. This formulation implies that when $\lambda(t) > \mu$, the threshold is adjusted downward to limit additional inflow, whereas a lower arrival rate permits an upward relaxation of throttling constraints. In more advanced models, the adjustment function may include higher-order terms or integrative components such that the throttle update is expressed as

$$T(t + \Delta t) = T(t) + K_p \left[\lambda(t) - \mu \right] \Delta t + K_i \int_t^{t+\Delta t} \left[\lambda(\tau) - \mu \right] d\tau,$$

where K_p and K_i are proportional and integral gain constants, respectively. The system's stability and responsiveness can be analyzed by inspecting the convergence properties and transient behavior of $T(t)$ as the system adapts to variable loads.

Control Theory and Feedback Mechanisms in Throttling

At the core of dynamic throttling strategies lies the application of feedback control theory. A feedback loop continuously measures system performance and adjusts the throttling parameters to minimize the error defined as

$$e(t) = \lambda(t) - \mu.$$

This error is processed through a control function that may incorporate elements analogous to a proportional-integral-derivative (PID) controller. In such systems, the control input $u(t)$ used to modulate the throttling threshold is given by

$$u(t) = K_p \, e(t) + K_i \int_0^t e(\tau) \, d\tau + K_d \frac{de(t)}{dt},$$

with K_d representing the derivative gain. Although the derivative term may be secondary in many throttling applications due to measurement noise, its inclusion can enhance stability in rapidly oscillating load conditions. The design challenge centers on selecting the gain parameters so that the system smoothly transitions between throttled and unthrottled states while avoiding excessive oscillations or overcorrections that could degrade overall service quality.

Implementation Considerations in Asynchronous API Services

In environments characterized by asynchronous event execution, the implementation of dynamic throttling logic must address issues of concurrency, state synchronization, and timing precision. The asynchrony inherent in modern API services implies that requests can arrive concurrently across multiple threads or event loops, making atomicity and non-blocking state management essential. Temporal inconsistencies due to scheduling delays or jitter necessitate that the throttling mechanism is resilient to irregular measurement intervals. In practice, the system continuously samples the instantaneous request rate $\lambda(t)$ and updates the throttling threshold in accordance with discrete approximations of the underlying continuous-time model. Furthermore, the integration of the throttling module into the overall system must be designed so as not to become a bottleneck in and of itself; this often involves employing lock-free data structures or fine-grained synchronization primitives to accurately maintain the current throttling state without imposing significant overhead.

Algorithmic Trade-Offs and Parameter Tuning

The efficacy of a dynamic throttling strategy is contingent upon the careful calibration of its algorithmic parameters. Robust adaptive throttling requires a balance between aggressiveness in suppressing overload and leniency sufficient to maintain high throughput under normal conditions. Overly rapid responses to transient load spikes may result in oscillations, whereas sluggish adjustments can permit the temporary saturation of service capacities. The choice of parameters for gain factors such as K_p, K_i, and K_d, as well as the interval Δt for control updates, must be informed by both theoretical stability analysis and empirical benchmarking. In designing the throttling algorithm, one must consider the trade-off between reducing the risk of service degradation during load surges and maintaining fairness in request processing. Parameter tuning is thus an iterative process that involves the systematic exploration of the control parameter space, often through simulation studies or in situ experimentation, to arrive at an optimal configuration that adapts gracefully over a wide range of operational scenarios.

Rust Code Snippet

```rust
use std::fmt::{Display, Formatter};

/// A struct representing the dynamic throttling mechanism using PID
↪   control.
/// It models the update equation:
///
///    T(t+t) = T(t) + [Kp * e(t) + Ki * e dt + Kd * de/dt] * t,
///
/// where the error is defined as:
///
///    e(t) = (t) - ,
///
/// with (t) being the instantaneous arrival rate,  the processing
↪   capacity,
/// and t the discrete time step.
struct Throttler {
    /// Current throttling threshold T(t)
    threshold: f64,
    /// Proportional gain (K_p)
    kp: f64,
    /// Integral gain (K_i)
    ki: f64,
    /// Derivative gain (K_d)
    kd: f64,
    /// Accumulated error used for the integral term (e dt)
    integral: f64,
    /// Previous error used to compute the derivative term (de/dt)
    previous_error: Option<f64>,
}

impl Throttler {
    /// Constructs a new Throttler with an initial threshold and PID
    ↪   gains.
    fn new(initial_threshold: f64, kp: f64, ki: f64, kd: f64) ->
    ↪   Throttler {
```

```rust
    Throttler {
        threshold: initial_threshold,
        kp,
        ki,
        kd,
        integral: 0.0,
        previous_error: None,
    }
}

/// Updates the throttling threshold using the discrete PID
↪   control formula.
///
/// # Arguments
///
/// * `arrival_rate` - The current arrival rate (t) (requests
↪   per unit time).
/// * `capacity`     - The maximum processing capacity .
/// * `dt`           - The time increment t.
///
/// # Returns
///
/// The updated threshold T(t+t).
fn update(&mut self, arrival_rate: f64, capacity: f64, dt: f64)
↪   -> f64 {
    // Compute the error: e(t) = (t) -
    let error = arrival_rate - capacity;

    // Update the integrated error term: e dt
    self.integral += error * dt;

    // Compute the derivative term: de/dt
    let derivative = if let Some(prev_err) = self.previous_error
    ↪   {
        (error - prev_err) / dt
    } else {
        0.0
    };
    self.previous_error = Some(error);

    // PID control input: u(t) = Kp * e + Ki * e dt + Kd * de/dt
    let control_input = self.kp * error + self.ki *
    ↪   self.integral + self.kd * derivative;

    // Update the threshold using the control input:
    // T(t+t) = T(t) + u(t) * t
    self.threshold += control_input * dt;

    self.threshold
    }
}

fn main() {
```

```rust
// Simulation parameters
let capacity = 100.0;           // Maximum processing capacity
let dt = 0.1;                   // Time step t in seconds
let simulation_duration = 10.0; // Total simulation time in
↪   seconds
let steps = (simulation_duration / dt) as usize;

// PID parameters for dynamic throttling
let initial_threshold = 150.0;  // Initial threshold T(0)
let kp = 0.5;   // Proportional gain
let ki = 0.1;   // Integral gain
let kd = 0.05;  // Derivative gain

// Initialize the throttler with the specified parameters
let mut throttler = Throttler::new(initial_threshold, kp, ki,
↪   kd);

// Print header for simulation output: Time, ArrivalRate, and
↪   Threshold
println!("Time\tArrivalRate\tThreshold");

// Simulation loop: Update the throttler at each discrete time
↪   step
for step in 0..steps {
    let current_time = step as f64 * dt;
    // Simulate an arrival rate (t) that includes an oscillatory
    ↪   component and a surge after 5 seconds.
    let arrival_rate = capacity
        + 20.0 * (current_time).sin()
        + if current_time > 5.0 { 30.0 } else { 0.0 };

    // Update the throttling threshold based on the current
    ↪   arrival rate
    let updated_threshold = throttler.update(arrival_rate,
    ↪   capacity, dt);

    // Output the current time, simulated arrival rate, and
    ↪   computed threshold
    println!("{:.2}\t{:.2}\t\t{:.2}", current_time,
    ↪   arrival_rate, updated_threshold);
}
}
```

336

Chapter 54

High-Volume Traffic Handling with Async Stream Combinators

Theoretical Foundations of Asynchronous Stream Combinators

High-volume network traffic is modeled as a continuous sequence of events that, when abstracted, forms an asynchronous stream. Such streams are conceived as potentially unbounded sequences of data items generated in a non-blocking fashion. The abstraction facilitates the application of functional operators that manipulate these streams through composition. Given asynchronous streams $S_1, S_2, \ldots, S_n$, it is natural to define a merger operator M as a mapping

$$M(S_1, S_2, \ldots, S_n) = S,$$

where S represents the unified flow of events that preserves the inherent timing and ordering properties intrinsic to the original streams. The composability of these operators supports the theoretical framework of monadic transformations, ensuring that the successive application of operators yields predictable and mathematically tractable behaviors even under conditions of high concurrency.

Merging Multiple Asynchronous Data Streams

The integration of inputs from diverse network sources requires precise mechanisms to combine concurrent data flows. Merging, in this context, transcends simple concatenation; it involves the interleaving of events based on temporal criteria or priority policies dictated by the network protocol. The merging operator must guarantee that the relative order of events, as determined by their arrival timestamps, is either maintained or deterministically restructured. In scenarios where network packets are subject to unpredictable delays or sudden bursts, merging operators must contend with synchronization challenges by employing robust scheduling algorithms that dynamically adjust the interleaving strategy. The mathematical representation of a merging operator inherently supports a probabilistic model wherein events from streams S_i occur with an associated probability measure, and the unified stream S is characterized by a rate function that amalgamates these individual measures.

Rate Limiting and Flow Control in High-Volume Environments

Efficient handling of asynchronous streams in high-volume contexts inherently requires the implementation of limiting operators that impose strict flow control. Rate limiting acts to constrain the throughput of events in order to balance the processing load with the finite computational resources available. In a formal setting, let λ denote the arrival rate of events within the unified stream, and let L represent an upper bound on the sustainable processing rate. The limiting operator can be expressed as a filtering function $F : S \to S'$, defined by

$$F(s) = \begin{cases} s, & \text{if } \lambda(s) \leq L, \\ , & \text{if } \lambda(s) > L, \end{cases}$$

where   indicates that the event is either temporarily buffered or discarded in order to enforce the imposed rate limit. The deployment of such operators ensures that downstream processing components are not overwhelmed during transient spikes in network load. Moreover, the incorporation of backpressure mechanisms allows the system to dynamically adjust the flow, thereby maintaining the equilibrium between arrival rates and processing capacity.

Design Considerations for Efficient Processing Pipelines

In high-throughput environments, the design of processing pipelines encompasses the chaining of multiple asynchronous stream combinators to achieve both high performance and low latency. Each combinator is responsible for a distinct transformation such as mapping, filtering, batching, or windowing, and the overall pipeline is characterized by the sequential composition of these functionally pure transformations. The partitioning of a volatile data stream into independent substreams permits parallel processing strategies that distribute the computational load across multiple processing units. Subsequent reassembly of these substreams leverages merging operators that preserve semantic order while ensuring balanced resource utilization.

The pipeline must further address synchronization challenges by incorporating atomic state transitions and non-blocking coordination primitives. This is particularly critical when adaptive mechanisms, such as dynamic rate limiting, are introduced into the data flow. The architecture benefits from the clear separation between computational logic and flow control, a separation that is achieved by the declarative nature of asynchronous stream combinators. When designing such pipelines, careful consideration is given to both the temporal dynamics of the input streams and the operational characteristics of downstream processing elements. The result is a robust design that facilitates efficient handling of large volumes of network traffic, achieved through the seamless integration of merging, limiting, and parallel processing operators within a highly modular and scalable framework.

Rust Code Snippet

```
//! This code snippet demonstrates key concepts from the chapter by
↪    implementing:
//! 1. A merging operator M(S, S, ..., S) = S that combines multiple
↪    asynchronous streams.
//! 2. A rate limiting operator F(s) defined as:
//!      F(s) = { s, if (s)  L; , if (s) > L }
```

```
//!    where (s) represents the arrival rate of events and L is the
↪    processing limit.
//!
//! The merged stream simulates high-volume network traffic, and the
↪    rate limiter
//! uses a token bucket approach to enforce a maximum of 3 events
↪    per second.

use tokio::time::{Duration, Instant, sleep, interval};
use futures::stream::{Stream, StreamExt, select_all};
use tokio_stream::wrappers::IntervalStream;
use async_stream::stream;
use std::pin::Pin;

// Define a simple Event structure.
#[derive(Debug)]
struct Event {
    timestamp: Instant,
    data: String,
}

// simulate_stream creates an asynchronous stream that produces
↪    events at regular intervals.
fn simulate_stream(source: &'static str, interval_duration:
↪    Duration) -> impl Stream<Item = Event> + Unpin {
    let ticker = interval(interval_duration);
    let interval_stream = IntervalStream::new(ticker);
    interval_stream.enumerate().map(move |(i, _)| {
        Event {
            timestamp: Instant::now(),
            data: format!("{} event {}", source, i),
        }
    })
}

// merge_streams implements the merging operator M(S, S, ..., S) = S
↪    by interleaving events
// from multiple input streams. This operation preserves the
↪    temporal characteristics of the events.
fn merge_streams<T, S>(streams: Vec<S>) -> impl Stream<Item = T>
where
    S: Stream<Item = T> + Unpin,
{
    select_all(streams)
}

// rate_limited_stream implements a token-bucket-like rate limiter
↪    which ensures that the stream
// does not exceed a specified rate (limit events per
↪    refill_interval).
// This corresponds to the rate limiting equation F(s) as described.
fn rate_limited_stream<S>(
    input_stream: S,
```

```
        limit: usize,
        refill_interval: Duration,
) -> Pin<Box<dyn Stream<Item = Event> + Send>>
where
        S: Stream<Item = Event> + Send + 'static + Unpin,
{
        Box::pin(stream! {
            let mut tokens = limit;
            let mut last_refill = Instant::now();
            tokio::pin!(input_stream);

            while let Some(event) = input_stream.next().await {
                let now = Instant::now();
                // Refill tokens if the refill interval has passed.
                if now.duration_since(last_refill) >= refill_interval {
                    tokens = limit;
                    last_refill = now;
                }
                // If tokens are available, yield the event, simulating
                ↪   F(s) = s when (s)   L.
                if tokens > 0 {
                    tokens -= 1;
                    yield event;
                } else {
                    // When tokens are exhausted, wait until tokens are
                    ↪   refilled, i.e., simulate F(s) = .
                    let wait_time = refill_interval -
                    ↪   now.duration_since(last_refill);
                    sleep(wait_time).await;
                    tokens = limit - 1; // Consume one token for the
                    ↪   current event after refill.
                    last_refill = Instant::now();
                    yield event;
                }
            }
        })
}

#[tokio::main]
async fn main() {
    // Create two simulated asynchronous streams representing
    ↪   different network sources.
    let stream1 = simulate_stream("Source1",
    ↪   Duration::from_millis(300));
    let stream2 = simulate_stream("Source2",
    ↪   Duration::from_millis(500));

    // Merge the streams using the merging operator M(S, S) = S.
    let merged_stream = merge_streams(vec![stream1, stream2]);

    // Apply the rate limiter to ensure only 3 events are processed
    ↪   per second.
```

341

```rust
    let limited_stream = rate_limited_stream(merged_stream, 3,
    ↪  Duration::from_secs(1));

    // Process each event from the limited stream.
    limited_stream.for_each(|event| async move {
        // Print the elapsed time in milliseconds along with event
        ↪  details.
        println!("[{} ms] {}",
        ↪  event.timestamp.elapsed().as_millis(), event.data);
    }).await;
}
```

Chapter 55

Efficient Batch Processing in Asynchronous Workflows

Foundations of Asynchronous Batch Processing

Batch processing within asynchronous environments constitutes a pivotal mechanism for managing high-throughput requests. This paradigm rests upon the aggregation of multiple individual requests into discrete batches, thereby reducing overhead associated with per-request scheduling and execution. In these systems, requests are characterized by sporadic arrival patterns and non-deterministic timing, which necessitates a robust approach to grouping tasks. By consolidating requests, the system is able to amortize fixed processing costs, minimize context switching, and better utilize computational resources. The conceptual framework is built upon the assumption that each incoming request r_i contributes a processing cost C_i, and that a fixed overhead cost C_b is incurred whenever a new batch is initialized. Consequently, the effective per-request cost when employing batch processing is modeled as

$$C_{\text{eff}} = \frac{B \times C_i + C_b}{B},$$

where B denotes the batch size. This formulation underscores the advantage of batch processing, as the overhead C_b is distributed over multiple requests.

Design Patterns for Request Batching

A spectrum of design patterns has evolved to facilitate the grouping of requests in asynchronous workflows. Among these, fixed-size batching, adaptive batching, and time-window-based aggregation are prominent. Fixed-size batching accumulates a predetermined number of requests before processing, while adaptive batching dynamically adjusts the batch size based on real-time metrics such as instantaneous load and system latency. Time-window-based aggregation, in contrast, gathers all incoming requests within a specified interval Δt, thereby forming a batch that inherently reflects both the frequency and temporal proximity of events. In many systems, the chosen strategy must account for the variability in request arrival rates. For example, if N requests are received over a time period Δt, the effective batch size is determined by

$$B = \min\left(N, \ B_{\max}\right),$$

with $B_{\max}$ representing the upper bound on batch capacity. This design decision plays a critical role in aligning the batching mechanism with the performance objectives of the system.

Theoretical Analysis of Throughput Enhancement

The mathematical analysis of batching techniques elucidates the conditions under which throughput is maximized. Batch processing enhances throughput by mitigating the impact of per-request overhead. If T_p denotes the processing time for an individual request and T_w the waiting time incurred while batching, then the overall system throughput X can be expressed as

$$X = \frac{B}{T_p + T_w}.$$

As the batch size B increases, the fixed overhead associated with batch initialization is mitigated, thus improving the effective throughput. The optimization of B involves achieving a balance between the benefits of reduced overhead and the potential penalty of increased waiting times. This trade-off is formalized by analyzing the derivative of the effective cost function with respect to B, as in

$$\frac{d}{dB}\left(\frac{B \times C_i + C_b}{B}\right) = 0,$$

which yields the optimal batch size B^* under given system constraints. Such theoretical models serve as a foundation for designing batching strategies that maximize resource utilization while preserving acceptable latency bounds.

Trade-offs and Concurrency Considerations

The integration of batch processing into asynchronous workflows introduces trade-offs that are pivotal to system performance. While the aggregation of requests can significantly decrease per-request overhead, it may also introduce additional latency as individual requests await inclusion in a batch. The latency induced by batching, denoted by Δt, must be carefully managed so as not to compromise system responsiveness, particularly in environments where timely processing is critical. Concurrency considerations further complicate the design. As multiple asynchronous tasks operate simultaneously, ensuring that batches are formed, dispatched, and processed without contention requires the use of non-blocking coordination mechanisms. Techniques such as lock-free data structures and atomic counters enable the maintenance of consistency in the presence of high concurrency. Moreover, batch expiry conditions are typically defined by a dual threshold: either the batch achieves a target size B_{target} or the waiting time exceeds the limit Δt. In such cases, the system triggers batch dispatch, thereby guaranteeing that the throughput gains obtained by batching do not come at an unacceptable cost to latency.

Rust Code Snippet

```
use std::sync::Arc;
use tokio::sync::Mutex;
use std::time::{Duration, Instant};

/// Calculate effective per-request cost given batch size (B), cost
↪    per request (C_i) and batch overhead (C_b)
```

```
/// Formula: C_eff = (B * C_i + C_b) / B
fn effective_cost(batch_size: f64, cost_ind: f64, overhead: f64) ->
↪    f64 {
    (batch_size * cost_ind + overhead) / batch_size
}

/// Calculate throughput given batch size (B), processing time (T_p)
↪    and waiting time (T_w)
/// Formula: X = B / (T_p + T_w)
fn throughput(batch_size: f64, processing_time: f64, waiting_time:
↪    f64) -> f64 {
    batch_size / (processing_time + waiting_time)
}

/// Overall cost function combining the effective cost and a waiting
↪    penalty factor.
/// Here we define an overall cost as:
///     F(B) = (B * C_i + C_b) / B +  * B
/// where  (wait_penalty) models the cost of increased waiting time
↪    for larger batches.
fn overall_cost(B: usize, cost_ind: f64, overhead: f64,
↪    wait_penalty: f64) -> f64 {
    let eff = effective_cost(B as f64, cost_ind, overhead);
    eff + wait_penalty * (B as f64)
}

/// Optimize batch size by scanning candidate batch sizes from 1 to
↪    max_batch.
/// Returns the optimal batch size and its corresponding overall
↪    cost.
fn optimize_batch_size(cost_ind: f64, overhead: f64, wait_penalty:
↪    f64, max_batch: usize) -> (usize, f64) {
    let mut best_batch = 1;
    let mut min_cost = overall_cost(1, cost_ind, overhead,
↪    wait_penalty);
    for B in 2..=max_batch {
        let cost = overall_cost(B, cost_ind, overhead,
↪    wait_penalty);
        if cost < min_cost {
            min_cost = cost;
            best_batch = B;
        }
    }
    (best_batch, min_cost)
}

/// Represents a request in the batch processing simulation.
#[derive(Debug)]
struct Request {
    id: usize,
    arrival: Instant,
}
```

```rust
/// A simple asynchronous batch processor that demonstrates batching
↪   logic.
///
/// It aggregates incoming requests (which arrive sporadically)
↪   until either:
/// - The number of requests reaches the batch target (B_target), or
/// - The waiting time of the oldest request exceeds max_wait_time
↪   (t)
///
/// At batch processing, it computes the effective per-request cost
↪   using:
///   C_eff = (B * C_i + C_b) / B
struct BatchProcessor {
    batch_target: usize,
    max_wait_time: Duration,
    cost_ind: f64,      // C_i: cost per individual request
    overhead: f64,      // C_b: fixed batch initialization overhead
    wait_penalty: f64, // penalty factor for waiting (used in
    ↪   optimization)
    requests: Mutex<Vec<Request>>,
}

impl BatchProcessor {
    /// Create a new BatchProcessor with the specified parameters.
    fn new(batch_target: usize, max_wait_time: Duration, cost_ind:
    ↪   f64, overhead: f64, wait_penalty: f64) -> Self {
        BatchProcessor {
            batch_target,
            max_wait_time,
            cost_ind,
            overhead,
            wait_penalty,
            requests: Mutex::new(Vec::new()),
        }
    }

    /// Add a new request to the batching queue.
    async fn add_request(&self, req: Request) {
        let mut reqs = self.requests.lock().await;
        reqs.push(req);
    }

    /// The main loop that checks and processes batches when either
    ↪   the batch size target is met
    /// or the oldest request has waited longer than max_wait_time.
    async fn run(&self) {
        loop {
            let maybe_batch = {
                let mut reqs = self.requests.lock().await;
                if !reqs.is_empty() {
                    let now = Instant::now();
                    // If batch size has reached the target or the
                    ↪   oldest request's waiting time exceeds t:
```

```rust
                if reqs.len() >= self.batch_target ||
                    now.duration_since(reqs[0].arrival) >=
                    ↪   self.max_wait_time {
                        Some(std::mem::take(&mut *reqs))
                } else {
                        None
                }
            } else {
                None
            }
        };

        if let Some(batch) = maybe_batch {
            let b_size = batch.len();
            let eff = effective_cost(b_size as f64,
            ↪   self.cost_ind, self.overhead);
            println!(
                "Processing batch of size {}: Effective cost per
                ↪   request = {:.4}",
                b_size, eff
            );
            // Simulate processing delay (e.g., non-blocking
            ↪   asynchronous I/O operations)

            ↪   tokio::time::sleep(Duration::from_millis(200)).await;
        } else {
            // No batch yet; sleep briefly before rechecking.
            tokio::time::sleep(Duration::from_millis(50)).await;
        }
    }
}
}

#[tokio::main]
async fn main() {
    // Simulation parameters:
    // C_i (cost per individual request), C_b (batch overhead), and
    ↪   wait_penalty ()
    let cost_ind = 1.0;        // Example cost per request
    let overhead = 10.0;       // Example fixed overhead cost per
    ↪   batch
    let wait_penalty = 0.05; // Waiting penalty factor
    let batch_target = 5;      // Target batch size (B_target)
    let max_wait_time = Duration::from_millis(300); // Maximum
    ↪   waiting time t

    // Demonstrate the important equations.
    let batch_size_example = 5.0;
    let eff = effective_cost(batch_size_example, cost_ind,
    ↪   overhead);
    let proc_time = 0.2;  // Processing time in seconds (example
    ↪   T_p)
    let wait_time = 0.1;  // Waiting time in seconds (example T_w)
```

348

```rust
    let x = throughput(batch_size_example, proc_time, wait_time);
    println!("Effective cost (for batch size {:.0}): {:.4}",
    ↪  batch_size_example, eff);
    println!("Throughput (for batch size {:.0}): {:.4}
    ↪  requests/sec", batch_size_example, x);

    // Optimize the batch size over a candidate range (e.g., 1 to
    ↪  20) using the overall cost function.
    let max_candidate = 20;
    let (optimal_batch, min_cost) = optimize_batch_size(cost_ind,
    ↪  overhead, wait_penalty, max_candidate);
    println!("Optimal batch size: {} with overall cost: {:.4}",
    ↪  optimal_batch, min_cost);

    // Create an instance of the BatchProcessor.
    let processor = Arc::new(BatchProcessor::new(batch_target,
    ↪  max_wait_time, cost_ind, overhead, wait_penalty));

    // Spawn the batch processing loop.
    let processor_clone = processor.clone();
    tokio::spawn(async move {
        processor_clone.run().await;
    });

    // Simulate sporadic arrival of requests.
    // For demonstration, we generate 50 requests with an interval
    ↪  of 80 milliseconds.
    for id in 1..=50 {
        let req = Request { id, arrival: Instant::now() };
        let proc_clone = processor.clone();
        tokio::spawn(async move {
            proc_clone.add_request(req).await;
        });
        tokio::time::sleep(Duration::from_millis(80)).await;
    }

    // Allow time for processing of any remaining requests before
    ↪  shutting down.
    tokio::time::sleep(Duration::from_secs(5)).await;
}
```

Chapter 56

Zero-Copy Techniques for Optimized Data Transfer

Foundations of Memory Copy Overhead and the Zero-Copy Paradigm

Traditional data transfer methodologies typically require explicit memory copying, an operation whose computational cost scales linearly with the size of the data; that is, the time complexity can be characterized as $O(n)$ where n denotes the number of bytes transferred. Such copying incurs additional latency and increases processor usage, both of which are detrimental in high-throughput environments. The zero-copy paradigm seeks to eliminate these redundant data moves by enabling direct data transfers, thus preserving the original memory location during transfer. In essence, zero-copy mechanisms leverage reference-based sharing, where data is transmitted without duplicative memory operations, thereby reducing both CPU intervention and unnecessary buffer reallocation. This approach is particularly beneficial in scenarios where minimizing memory overhead directly correlates with maximizing overall transfer speeds.

Rust's Ownership Model and Zero-Copy Semantics

Rust's programming model, with its rigorous ownership and borrowing rules, provides an ideal foundation for zero-copy techniques. The language's emphasis on memory safety and zero-cost abstractions allows for the creation of highly efficient data structures that operate via reference semantics rather than duplicative copies. Data can be shared between concurrent processes through immutable or mutable references—mechanisms that completely avoid the overhead of copying large amounts of data. Instead, slices, views, and other lightweight abstractions are employed, preserving the integrity of the original memory block while providing safe access to its content. The absence of a garbage collection runtime further contributes to the performance gains achievable through such strategies, as memory management is handled at compile time, ensuring that the system benefits from minimal runtime overhead during zero-copy operations.

Leveraging Operating System-Level Zero-Copy Mechanisms

Operating systems offer built-in facilities for zero-copy data transfer, which can be directly harnessed in Rust through appropriate system call wrappers. Techniques such as memory mapping with *mmap* allow a file's contents to be mapped directly into the process's address space, thereby eliminating the need for additional data copying between buffers. Similarly, system calls like *sendfile* enable direct transmission of data from a file descriptor to a socket, bypassing intermediaries in userspace entirely. These methods permit the operating system to manage data transfers more efficiently, reducing the overhead associated with explicit, application-level copying. The correct orchestration of these low-level mechanisms requires a thorough grasp of file descriptor management, memory protection attributes, and synchronization between user and kernel space. In Rust, safe wrappers around these inherently unsafe operations encapsulate the complexity, allowing developers to implement zero-copy strategies while preserving the language's guarantees of memory safety.

Optimization Strategies and Performance Considerations

In high-performance applications, the cumulative effect of eliminating per-transfer memory copying is significant. Zero-copy techniques directly impact the effective transfer time, which can be conceptualized by the relationship

$$T_{\text{eff}} = T_{\text{transfer}} + \frac{T_{\text{copy}}}{B},$$

where T_{transfer} represents the intrinsic data transmission time, T_{copy} denotes the total overhead due to copying operations, and B is the factor representing the number of transfers combined or batched. By obviating the copy overhead, the effective transfer time is reduced to primarily the direct transmission component, thereby substantially increasing throughput. Moreover, the reduction in extraneous memory operations minimizes pressure on system caches and reduces contention for memory bandwidth, a crucial performance consideration in systems handling large volumes of data. Advanced optimization strategies further entail careful management of buffer lifecycles and alignment, ensuring that data structures are constructed to exploit memory locality and to take full advantage of the underlying hardware capabilities. The careful orchestration of these techniques culminates in a system architecture that exhibits markedly lower latencies and higher overall efficiency in data transfer scenarios.

Rust Code Snippet

```
use std::fs::File;
use std::io;
use std::os::unix::io::AsRawFd;

use memmap2::Mmap;
use nix::sys::sendfile::sendfile;

/// Computes the effective transfer time based on the equation:
/// T_eff = T_transfer + (T_copy / B)
fn compute_effective_time(t_transfer: f64, t_copy: f64, b: f64) ->
↪    f64 {
    t_transfer + (t_copy / b)
}
```

```rust
fn main() -> io::Result<()> {
    // ----------------------------------------------------
    // Part 1: Demonstrate the Effective Transfer Time Calculation
    // ----------------------------------------------------
    let t_transfer: f64 = 2.0;        // Intrinsic data transmission
    ↪    time in seconds
    let t_copy: f64 = 3.0;            // Overhead due to copying
    ↪    (seconds)
    let batch_factor: f64 = 5.0;      // Number of transfers batched
    ↪    together to amortize copy cost
    let t_eff = compute_effective_time(t_transfer, t_copy,
    ↪    batch_factor);
    println!("Effective Transfer Time: {:.6} seconds", t_eff);

    // ----------------------------------------------------
    // Part 2: Zero-Copy Data Transfer using Memory Mapping and
    ↪    sendfile
    // ----------------------------------------------------

    // Open a source file - in production, this could be a large
    ↪    data file.
    let file = File::open("example.dat")?;
    let file_size = file.metadata()?.len();

    // Memory-map the file to allow zero-copy access. The OS maps
    ↪    the file contents
    // directly into the process address space without duplicative
    ↪    memory copying.
    // Safety: This is safe as long as the file is not concurrently
    ↪    modified.
    let mmap = unsafe { Mmap::map(&file)? };
    println!("Memory-mapped file of size {} bytes", file_size);

    // Simulate a network socket by creating an output file.
    // In real scenarios, this would be a socket file descriptor.
    let output_file = File::create("output.dat")?;

    // Retrieve raw file descriptors for the input (memory-mapped
    ↪    file) and output.
    let input_fd = file.as_raw_fd();
    let output_fd = output_file.as_raw_fd();

    // Initialize offset for the sendfile call. Offset is of type
    ↪    i64.
    let mut offset: i64 = 0;

    // Loop until all bytes are transferred.
    while (offset as u64) < file_size {
        // The sendfile function enables direct data transfer
        ↪    between file descriptors,
        // bypassing user-space copying and leveraging the OS's
        ↪    zero-copy mechanism.
```

```rust
    match sendfile(output_fd, input_fd, Some(&mut offset),
    ↪  file_size - (offset as u64)) {
        Ok(bytes_sent) => {
            if bytes_sent == 0 {
                // Transfer complete if no more bytes were sent.
                break;
            }
            println!("Sent {} bytes using zero-copy mechanism",
            ↪  bytes_sent);
        }
        Err(e) => {
            eprintln!("Error during sendfile: {:?}", e);
            break;
        }
    }
}

println!("Zero-copy data transfer complete.");
Ok(())
}
```

Chapter 57

Deep Dive into DNS Query Implementation

DNS Query Packet Anatomy

The Domain Name System protocol, in its query phase, is founded upon a binary message format that encapsulates a variety of fields essential for ensuring accurate and efficient name resolution. The foremost segment, known as the header, comprises several subfields: a 16-bit identification number, flags that encode the query parameters, and counters for questions, answers, authority, and additional records. The question section follows, where the queried domain name is encoded using a length-prefixed format. Subsequent fields such as the type and class of the query are appended in a standard format, adhering to network byte order. The precise delineation of these segments permits systematic unpacking of the incoming data while preserving the integrity of each field. This structural standardization not only facilitates interoperability among diverse systems but also provides a deterministic framework in which further packet processing may be realized.

Asynchronous Processing of Query Packets

The resolution of DNS queries within an asynchronous framework necessitates a design that is both concurrency-enabled and non-blocking in nature. The asynchronous approach capitalizes on event-driven architectures wherein individual query packets are handled via a scheduling mechanism that minimizes latency by avoiding traditional blocking I/O operations. In such an implementation, each incoming DNS query is encapsulated within a discrete task, an instance of the underlying asynchronous abstraction. These tasks are coordinated by an event loop that monitors multiple file descriptors or socket channels simultaneously, thereby providing the means to interleave processing without incurring waiting penalties. The transformation of the blocking paradigm into an asynchronous structure is achieved through the use of futures and promises, which abstract the underlying computations and allow their results to be resolved at a later instance, once the requisite I/O operations complete. Consequently, the system is able to sustain a high throughput of concurrent queries while maintaining the overall responsiveness and scalability typical of modern networked applications.

Caching Strategies in DNS Resolver Architectures

The high frequency of repetitive queries in DNS operations highlights the necessity for an efficient caching mechanism, aimed at mitigating latency and reducing the computational overhead associated with each query resolution. A sophisticated caching strategy typically involves the construction of a data store—often implemented as a hash table—that maps domain names to their corresponding response packets. Each cache entry is annotated with a time-to-live (TTL) value, which defines the period during which the cached response remains valid. The implementation must ensure adherence to the TTL constraints to prevent the dissemination of stale data. In an asynchronous framework, the cache management duty is performed concurrently with other non-blocking operations, enabling real-time updates and invalidation of cache entries as dictated by dynamic network conditions. Furthermore, the caching mechanism must incorporate measures for concurrency control to prevent race conditions and ensure that cache coherence is maintained across simultaneous accesses. This is often achieved through the use of lock-free data structures or atomic operations that complement the overall asynchronous paradigm.

Integration with an Asynchronous Framework for Scalable Query Handling

The amalgamation of DNS query processing and caching techniques within a cohesive asynchronous framework underpins the development of a custom DNS resolver that is both robust and scalable. The design architecture leverages asynchronous task scheduling to permit concurrent handling of network I/O, while the caching subsystem reduces the frequency of redundant external queries. The interplay between these components is orchestrated in such a manner that the resolution logic remains decoupled from the underlying transport mechanisms. Each query packet is subject to a rigorous validation and parsing routine, after which it is either immediately resolved via the cache or forwarded for further processing. This modular approach ensures that each layer of the implementation operates within clearly defined boundaries, facilitating both maintainability and extensibility. The confluence of low-level packet parsing, concurrent processing of asynchronous tasks, and dynamic cache updates coalesces into an architecture that maximally exploits available system resources, thereby delivering a performance-efficient and resilient DNS resolving service.

Rust Code Snippet

```
extern crate tokio;

use std::collections::HashMap;
use std::sync::Arc;
use std::time::{Duration, Instant};
use tokio::net::UdpSocket;
use tokio::sync::RwLock;
use tokio::time;

/// DNS Header Structure representing the first 12 bytes part of a
↪   DNS query packet.
#[derive(Debug)]
struct DnsHeader {
    id: u16,
    flags: u16,
    qdcount: u16,
    ancount: u16,
    nscount: u16,
    arcount: u16,
}
```

```rust
/// DNS Question Structure which holds the queried domain name and
↪ its type and class.
/// The domain name is encoded using a length-prefixed format.
#[derive(Debug)]
struct DnsQuestion {
    qname: String,
    qtype: u16,
    qclass: u16,
}

/// Complete DNS Query structure combining header and question.
#[derive(Debug)]
struct DnsQuery {
    header: DnsHeader,
    question: DnsQuestion,
}

/// Parses a raw DNS packet and returns a DnsQuery if the packet is
↪ valid.
/// It decodes the header, extracts the domain name from the
↪ question section,
/// and reads the query type and class.
fn parse_dns_packet(packet: &[u8]) -> Option<DnsQuery> {
    // Packet must be at least 12 bytes for the header.
    if packet.len() < 12 {
        return None;
    }

    // Parse the DNS header (fields are in network byte order i.e.,
    ↪ big-endian)
    let header = DnsHeader {
        id: u16::from_be_bytes([packet[0], packet[1]]),
        flags: u16::from_be_bytes([packet[2], packet[3]]),
        qdcount: u16::from_be_bytes([packet[4], packet[5]]),
        ancount: u16::from_be_bytes([packet[6], packet[7]]),
        nscount: u16::from_be_bytes([packet[8], packet[9]]),
        arcount: u16::from_be_bytes([packet[10], packet[11]]),
    };

    // For simplicity, we only handle packets with at least one
    ↪ question.
    if header.qdcount < 1 {
        return None;
    }

    // Decode the queried domain name using length-prefixed labels.
    let mut idx = 12;
    let mut qname = String::new();
    loop {
        if idx >= packet.len() {
            return None;
        }
```

```rust
        let len = packet[idx] as usize;
        idx += 1;
        // A zero-length label indicates the end of the domain name
        ↪  field.
        if len == 0 {
            break;
        }
        if idx + len > packet.len() {
            return None;
        }
        let label = match std::str::from_utf8(&packet[idx..idx +
        ↪  len]) {
            Ok(text) => text,
            Err(_) => return None,
        };
        if !qname.is_empty() {
            qname.push('.');
        }
        qname.push_str(label);
        idx += len;
    }

    // Verify there is enough space remaining for qtype and qclass.
    if idx + 4 > packet.len() {
        return None;
    }
    let qtype = u16::from_be_bytes([packet[idx], packet[idx + 1]]);
    let qclass = u16::from_be_bytes([packet[idx + 2], packet[idx +
    ↪  3]]);

    let question = DnsQuestion { qname, qtype, qclass };
    Some(DnsQuery { header, question })
}

/// Represents a cache entry for DNS responses with a TTL.
/// The 'expires_at' field defines the expiration instant calculated
↪  as start time plus TTL.
#[derive(Clone, Debug)]
struct CacheEntry {
    response: Vec<u8>,
    expires_at: Instant,
}

/// DNS Cache based on a HashMap guarded by an asynchronous RwLock
↪  for concurrent access.
#[derive(Clone, Debug)]
struct DnsCache {
    store: Arc<RwLock<HashMap<String, CacheEntry>>>,
}

impl DnsCache {
    fn new() -> Self {
        DnsCache {
```

```rust
            store: Arc::new(RwLock::new(HashMap::new())),
        }
    }

    /// Asynchronously retrieves a cached response for the given
    ↪  domain if it has not expired.
    async fn get(&self, key: &str) -> Option<Vec<u8>> {
        let store = self.store.read().await;
        if let Some(entry) = store.get(key) {
            if Instant::now() < entry.expires_at {
                return Some(entry.response.clone());
            }
        }
        None
    }

    /// Inserts a DNS response into the cache with the provided TTL
    ↪  (in seconds).
    async fn insert(&self, key: String, response: Vec<u8>,
    ↪  ttl_seconds: u64) {
        let mut store = self.store.write().await;
        let expires_at = Instant::now() +
        ↪  Duration::from_secs(ttl_seconds);
        store.insert(key, CacheEntry { response, expires_at });
    }
}

/// Asynchronously handles incoming DNS queries using a UDP socket.
/// For each query, it parses the packet, checks the cache for an
↪  existing response,
/// and either returns the cached result or processes the packet to
↪  generate a dummy response.
/// This non-blocking implementation leverages Tokio's async runtime
↪  along with futures.
async fn handle_dns_query(socket: Arc<UdpSocket>, cache: DnsCache)
↪  -> Result<(), Box<dyn std::error::Error>> {
    let mut buf = [0u8; 512];
    loop {
        let (len, addr) = socket.recv_from(&mut buf).await?;
        let packet = &buf[..len];

        if let Some(query) = parse_dns_packet(packet) {
            println!("Received query for domain: {}",
            ↪  query.question.qname);

            // Check if a valid cached response exists.
            if let Some(cached_response) =
            ↪  cache.get(&query.question.qname).await {
                println!("Serving cached response for: {}",
                ↪  query.question.qname);
                socket.send_to(&cached_response, &addr).await?;
                continue;
            }
```

```rust
        // Simulate asynchronous DNS resolution with a
        ↪  processing delay.
        time::sleep(Duration::from_millis(100)).await;

        // For demonstration, we echo back the query packet as a
        ↪  dummy response.
        let mut response = packet.to_vec();
        // In a real implementation, response would be modified
        ↪  to include answer records,
        // use proper header flags, and encode additional
        ↪  sections.

        // Cache the response with a TTL of 30 seconds.
        cache.insert(query.question.qname.clone(),
        ↪  response.clone(), 30).await;
        socket.send_to(&response, &addr).await?;
    }
  }
}

#[tokio::main]
async fn main() -> Result<(), Box<dyn std::error::Error>> {
    // Bind the UDP socket to a local address and non-standard port
    // for demonstration since privileged ports may require special
    ↪  rights.
    let socket = Arc::new(UdpSocket::bind("127.0.0.1:8053").await?);
    println!("DNS server listening on 127.0.0.1:8053");

    let cache = DnsCache::new();

    // Spawn the asynchronous DNS query handler.
    tokio::spawn(handle_dns_query(socket.clone(), cache.clone()));

    // Run indefinitely keeping the server alive; in real
    ↪  applications this could run as a service.
    loop {
        time::sleep(Duration::from_secs(60)).await;
    }
}
```

Chapter 58

Custom Domain Name Resolution Modules

Architectural Overview

Domain name resolution in distributed systems necessitates an architecture that amalgamates precision, speed, and modularity. Advanced modules are constructed to isolate the resolution logic from lower-level network abstractions while ensuring interoperability and efficient data flow. The design employs a layered approach in which the initial phase is dedicated to the ingestion and preliminary parsing of domain name queries, followed by a structured resolution pipeline that is integrated with an asynchronous runtime. This architecture leverages Rust's robust type system and memory safety guarantees to maintain integrity during high-frequency operations. Each component is meticulously defined to operate independently yet cohesively, thereby facilitating targeted optimization, extensibility, and resource modularity in environments where rapid query resolution is imperative.

Asynchronous Domain Name Resolution Pipeline

The domain name resolution process is executed through an asynchronous pipeline that transforms conventional synchronous I/O into a flow of non-blocking operations. At the heart of this pipeline lies an event-driven framework that encapsulates each DNS query within a future, thereby deferring the computation and enabling a seamless concurrency model. The pipeline commences with the precise parsing of binary message formats, which encapsulate multiple fields such as the identification number, flags, and query counters. Subsequent stages involve validation and dynamic dispatching to authoritative services, all orchestrated by an event loop optimized for simultaneous operation on multiple sockets. The conversion of blocking calls into asynchronous tasks is underpinned by mechanisms that synchronize computation with I/O readiness. This ensures that resource allocation is conducted in a fine-grained manner, reducing latency and expediting overall throughput.

Efficient Caching and Time-to-Live Management

Central to the performance paradigm of the module is the integration of an efficient caching subsystem, designed to mitigate redundant resolution efforts and minimize network latency. The caching mechanism is architected as a concurrent key-value repository, wherein each key represents a fully qualified domain name and each value contains the corresponding response, annotated with a TTL (Time-to-Live) value. This TTL parameter is pivotal, as it governs the temporal validity of the cache entries and ensures that stale data is not propagated through subsequent queries. The asynchronous nature of Rust's execution model facilitates simultaneous cache reads and writes without impeding the resolution process. Advanced concurrency techniques, including atomic operations and lock-free data structures, are employed to preserve cache coherence and mitigate the risks of race conditions. The cache module is thereby optimized for rapid lookup and timely invalidation, ensuring that dynamic changes in network conditions are promptly reflected within the resolution modules.

Concurrency and Resource Management in Rust

The implementation of custom domain name resolution modules in Rust involves exploiting the language's intrinsic guarantees about memory safety and concurrency. The design is predicated on the efficient management of resources via Rust's ownership model, which prevents data races and minimizes the need for explicit synchronization in most cases. Asynchronous operations are managed through futures and task pooling, where each task is allocated a discrete piece of computational work corresponding to a segment of the resolution process. Concurrency is achieved through the careful orchestration of these tasks, ensuring that I/O operations, cache access, and computation are executed concurrently yet reliably. The emphasis is on zero-cost abstractions, wherein the performance overhead introduced by the asynchronous runtime is kept to an absolute minimum. The cumulative effect of these design choices is a system that is both scalable and resilient, capable of processing a high volume of domain queries with minimal latency while preserving the integrity and reliability expected from high-performance network services.

Rust Code Snippet

```rust
use std::collections::HashMap;
use std::sync::Arc;
use std::time::{Duration, Instant};

use tokio::sync::RwLock;
use tokio::time::sleep;
use tokio::spawn;

/// Represents a simplified DNS query parsed from binary data.
#[derive(Clone, Debug)]
struct DNSQuery {
    id: u16,
    flags: u16,
    query_name: String,
}

/// Represents a DNS response containing the resolved IP address.
#[derive(Clone, Debug)]
struct DNSResponse {
    query_name: String,
    ip_address: String,
}

/// A single cache entry holding the DNS response and its expiry
↪    time.
#[derive(Debug)]
struct CacheEntry {
    response: DNSResponse,
```

364

```rust
        expiry: Instant,
}

/// A concurrent cache for DNS responses using an asynchronous
↪    RwLock.
/// The cache maps fully qualified domain names to their DNS
↪    responses with TTL.
#[derive(Clone)]
struct DnsCache {
    store: Arc<RwLock<HashMap<String, CacheEntry>>>,
}

impl DnsCache {
    /// Creates a new empty DNS cache.
    fn new() -> Self {
        DnsCache {
            store: Arc::new(RwLock::new(HashMap::new())),
        }
    }

    /// Attempts to get a cached DNS response for a given domain.
    /// Returns None if the domain is not present or its TTL has
    ↪    expired.
    async fn get(&self, domain: &str) -> Option<DNSResponse> {
        let store = self.store.read().await;
        if let Some(entry) = store.get(domain) {
            if Instant::now() < entry.expiry {
                return Some(entry.response.clone());
            }
        }
        None
    }

    /// Inserts or updates the cache with a given DNS response,
    ↪    associating it with a TTL.
    async fn set(&self, domain: String, response: DNSResponse, ttl:
    ↪    Duration) {
        let expiry = Instant::now() + ttl;
        let entry = CacheEntry { response, expiry };
        let mut store = self.store.write().await;
        store.insert(domain, entry);
    }

    /// Periodically cleans up expired cache entries.
    async fn cleanup(&self) {
        let mut store = self.store.write().await;
        let now = Instant::now();
        store.retain(|_, entry| now < entry.expiry);
    }
}

/// Asynchronously parses a binary DNS query into a DNSQuery struct.
/// For simplicity, the first 2 bytes are treated as the query ID,
```

```rust
/// the next 2 bytes as flags, and the remaining bytes as the domain
↪    name in ASCII.
async fn parse_dns_query(bytes: &[u8]) -> DNSQuery {
    let id = ((bytes.get(0).cloned().unwrap_or(0) as u16) << 8)
           | (bytes.get(1).cloned().unwrap_or(0) as u16);
    let flags = ((bytes.get(2).cloned().unwrap_or(0) as u16) << 8)
              | (bytes.get(3).cloned().unwrap_or(0) as u16);
    let query_name =
    ↪    String::from_utf8_lossy(&bytes[4..]).to_string();

    DNSQuery { id, flags, query_name }
}

/// Simulates network resolution of a DNS query.
/// In a real-world scenario, this would involve sending the query
↪    to an external resolver.
/// Here, it waits for a short duration and produces a dummy IP
↪    address.
async fn network_resolve(query: &DNSQuery) -> DNSResponse {
    // Simulate network delay representing I/O wait times.
    sleep(Duration::from_millis(100)).await;
    // For demonstration purposes, generate a dummy IP.
    let ip_address = "192.0.2.1".to_string();
    DNSResponse {
        query_name: query.query_name.clone(),
        ip_address,
    }
}

/// Resolves a DNS query using an asynchronous pipeline that first
↪    checks the cache.
/// If a cache miss occurs, it performs a simulated network
↪    resolution and caches the result.
/// The TTL is set using a computed value (here hardcoded as 60
↪    seconds for simplicity).
async fn resolve_domain(query: DNSQuery, cache: DnsCache) ->
↪    DNSResponse {
    // Attempt to retrieve a cached response.
    if let Some(cached_response) =
    ↪    cache.get(&query.query_name).await {
        println!("Cache hit for {}", query.query_name);
        return cached_response;
    }

    println!("Cache miss for {}. Resolving...", query.query_name);
    let response = network_resolve(&query).await;
    // The TTL could be computed using a formula based on query
    ↪    characteristics.
    // For this example, we set TTL = 60 seconds.
    let ttl = Duration::from_secs(60);
    cache.set(query.query_name.clone(), response.clone(),
    ↪    ttl).await;
    response
```

```rust
}

/// The asynchronous main function simulates the full DNS resolution
↪   pipeline.
/// It spawns a periodic cache cleanup task and processes both a
↪   single query
/// and multiple concurrent queries to illustrate the asynchronous
↪   handling.
#[tokio::main]
async fn main() {
    let cache = DnsCache::new();

    // Spawn a background task to periodically clean up expired
    ↪   cache entries.
    let cache_cleanup = cache.clone();
    spawn(async move {
        loop {
            cache_cleanup.cleanup().await;
            sleep(Duration::from_secs(30)).await;
        }
    });

    // Simulate a binary DNS query.
    // The byte array is structured as follows:
    // [0, 1]          -> Query ID (0x0001)
    // [129, 128]      -> Flags (0x8180)
    // ["example.com"]-> Domain name in ASCII.
    let query_prefix = [0x00, 0x01, 0x81, 0x80];
    let mut query_bytes = query_prefix.to_vec();
    query_bytes.extend_from_slice(b"example.com");

    // Parse the DNS query.
    let dns_query = parse_dns_query(&query_bytes).await;

    // Resolve the DNS query and handle the response.
    let response = resolve_domain(dns_query.clone(),
    ↪   cache.clone()).await;
    println!("Response: {:?}", response);

    // Simulate processing multiple concurrent queries.
    let mut handles = Vec::new();
    for _ in 0..5 {
        let cache_clone = cache.clone();
        let query_clone = dns_query.clone();
        let handle = spawn(async move {
            let resp = resolve_domain(query_clone,
            ↪   cache_clone).await;
            println!("Concurrent Response: {:?}", resp);
        });
        handles.push(handle);
    }

    for handle in handles {
```

```
        let _ = handle.await;
    }
}
```

Chapter 59

Low-Level Network API Wrappers

Abstraction Design Principles

The design of the network API wrappers emphasizes minimalism by constructing an abstraction layer that preserves the idiosyncrasies of the underlying raw network interfaces while imposing a coherent, statically verifiable structure. The wrappers adhere to a one-to-one mapping with system-level calls, ensuring that each operation—whether it involves the manipulation of file descriptors or the setting of protocol-specific flags—remains as unobtrusive as possible. This approach allows the encapsulated functionality to mimic native behavior, transforming direct system calls such as *socket*, *bind*, and *connect* into thin abstractions that facilitate nuanced control over network communications. The abstraction strategy intentionally avoids extraneous logic, thereby ensuring that performance and predictability are not compromised by the overhead of additional layers.

Safety and Memory Management

The bijective relationship between the wrappers and raw network APIs is carefully balanced with stringent safety guarantees. Fundamental security challenges, including the mitigation of null pointer dereferences and the prevention of buffer overflows, are addressed by enforcing strict invariants during resource acquisition and release. The wrappers integrate a refined management of memory that leverages compile-time type checking alongside runtime verifications. By embedding the characteristics of the operating system's error signaling mechanisms into these abstractions, the wrappers ensure that each network resource is associated with an unequivocal lifecycle. This methodology minimizes the occurrence of resource leaks and promotes disciplined error propagation, where exceptional scenarios are handled through well-defined state transitions that respect both the needs of system-level performance and the principles of safe memory management.

Fine-Grained Control over Socket Operations

Fine-grained control is achieved by exposing the granular details inherent in the low-level network stack. The design provides direct access to the precise parameters and flags used by system calls, thereby allowing each network operation to be governed with exacting precision. Operations such as *bind*, *listen*, *accept*, and *connect* are deconstructed into their elemental components, enabling explicit management of socket options and protocol-specific configurations. This level of control facilitates the manipulation of asynchronous I/O events and non-blocking operations, ensuring that each call to a wrapper not only emulates the desired system behavior but also provides hooks for fine-tuning based on dynamic runtime conditions. The resulting interface, by relinquishing superfluous abstraction layers, yields a mechanism for directly interfacing with the operating system's network functionalities while maintaining a minimal performance overhead.

Error Handling and Resource Safety

Robust error handling is a cornerstone of the wrapper design, where the translation of low-level error codes into semantically rich abstractions is performed with meticulous attention to detail. Each system call's potential failure modes are captured, and error states are propagated through a sophisticated mechanism that discriminates between transient and fatal conditions. The wrappers employ a model in which errors are paired with explicit recovery strategies, ensuring that the integrity of network operations is preserved even in the face of anomalous system behaviors. Resource safety is enforced through a deterministic deallocation process whereby resources such as file descriptors and dynamically allocated buffers are reclaimed in harmony with the execution of the network protocol. This intricate interplay between error signaling and resource management guarantees that even during extensive network operations, the system retains a consistent state free of dangling resources or improperly terminated connections.

Integration with System-Level Constructs

The integration of low-level network wrappers with the operating system's native constructs is achieved through a careful synthesis of direct system call exposure and stringent safety protocols. The wrappers are designed to serve as a conduit between raw network operations and higher-level abstractions, thereby preserving the semantics of the underlying system calls while endowing them with controlled execution behavior. File descriptor management, for example, is abstracted in such a way that the lifecycle of each descriptor is explicitly modeled, with start and end states that correspond directly to operating system events. Furthermore, the careful encapsulation of asynchronous event handling within these wrappers allows for the precise synchronization of input/output readiness with network operations. Such an integration ensures that the performance characteristics of the native operating system are retained, affording fine-grained control over network sockets without incurring significant overhead beyond that of the environment's inherent mechanisms.

Rust Code Snippet

```
use std::io;
use std::io::Error;
use std::os::unix::io::RawFd;
use std::mem;
use std::ptr;

// A thin wrapper around a low-level socket file descriptor.
// This structure encapsulates the raw socket with RAII for
↪    automatic closure.
pub struct Socket {
```

```rust
    fd: RawFd,
}

impl Socket {
    /// Create a new socket using libc::socket.
    /// This function wraps the system call and converts error codes
    /// ↪ to io::Error.
    pub fn new(domain: i32, sock_type: i32, protocol: i32) ->
    ↪ io::Result<Self> {
        let fd = unsafe { libc::socket(domain, sock_type, protocol)
        ↪ };
        if fd < 0 {
            return Err(Error::last_os_error());
        }
        Ok(Socket { fd })
    }

    /// Set the socket to non-blocking mode using fcntl.
    /// This demonstrates fine-grained control over file descriptor
    ↪ flags.
    pub fn set_nonblocking(&self, nonblocking: bool) ->
    ↪ io::Result<()> {
        // Retrieve current flags
        let flags = unsafe { libc::fcntl(self.fd, libc::F_GETFL, 0)
        ↪ };
        if flags < 0 {
            return Err(Error::last_os_error());
        }

        // Compute new flags with or without O_NONBLOCK.
        let new_flags = if nonblocking {
            flags | libc::O_NONBLOCK
        } else {
            flags & !libc::O_NONBLOCK
        };

        let ret = unsafe { libc::fcntl(self.fd, libc::F_SETFL,
        ↪ new_flags) };
        if ret < 0 {
            return Err(Error::last_os_error());
        }
        Ok(())
    }

    /// Enable or disable address reuse on the socket.
    /// This function maps the SO_REUSEADDR option to a thin
    ↪ abstraction.
    pub fn set_reuseaddr(&self, flag: bool) -> io::Result<()> {
        let optval: libc::c_int = flag as libc::c_int;
        let ret = unsafe {
            libc::setsockopt(
                self.fd,
                libc::SOL_SOCKET,
```

372

```
            libc::SO_REUSEADDR,
            &optval as *const _ as *const libc::c_void,
            mem::size_of_val(&optval) as libc::socklen_t,
        )
    };
    if ret < 0 {
        return Err(Error::last_os_error());
    }
    Ok(())
}

/// Bind the socket to the provided address.
/// This is a one-to-one mapping with the underlying bind system
↪  call.
pub fn bind(&self, addr: &libc::sockaddr, addr_len:
↪  libc::socklen_t) -> io::Result<()> {
    let ret = unsafe { libc::bind(self.fd, addr as *const _,
    ↪  addr_len) };
    if ret < 0 {
        return Err(Error::last_os_error());
    }
    Ok(())
}

/// Listen for incoming connections with the specified backlog.
/// This thin abstraction emulates the listen system call.
pub fn listen(&self, backlog: i32) -> io::Result<()> {
    let ret = unsafe { libc::listen(self.fd, backlog) };
    if ret < 0 {
        return Err(Error::last_os_error());
    }
    Ok(())
}

/// Accept an incoming connection.
/// Returns a new Socket that wraps the file descriptor for the
↪  accepted connection.
pub fn accept(&self) -> io::Result<Socket> {
    let fd = unsafe { libc::accept(self.fd, ptr::null_mut(),
    ↪  ptr::null_mut()) };
    if fd < 0 {
        return Err(Error::last_os_error());
    }
    Ok(Socket { fd })
}

/// Establish a connection to a remote address.
/// Wraps the connect system call with error conversion.
pub fn connect(&self, addr: &libc::sockaddr, addr_len:
↪  libc::socklen_t) -> io::Result<()> {
    let ret = unsafe { libc::connect(self.fd, addr as *const _,
    ↪  addr_len) };
    if ret < 0 {
```

```rust
            return Err(Error::last_os_error());
        }
        Ok(())
    }
}

// Ensure that the socket is properly closed when it goes out of
↪   scope.
impl Drop for Socket {
    fn drop(&mut self) {
        unsafe {
            libc::close(self.fd);
        }
    }
}

fn main() -> io::Result<()> {
    // Create a TCP socket for IPv4 communication (AF_INET,
    ↪   SOCK_STREAM).
    let server_socket = Socket::new(libc::AF_INET,
    ↪   libc::SOCK_STREAM, 0)?;

    // Set socket options: enable address reuse and non-blocking
    ↪   mode.
    server_socket.set_reuseaddr(true)?;
    server_socket.set_nonblocking(true)?;

    // Prepare a sockaddr_in structure for binding to port 8080 on
    ↪   all interfaces.
    let mut addr_in: libc::sockaddr_in = unsafe { mem::zeroed() };
    addr_in.sin_family = libc::AF_INET as libc::sa_family_t;
    addr_in.sin_port = 8080u16.to_be(); // Convert port to network
    ↪   byte order.
    addr_in.sin_addr.s_addr = libc::INADDR_ANY; // Bind to all
    ↪   available interfaces.

    // Convert the sockaddr_in pointer to a generic sockaddr
    ↪   pointer.
    let addr_ptr = &addr_in as *const libc::sockaddr_in as *const
    ↪   libc::sockaddr;
    let addr_len = mem::size_of::<libc::sockaddr_in>() as
    ↪   libc::socklen_t;

    // Bind the socket to the specified address and port.
    server_socket.bind(addr_ptr, addr_len)?;

    // Transition the socket into listening mode with a backlog of
    ↪   128.
    server_socket.listen(128)?;

    println!("Server listening on port 8080...");

    // Accept an incoming connection.
```

374

```rust
    // This demonstrates error handling where transient errors might
    ↪   be retried.
    match server_socket.accept() {
        Ok(client_socket) => {
            println!("Accepted client connection with FD: {}",
            ↪   client_socket.fd);
            // Further processing such as asynchronous I/O could be
            ↪   implemented here.
        }
        Err(e) => {
            eprintln!("Failed to accept a client connection: {}",
            ↪   e);
        }
    }

    Ok(())
}
```

Chapter 60

Custom Load Balancing Algorithms in Rust

Architectural Foundations

The design of custom load balancing algorithms in Rust is predicated on the tight integration of low-level control with high-level abstractions. At its core, the load balancing module is constructed as an abstraction over network traffic distribution across multiple service instances. This approach necessitates an architecture that can efficiently manage hardware-level and operating system-level resources, while simultaneously providing flexibility through Rust's robust type system and ownership semantics. The abstraction is designed to encapsulate the underlying network sockets and asynchronous event notifications, ensuring that each load balancing decision is made with full visibility of the resource state. The architectural pattern adheres to a modular structure, where core components are clearly demarcated: a decision engine for traffic routing, a state monitor for instance metrics, and a scheduler that coordinates the real-time redistribution of load.

Algorithmic Strategies for Traffic Distribution

Central to the module is the implementation of algorithmic strategies that underpin effective traffic distribution. The algorithms are developed to address key challenges, such as balancing load across heterogeneous instances with varying computational capacities and response latencies. Multiple strategies are considered, including variations of round robin, weighted distributions, and dynamic least connections. Each algorithm is rigorously defined by a set of stateful parameters S, where decisions are computed as functions $f : S \to D$ mapping the current system state to distribution decisions D. These strategies involve the continuous measurement of metrics such as average response time, error rates, and throughput, which are then normalized and mathematically combined to yield an aggregated performance score. The decision criteria are dynamically adjusted to optimize resource utilization while maintaining minimal processing overhead.

Dynamic Reallocation and Feedback Loops

A prominent feature of the proposed load balancing design is the incorporation of dynamic reallocation mechanisms based on feedback loops. These mechanisms are engineered to adapt to transient variations in network traffic and service capacity, ensuring that the distribution of requests is continuously optimized. The system employs moving averages and exponential smoothing techniques to filter noise from rapidly fluctuating metrics. A sequence of control signals, denoted by $C(t)$ at time t, is generated and used to modulate the assignment of incoming requests to service instances. In constructing robust feedback loops, the design leverages Rust's concurrency primitives to ensure that state updates and decision computations occur in a non-blocking manner, thus preserving the overall responsiveness of the system. The interplay between real-time metric collection and algorithmic adjustment constitutes a closed-loop control system that minimizes latency and prevents overload conditions.

Performance Considerations and Scalability

Efficiency is achieved by minimizing the overhead associated with load balancing decisions while maintaining a high degree of precision in distribution. The underlying design implements a lightweight scheduling mechanism that scales linearly with the number of service instances. Memory safety guarantees are enforced by rigorous compile-time checks combined with runtime verifications such that state inconsistencies are precluded. Data structures employed within the decision engine are optimized for fast access and modification, featuring lock-free or fine-grained locking mechanisms where necessary. The computational complexity of the balancing algorithms is carefully analyzed, ensuring that the worst-case time complexity remains bounded within acceptable limits. Emphasis is placed on the reduction of allocation and deallocation overheads by utilizing Rust's zero-cost abstractions, thereby achieving performance parity with direct system-level calls.

Integration with Asynchronous and Distributed Systems

The load balancing algorithms are designed as a critical component within a broader asynchronous and distributed system. The communication between load balancers and service instances is facilitated by well-defined interfaces that leverage Rust's futures and async/await paradigms. This integration ensures that the load balancing logic does not impede the throughput of the system, even under conditions of high concurrency. The abstraction layer also supports the extension of the algorithms to accommodate distributed environments, where balancing decisions may consider not only local instance metrics but also global state information disseminated via inter-process communication channels. As such, the load balancer is capable of responding to shifts in both local and distributed workloads, adjusting its decision parameters in real time to achieve a harmonious distribution of network traffic.

Theoretical Underpinnings and Design Trade-Offs

The formal design of custom load balancing algorithms in Rust is deeply rooted in both theory and practical considerations. By deriving the algorithmic models from principles found in queuing theory and control systems, the implementation ensures that theoretical optimality is balanced with practical constraints such as system latency and resource contention. The design process involves a careful analysis of trade-offs between fairness, responsiveness, and computational overhead. In particular, the decision functions are crafted to remain robust under conditions of rapid load changes, while avoiding over-reactive behavior that might lead to oscillatory dynamics. Trade-offs are also encountered in the selection of metrics to prioritize, culminating in a multi-criteria optimization problem that reconciles the needs for low latency, high throughput, and equitable resource distribution. This rigorous analytical framework underpins the reliability and efficiency of the resultant load balancing algorithms.

Rust Code Snippet

```rust
//! This code snippet demonstrates a custom load balancing module in
↪    Rust.
//! It includes definitions for service instances, exponential
↪    smoothing for metric
//! updates, and a decision engine that selects the best instance
↪    based on a computed
//! performance score. The score function implements an algorithm
↪    that combines
//! average response time, error rate, and active connection count
↪    in a weighted formula.
//!
//! The load balancer is integrated into an asynchronous environment
↪    using Tokio,
//! where simulated metric updates and periodic decision-making are
↪    performed concurrently.

use std::sync::{Arc, Mutex};
use std::time::{Duration, Instant};
use tokio::sync::mpsc;
use tokio::time;

/// Represents a service instance in the load balancing pool.
#[derive(Debug, Clone)]
```

```rust
struct ServiceInstance {
    id: u32,
    weight: f64,
    active_connections: u32,
    average_response_time: f64, // in milliseconds
    error_rate: f64,            // as a fraction, e.g., 0.01 for 1%
    last_updated: Instant,
}

impl ServiceInstance {
    /// Updates instance metrics using an exponential smoothing
    ↪   technique.
    ///
    /// The smoothing is defined as: s(t) =  * new_value + (1 - ) *
    ↪   old_value.
    fn update_metrics(&mut self, new_response_time: f64,
    ↪   new_error_rate: f64, alpha: f64) {
        self.average_response_time =
            alpha * new_response_time + (1.0 - alpha) *
            ↪   self.average_response_time;
        self.error_rate = alpha * new_error_rate + (1.0 - alpha) *
        ↪   self.error_rate;
        self.last_updated = Instant::now();
    }

    /// Computes a performance score for the service instance.
    ///
    /// The score is computed as:
    ///    score = (0.7 * average_response_time + 0.3 * error_rate *
    ↪   100)
    ///             / (weight / (active_connections + 1))
    ///
    /// Lower scores represent more desirable candidates for
    ↪   handling requests.
    fn performance_score(&self) -> f64 {
        let base_score = 0.7 * self.average_response_time + 0.3 *
        ↪   self.error_rate * 100.0;
        // Ensure we avoid division by zero by adding 1 to
        ↪   active_connections.
        base_score / (self.weight / ((self.active_connections as
        ↪   f64) + 1.0))
    }
}

/// The load balancer holds multiple service instances and makes
↪   routing decisions.
struct LoadBalancer {
    instances: Vec<ServiceInstance>,
}

impl LoadBalancer {
    /// Creates a new LoadBalancer with the given service instances.
    fn new(instances: Vec<ServiceInstance>) -> Self {
```

```rust
        LoadBalancer { instances }
    }

    /// Decision engine function: f: S -> D.
    ///
    /// This function selects the best service instance (with the
    ↪  minimum performance score).
    fn select_instance(&self) -> Option<ServiceInstance> {
        self.instances
            .iter()
            .min_by(|a, b| a.performance_score().partial_cmp(
            &b.performance_score()).unwrap())
            .cloned()
    }

    /// Updates metrics for a specific service instance by ID.
    fn update_instance_metrics(&mut self, id: u32, response_time:
    ↪  f64, error_rate: f64, alpha: f64) {
        if let Some(instance) = self.instances.iter_mut().find(|s|
        ↪  s.id == id) {
            instance.update_metrics(response_time, error_rate,
            ↪  alpha);
        }
    }
}

/// The asynchronous main function simulates dynamic reallocation
↪  and decision-making in a load balancer.
#[tokio::main]
async fn main() {
    // Shared LoadBalancer wrapped in Arc and Mutex to allow safe
    ↪  concurrent access.
    let load_balancer = Arc::new(Mutex::new(LoadBalancer::new(vec![
        ServiceInstance {
            id: 1,
            weight: 1.5,
            active_connections: 10,
            average_response_time: 200.0,
            error_rate: 0.01,
            last_updated: Instant::now(),
        },
        ServiceInstance {
            id: 2,
            weight: 2.0,
            active_connections: 5,
            average_response_time: 180.0,
            error_rate: 0.02,
            last_updated: Instant::now(),
        },
        ServiceInstance {
            id: 3,
            weight: 1.0,
            active_connections: 8,
```

```rust
            average_response_time: 220.0,
            error_rate: 0.015,
            last_updated: Instant::now(),
        },
    ])));

    // Channel for simulating metric updates: (instance ID, new
    // ↪    response time, new error rate)
    let (tx, mut rx) = mpsc::channel::<(u32, f64, f64)>(100);

    // Spawn a task to periodically simulate metric updates.
    {
        let tx_clone = tx.clone();
        tokio::spawn(async move {
            let instance_ids = [1, 2, 3];
            let mut interval =
            ↪    time::interval(Duration::from_secs(2));
            loop {
                interval.tick().await;
                for &id in instance_ids.iter() {
                    // Simulated response time and error rate
                    // ↪    values.
                    let simulated_response = 150.0 + (id as f64) *
                    ↪    10.0; // in milliseconds
                    let simulated_error = 0.005 * (id as f64); //
                    ↪    error rate
                    tx_clone.send((id, simulated_response,
                    ↪    simulated_error)).await.unwrap();
                }
            }
        });
    }

    // Spawn a task to periodically select the best service instance
    // ↪    based on current metrics.
    {
        let lb_clone = Arc::clone(&load_balancer);
        tokio::spawn(async move {
            let mut interval =
            ↪    time::interval(Duration::from_secs(5));
            loop {
                interval.tick().await;
                let lb_guard = lb_clone.lock().unwrap();
                if let Some(selected) = lb_guard.select_instance() {
                    println!("Selected instance for routing: {:?}",
                    ↪    selected);
                }
            }
        });
    }

    // Process incoming simulated metric updates.
```

382

```
    while let Some((id, response_time, error_rate)) =
    ↪   rx.recv().await {
        let mut lb_guard = load_balancer.lock().unwrap();
        // Use an exponential smoothing factor alpha = 0.3.
        lb_guard.update_instance_metrics(id, response_time,
        ↪   error_rate, 0.3);
    }
}
```

Chapter 61

Service Composition with Tower Layers

Foundational Principles of Composable Services

Service composition within the Tower framework is underpinned by a rigorous abstraction that consolidates asynchronous communication into a unified request–response paradigm. At the core of this paradigm lies the concept of a Service, which is defined by the contract that any given service S can be expressed as a composable function, such that the overall service pipeline is equivalent to a composition $S = S_n \circ \cdots \circ S_2 \circ S_1$. This formulation emphasizes the role of individual service components as modular, self-contained units that can be seamlessly integrated to form a complex system. The theoretical foundation is deeply rooted in the principles of functional composition, where each middleware or endpoint layer adheres to strict type constraints and operational semantics dictated by the Rust programming language.

Modularity Through Middleware Layering

Middleware layers within Tower embody the principle of separation of concerns, enabling the isolation of cross-cutting concerns such as logging, authentication, and error handling from the core

384

business logic. Each middleware layer acts as a transparent interceptor that processes both incoming requests and outgoing responses. This design leverages established patterns such as the chain of responsibility and decorator paradigm, ensuring that each layer conforms to well-defined interface contracts. The modularity achieved through this layering allows for incremental assembly of services, where the addition or removal of middleware components can be accomplished without necessitating significant alterations to the system's overall structure. In this respect, the aggregation of middleware layers provides a robust mechanism for enforcing policy and behavior consistently across the service boundary.

Endpoint Abstraction and Service Pipelines

The abstraction of endpoints plays a critical role in the overall service composition strategy. Endpoints, which encapsulate the business logic of network request handling, are designed to interact harmoniously with preceding middleware layers. Within the Tower ecosystem, each endpoint is treated as an individual service whose operations conform to the same compositional principles that govern middleware. The resulting service pipeline is a concatenation of discrete processing stages, each responsible for transforming or refining the data as required. This architectural pattern ensures that complex request handling logic is decomposed into simpler, reusable units, thereby promoting both maintainability and scalability. Furthermore, the consistent use of interface contracts between endpoints and middleware layers reinforces the reliability of the overall system.

Inter-layer Coordination and Concurrency Semantics

The interaction between middleware layers and endpoints is mediated through carefully designed concurrency semantics that uphold the asynchronous nature of modern network services. Within Tower, each layer operates concurrently by leveraging Futures and asynchronous combinators, thereby allowing non-blocking execution of service components. These concurrency constructs ensure that each layer's execution context remains isolated while still participating in a cooperative processing pipeline. Inter-layer coordination is achieved through asynchronous protocols that govern state transitions and data flow, facilitating rapid feedback mechanisms and prompt error propagation. The result is a service composition that remains resilient under high-throughput conditions, where independent layers work in concert while respecting the integrity of the overall execution model.

Contract Enforcement and Error Management

Robust service composition necessitates strict adherence to interface contracts that define both data exchange formats and error propagation rules. In Tower, every middleware and endpoint layer is bound by a predefined protocol that governs the transmission of signals and the handling of anomalous conditions. When a layer encounters an exception or an unexpected state, the error management constructs embedded within the Tower framework ensure that such events are captured and conveyed in a controlled manner. This controlled propagation enables subsequent layers to enact appropriate recovery or fallback strategies, thereby preserving the stability of the entire service chain. The consistency with which these contracts are enforced across layers not only enhances modularity but also mitigates the risk of cascading failures within the composed service pipeline.

Scalability and Performance Considerations in Layered Architectures

The design of composable services using Tower inherently facilitates high scalability and optimum performance. By decomposing service functionality into discrete middleware and endpoint layers, the overhead associated with each processing stage can be independently analyzed and minimized. The sequential nature of layer composition typically exhibits linear complexity with respect to the number of layers, a characteristic that lends itself well to optimization through targeted profiling and fine-tuning. Moreover, the zero-cost abstractions provided by Rust ensure that the additional layer of indirection incurs minimal runtime penalty, enabling performance metrics that approach those of lower-level network service implementations. The meticulous structuring of the service pipeline, combined with stringent contract enforcement and asynchronous execution, culminates in a system that is both modular and capable of sustaining high levels of concurrent network traffic.

Rust Code Snippet

```
/*
  This example demonstrates a composable service architecture using
  ↪ Tower layers,
  encapsulating concepts of functional composition, middleware
  ↪ layering, error propagation,
  and asynchronous handling. The composable service pipeline is
  ↪ described by the formula:

      S = S_n   ...   S_2  S_1

  In this example, we build a pipeline composed of:
    - An Endpoint that implements the core business logic.
    - A TimeoutMiddleware that enforces a timeout constraint.
    - A LoggingMiddleware that logs requests and responses.

  Each component adheres to the Tower Service trait and uses
  ↪ asynchronous constructs (Futures)
  to support non-blocking execution across the composed layers.
*/

use std::error::Error;
use std::fmt;
use std::pin::Pin;
use std::task::{Context, Poll};
use std::future::Future;
use std::time::Duration;
use futures::task::noop_waker_ref;
use tower::Service;

// Custom error type for our service chain
#[derive(Debug)]
struct MyError(String);

impl fmt::Display for MyError {
    fn fmt(&self, f: &mut fmt::Formatter<'_>) -> fmt::Result {
        write!(f, "MyError: {}", self.0)
    }
}

impl Error for MyError {}

// Define a simple Request and Response types
#[derive(Clone, Debug)]
struct Request {
```

```rust
    pub payload: String,
}

#[derive(Clone, Debug)]
struct Response {
    pub result: String,
}

// Endpoint: the fundamental service that encapsulates business
↪   logic
struct Endpoint;

impl Service<Request> for Endpoint {
    type Response = Response;
    type Error = MyError;
    type Future = Pin<Box<dyn Future<Output = Result<Response,
↪   MyError>> + Send>>;

    fn poll_ready(&mut self, _cx: &mut Context<'_>) ->
↪   Poll<Result<(), Self::Error>> {
        // Always ready to process requests for simplicity
        Poll::Ready(Ok(()))
    }

    fn call(&mut self, req: Request) -> Self::Future {
        Box::pin(async move {
            // Simulate processing logic (business logic)
            let result = format!("Processed: {}", req.payload);
            Ok(Response { result })
        })
    }
}

// LoggingMiddleware: intercepts the request and response to log
↪   details.
struct LoggingMiddleware<S> {
    inner: S,
}

impl<S> LoggingMiddleware<S> {
    fn new(inner: S) -> Self {
        Self { inner }
    }
}

impl<S, Req> Service<Req> for LoggingMiddleware<S>
where
    S: Service<Req> + Send,
    S::Response: fmt::Debug,
    S::Error: fmt::Display,
    S::Future: Send + 'static,
    Req: fmt::Debug,
{
```

388

```
        type Response = S::Response;
        type Error = S::Error;
        type Future = Pin<Box<dyn Future<Output = Result<S::Response,
    ↪   S::Error>> + Send>>;

        fn poll_ready(&mut self, cx: &mut Context<'_>) ->
    ↪   Poll<Result<(), Self::Error>> {
            self.inner.poll_ready(cx)
        }

        fn call(&mut self, req: Req) -> Self::Future {
            println!("[LoggingMiddleware] Received request: {:?}", req);
            let fut = self.inner.call(req);
            Box::pin(async move {
                let res = fut.await;
                match &res {
                    Ok(success) => println!("[LoggingMiddleware]
    ↪       Response: {:?}", success),
                    Err(err) => println!("[LoggingMiddleware] Error:
    ↪       {}", err),
                }
                res
            })
        }
    }

// TimeoutMiddleware: enforces a timeout on service operations to
↪   ensure responsiveness.
struct TimeoutMiddleware<S> {
    inner: S,
    timeout_duration: Duration,
}

impl<S> TimeoutMiddleware<S> {
    fn new(inner: S, timeout_duration: Duration) -> Self {
        Self { inner, timeout_duration }
    }
}

impl<S, Req> Service<Req> for TimeoutMiddleware<S>
where
    S: Service<Req> + Send,
    S::Future: Send,
    Req: Send,
{
    type Response = S::Response;
    type Error = S::Error;
    type Future = Pin<Box<dyn Future<Output = Result<S::Response,
    ↪   S::Error>> + Send>>;

    fn poll_ready(&mut self, cx: &mut Context<'_>) ->
    ↪   Poll<Result<(), Self::Error>> {
        self.inner.poll_ready(cx)
```

```
    }

    fn call(&mut self, req: Req) -> Self::Future {
        let fut = self.inner.call(req);
        let timeout_duration = self.timeout_duration;
        Box::pin(async move {
            match tokio::time::timeout(timeout_duration, fut).await
            ↪   {
                Ok(result) => result,
                Err(_elapsed) => Err(MyError("Request timed
                ↪   out".into()))),
            }
        })
    }
}

// Main function illustrating the composed service pipeline
#[tokio::main]
async fn main() {
    // Instantiate the core endpoint service.
    let endpoint = Endpoint;

    // Compose the service pipeline:
    //   Composed Service = LoggingMiddleware
    //                          TimeoutMiddleware
    //                          Endpoint
    let service = LoggingMiddleware::new(
        TimeoutMiddleware::new(endpoint, Duration::from_secs(2))
    );

    // Create a mutable instance of the composed service.
    let mut service = service;

    // Prepare a sample request.
    let req = Request { payload: "Hello, Tower!".into() };

    // Ensure the service is ready by polling readiness.
    let waker = noop_waker_ref();
    let mut cx = Context::from_waker(waker);
    let _ = service.poll_ready(&mut cx);

    // Call the composed service and await the result.
    match service.call(req).await {
        Ok(response) => println!("[Main] Final Response: {:?}",
        ↪   response),
        Err(err) => println!("[Main] Service Error: {}", err),
    }
}
```

Chapter 62

Implementing Circuit Breaker Patterns in Code

Conceptual Foundations and Theoretical Motivation

The circuit breaker pattern originates from the necessity to mitigate the propagation of erroneous signals in complex, distributed systems. At its core, the pattern constitutes a control mechanism that monitors inter-component communications, with the explicit intent of detecting anomalies and halting further propagation of failure events. This architectural construct is predicated on the observation that sustained erroneous interactions may yield cascading failures, thereby compromising the integrity of resilient systems. Within this paradigm, a circuit breaker may be conceptualized as an autonomous agent that evaluates the health of a component based on pre-defined criteria, such as error rates or response latencies, and, upon detecting sustained degradation of performance, isolates the component pending recovery.

Designing Resilient Failure Detection Mechanisms

A crucial aspect of the circuit breaker pattern involves the implementation of robust failure detection strategies. Such mechanisms are designed to capture transient and sustained failure events by employing quantitative measures. For example, given a time interval T, the circuit breaker may monitor the number of errors $E(T)$, comparing these with a pre-determined threshold τ. When the condition $E(T) > \tau$ is satisfied, the system designates the monitored component as degraded, prompting the circuit breaker to trip. This quantitative threshold-based approach allows for a deterministic method of failure detection and fosters the integration of statistical analyses with operational metrics, thereby enhancing the fidelity of failure recognition in real time.

The Circuit Breaker State Machine and Transition Logic

The operational behavior of a circuit breaker is typically governed by a finite state machine with well-defined states and transitions. Formally, the set of states may be denoted as

$$S = \{closed, open, half\text{-}open\},$$

where the *closed* state indicates normal operational conditions, the *open* state signifies active isolation due to detected failures, and the *half-open* state represents an intermediary period that allows for cautious reactivation of the isolated component. Transitions between these states are governed by pre-configured criteria, such as the duration of error persistence and the results of health-check probes. The transition logic is designed to ensure that erroneous components remain isolated until empirical evidence indicates recovery, thereby minimizing the risk of reintroducing severe failure conditions into the broader system.

Isolation Mechanisms and Fallback Strategies

Once the circuit breaker transitions to the *open* state, the immediate objective is to prevent further processing requests from reaching a known-faulty component. This isolation is implemented by intercepting incoming requests and inhibiting their propagation until the component under scrutiny demonstrates signs of recovery. During the isolation period, fallback strategies are often employed to maintain service continuity; these may include rerouting requests to pre-determined backup components or invoking simplified versions of the failing logic. The design of such fallback mechanisms necessitates a careful balance between maintaining operational service levels and ensuring that degraded components are not prematurely re-integrated. In so doing, the system reinforces its overall resilience by dynamically adjusting to fluctuating operational conditions while safeguarding against systemic collapse.

Analytical Perspectives on System Resilience Through Circuit Breakers

The integration of a circuit breaker into a service architecture can be empirically analyzed by evaluating its impact on system resilience. The adoption of such patterns enables the dynamic isolation of malfunctioning components, which, in turn, reduces the propagation of localized errors across the network. This decoupling mechanism is quantitatively justifiable by measuring the variance reduction in system performance metrics post-implementation. Additionally, the circuit breaker facilitates a probabilistic analysis of recovery by providing clear demarcations of operational states. Such analyses often employ statistical models where the reliability of a component is expressed as a function $R(t)$ over time. The efficacy of the circuit breaker is thus underscored by its ability to maintain high values of $R(t)$ by actively shielding the system from aberrant behaviors, thereby ensuring the continuity and integrity of operational workflows.

Rust Code Snippet

```rust
use std::time::{Duration, Instant};
use std::thread;
use std::fmt;

/// CircuitBreakerState represents the finite state machine states:
///   - Closed: Normal operation
///   - Open: Component isolated due to excessive errors
///   - HalfOpen: Testing if the component has recovered.
#[derive(Debug, PartialEq)]
enum CircuitBreakerState {
    Closed,
    Open,
    HalfOpen,
}

impl fmt::Display for CircuitBreakerState {
    fn fmt(&self, f: &mut fmt::Formatter<'_>) -> fmt::Result {
        match self {
            CircuitBreakerState::Closed => write!(f, "Closed"),
            CircuitBreakerState::Open => write!(f, "Open"),
            CircuitBreakerState::HalfOpen => write!(f, "Half-Open"),
        }
    }
}

/// The CircuitBreaker struct implements the circuit breaker
↪   pattern.
/// It monitors the error count E(T) over a time window T and trips
↪   when E(T) > .
/// It follows the state transitions:
///   - Closed -> Open when errors exceed the threshold.
///   - Open -> HalfOpen when the open duration expires.
///   - HalfOpen -> Closed on successful call, or reverts to Open on
↪   failure.
struct CircuitBreaker {
    state: CircuitBreakerState,
    error_count: u32,
    threshold: u32,              //   : Maximum allowed errors within
    ↪   the time window.
    last_error_reset: Instant,
    error_window: Duration,      // T: Time interval over which errors
    ↪   E(T) are counted.
    open_duration: Duration,     // Duration to keep the breaker open
    ↪   before attempting a reset.
}

impl CircuitBreaker {
    /// Create a new CircuitBreaker with given threshold, error
    ↪   window, and open duration.
```

```rust
fn new(threshold: u32, error_window: Duration, open_duration:
↪  Duration) -> Self {
    CircuitBreaker {
        state: CircuitBreakerState::Closed,
        error_count: 0,
        threshold,
        last_error_reset: Instant::now(),
        error_window,
        open_duration,
    }
}

/// record_error increments the error counter. If the counter
↪  exceeds the threshold ,
/// i.e., if E(T) > , the breaker trips (transitions to the Open
↪  state).
fn record_error(&mut self) {
    if self.last_error_reset.elapsed() > self.error_window {
        // Reset the error count if the error window (T) has
        ↪  passed.
        self.error_count = 0;
        self.last_error_reset = Instant::now();
    }
    self.error_count += 1;
    println!("Error recorded. Count = {}", self.error_count);

    // Check the condition E(T) >  to trip the circuit breaker.
    if self.error_count > self.threshold {
        self.trip();
    }
}

/// Trip the circuit breaker by transitioning it to the Open
↪  state.
fn trip(&mut self) {
    if self.state != CircuitBreakerState::Open {
        println!(
            "Circuit Breaker tripped (E(T) > ). Transitioning
            ↪  from {} to Open.",
            self.state
        );
        self.state = CircuitBreakerState::Open;
        // Restart timer for the open duration.
        self.last_error_reset = Instant::now();
    }
}

/// Reset the circuit breaker back to the Closed state, clearing
↪  error count.
fn reset(&mut self) {
    println!("Circuit Breaker reset. Transitioning to Closed
    ↪  state.");
    self.error_count = 0;
```

```rust
        self.state = CircuitBreakerState::Closed;
        self.last_error_reset = Instant::now();
}

/// If in the Open state for longer than open_duration,
↪   transition to Half-Open state.
fn attempt_reset(&mut self) {
    if self.state == CircuitBreakerState::Open &&
        self.last_error_reset.elapsed() >= self.open_duration {
        println!("Open duration expired. Transitioning to
        ↪   Half-Open state.");
        self.state = CircuitBreakerState::HalfOpen;
    }
}

/// call executes a protected call (service request) wrapped
↪   with circuit breaker logic.
/// It uses the state machine to decide whether to allow the
↪   call or reject it.
/// On success, it resets the breaker if it was in Half-Open.
/// On failure, it records an error and may trip the circuit
↪   breaker.
fn call<F, T>(&mut self, func: F) -> Option<T>
where
    F: FnOnce() -> Result<T, ()>,
{
    // Before making a call, check if the breaker is in Open
    ↪   state:
    if self.state == CircuitBreakerState::Open {
        self.attempt_reset();
        if self.state == CircuitBreakerState::Open {
            println!("Call rejected; Circuit Breaker is in Open
            ↪   state.");
            return None;
        }
    }

    // Execute the service call.
    let result = func();
    match result {
        Ok(val) => {
            if self.state == CircuitBreakerState::HalfOpen {
                // Successful call in Half-Open state implies
                ↪   recovery.
                self.reset();
            }
            Some(val)
        }
        Err(_) => {
            self.record_error();
            if self.state == CircuitBreakerState::HalfOpen {
                // Failure during Half-Open state causes the
                ↪   breaker to trip again.
```

396

```rust
                    println!("Failure in Half-Open state.
                    ↪   Transitioning back to Open.");
                    self.trip();
                }
                None
            }
        }
    }

    /// Compute a simple reliability function R(t) defined as:
    /// R(t) = 1 - min( E(t) / , 1 )
    /// This represents the component's reliability based on the
    ↪   error rate.
    fn reliability(&self) -> f64 {
        let error_ratio = (self.error_count as f64) /
        ↪   (self.threshold as f64);
        1.0 - error_ratio.min(1.0)
    }
}

/// A simulated external service call; returns Ok() for a successful
↪   service call
/// or Err() for a failure. This function helps in testing the
↪   circuit breaker.
fn simulated_service_call(success: bool) -> Result<&'static str, ()>
↪   {
    if success {
        Ok("Service call succeeded")
    } else {
        Err(())
    }
}

fn main() {
    // Initialize the CircuitBreaker with:
    //   - threshold   = 3 errors,
    //   - error window T = 5 seconds,
    //   - open duration = 3 seconds.
    let mut circuit_breaker = CircuitBreaker::new(3,
    ↪   Duration::new(5, 0), Duration::new(3, 0));

    // Simulate service call attempts with alternating successes and
    ↪   failures.
    // Even numbered calls are successful; odd numbered calls fail.
    for i in 0..10 {
        let success = i % 2 == 0;
        println!("\nAttempt {}: Circuit Breaker State: {}", i,
        ↪   circuit_breaker.state);
        match circuit_breaker.call(||
        ↪   simulated_service_call(success)) {
            Some(response) => println!("Call {}: {}", i, response),
            None => println!("Call {}: Rejected by Circuit
            ↪   Breaker.", i),
```

397

```
        }
        println!("Current Reliability R(t): {:.2}",
        ↪   circuit_breaker.reliability());
        // Wait for 500 milliseconds between calls to simulate time
        ↪   passing.
        thread::sleep(Duration::from_millis(500));
    }
}
```

Chapter 63

Atomic Operations and Concurrency Control

Atomic Types in High-Concurrency Systems

Atomic operations are fundamental constructs in the design of concurrent systems, providing the essential guarantee that operations on shared data occur indivisibly, without interleaving by other threads. An atomic type is characterized by its ability to perform read-modify-write sequences that are observed in their entirety, thereby eliminating the possibility of intermediate inconsistent states. In theoretical terms, an atomic operation can be modeled as executing instantaneously at a single, well-defined point in time. This property facilitates the construction of lock-free algorithms, wherein the strict mutual exclusion provided by traditional locking mechanisms is supplanted by lower-level guarantees that directly leverage hardware capabilities. The study of atomic types reveals that even simple state modifications, such as counter increments or flag toggling, demand careful attention to ensure that these updates are both visible and correctly ordered with respect to other concurrent operations. Such considerations are essential in the context of network service components, where high throughput and responsiveness are paramount.

399

Memory Ordering Primitives and Their Semantics

Memory ordering primitives establish a formal framework for specifying the constraints that govern the visibility and ordering of memory operations in a concurrent environment. Since enforcing global sequential consistency across all cores or threads is typically inefficient, modern architectures and programming languages introduce relaxed memory models that allow selective reordering. Memory ordering specifications, such as *memory_order_relaxed*, *memory_order_acquire*, *memory_order_release*, *memory_order_acq_rel*, and *memory_order_seq_cst*, provide precise annotations that delineate the required synchronization boundaries. The *memory_order_acquire* and *memory_order_release* operations, for instance, ensure that a set of memory accesses prior to and following the respective operations maintain a well-defined ordering relationship. In formal analysis, these primitives constitute the basis of the happens-before relation, which is vital for proving the absence of data races within a system. By rigorously applying these memory ordering constraints, a system ensures that updates to shared state are not only atomic but also globally consistent in the presence of concurrent modifications. Such formal guarantees underpin the reliability of network services operating under extreme levels of parallelism.

Integrating Atomic Operations into Concurrent Network Service Components

The incorporation of atomic types and memory ordering primitives into network service components is a central strategy for constructing scalable and robust concurrent systems. In environments characterized by high degrees of contention and frequent state updates, the adoption of lock-free techniques allows the system to maintain high throughput without incurring the performance penalties associated with heavyweight synchronization mechanisms. Atomic operations enable isolated updates to critical sections, such as session counters, request flags, or state indicators, thereby providing a deterministic behavior that is essential for maintaining overall service integrity. Concurrent network services are often architected to operate across multiple cores and threads; hence, the deliberate application of memory ordering rules ensures that all participating components observe consistent state transitions. By leveraging these low-level primitives, designers are able to implement fine-grained concurrency control that reduces latency and avoids the pitfalls of blocking operations. The synthesis of atomicity with carefully chosen memory barriers yields a design in which safe, concurrent operations become an intrinsic feature of the network service, rather than an afterthought in the face of rising contention levels.

Rust Code Snippet

```rust
use std::sync::atomic::{AtomicUsize, AtomicBool, Ordering};
use std::sync::Arc;
use std::thread;
use std::time::Duration;

// ConcurrentState encapsulates shared state for network service
↪   components.
// It demonstrates the use of atomic operations with defined memory
↪   ordering
// to safely update state in a high-concurrency scenario.
struct ConcurrentState {
    counter: AtomicUsize,
    flag: AtomicBool,
}

impl ConcurrentState {
    // Creates a new instance with the counter initialized to 0
    // and the flag set to false.
    fn new() -> Self {
        ConcurrentState {
            counter: AtomicUsize::new(0),
            flag: AtomicBool::new(false),
        }
    }

    // Atomically increments the counter.
    // Using Ordering::SeqCst to enforce a strong total order across
    ↪   threads.
    fn increment(&self) {
        self.counter.fetch_add(1, Ordering::SeqCst);
    }

    // Attempts to update the counter using a compare-and-swap
    ↪   operation.
    // Returns true if the counter was equal to 'expected' and
    ↪   updated to 'new'.
    // Ordering::AcqRel ensures both acquire and release semantics
    ↪   on success,
```

```
    // while Ordering::Relaxed is used for the failure case.
    fn try_update(&self, expected: usize, new: usize) -> bool {
        self.counter.compare_exchange(expected, new,
        ↪   Ordering::AcqRel, Ordering::Relaxed).is_ok()
    }

    // Sets the flag to true using Ordering::Release,
    // ensuring that all writes before this call are visible to
    ↪   threads that acquire the flag.
    fn set_flag(&self) {
        self.flag.store(true, Ordering::Release);
    }

    // Loads the flag value using Ordering::Acquire to ensure proper
    // synchronization with the corresponding store in set_flag.
    fn check_flag(&self) -> bool {
        self.flag.load(Ordering::Acquire)
    }

    // Retrieves the current value of the counter.
    fn get_counter(&self) -> usize {
        self.counter.load(Ordering::SeqCst)
    }
}

fn main() {
    // Wrap the shared state in an Arc to enable safe sharing across
    ↪   threads.
    let state = Arc::new(ConcurrentState::new());
    let mut handles = Vec::new();

    // Spawn 10 threads, each performing 1000 atomic increments on
    ↪   the counter.
    for _ in 0..10 {
        let state_clone = Arc::clone(&state);
        let handle = thread::spawn(move || {
            for _ in 0..1000 {
                state_clone.increment();
            }
        });
        handles.push(handle);
    }

    // Spawn an additional thread that simulates an asynchronous
    ↪   event by
    // setting the flag after a short delay.
    let state_flag = Arc::clone(&state);
    let flag_handle = thread::spawn(move || {
        thread::sleep(Duration::from_millis(10));
        state_flag.set_flag();
    });

    // Wait for all increment threads to complete.
```

402

```rust
    for handle in handles {
        handle.join().expect("Increment thread panicked");
    }

    // Wait for the flag thread to complete.
    flag_handle.join().expect("Flag thread panicked");

    // Retrieve and display the flag status and the final counter
    ↪   value.
    let flag_set = state.check_flag();
    let counter_val = state.get_counter();
    println!("Flag is set: {}", flag_set);
    println!("Final counter value from concurrent increments: {}",
    ↪   counter_val);

    // Demonstrate a compare-and-swap operation using try_update.
    // Attempt to update the counter from its current value to a new
    ↪   value.
    let expected = counter_val;
    let new_value = counter_val + 1;
    let update_success = state.try_update(expected, new_value);
    println!("Attempted compare_exchange update:");
    println!("  Expected: {}", expected);
    println!("  New Value: {}", new_value);
    println!("Update success: {}", update_success);
    println!("Counter value after try_update: {}",
    ↪   state.get_counter());
}
```

Chapter 64

Macro-Based Code Generation for Uniform APIs

Overview of the Rust Macro System

The Rust macro system is founded on two principal paradigms: declarative macros and procedural macros. Declarative macros, defined using the conventional macro syntax, employ pattern matching against token trees to recognize input patterns and generate corresponding code constructs. In contrast, procedural macros operate by receiving token streams, processing these streams into abstract syntax trees, and subsequently emitting transformed code. Both paradigms integrate with the Rust type system to enforce syntactic and semantic validity during the compile-time expansion phase. The intrinsic design of these macros underpins the capacity to generate consistent and predictable code structures, which is pivotal in the development of uniform application programming interfaces across diverse service domains.

Mechanisms of Compile-Time Expansion

Central to the efficacy of macro-based code generation is the process of compile-time expansion. During this phase, macro invocations are systematically analyzed and expanded in accordance with predefined transformation rules. The macro expansion mechanism leverages token stream manipulation to ensure that input patterns are converted into syntactically valid Rust code. This expansion is conducted within the compiler's early processing stages, thereby circumventing any runtime overhead. Critical characteristics, such as hygiene and scope fidelity, are rigorously maintained to ensure that the expanded code operates seamlessly within the ambient context without introducing unintended interactions. In this manner, the compile-time expansion process enforces strict invariants, facilitating the reliable synthesis of interface constructs that are consistent across multiple APIs.

Uniform API Synthesis via Macro Rules

Uniform API synthesis through macro rules embodies an approach wherein recurring design patterns are encapsulated within compact macro definitions. These definitions provide a blueprint that articulates the invariant structure and behavior expected of the generated interfaces. By specifying a set of transformation rules, macros produce API components that adhere to a uniform architectural guideline, thereby ensuring consistency in function signatures, error handling paradigms, and data representations. The systematic application of these transformation rules guarantees that each generated API segment conforms to predetermined structural invariants, thereby reducing the potential for discrepancies that may arise from manual code duplication. This mechanism not only streamlines the interface generation process but also reinforces contractual consistency across the service landscape.

Reduction of Boilerplate and Enhancement of Code Uniformity

The reduction of boilerplate code is an immediate and significant benefit derived from the macro-based approach to API generation. By abstracting common patterns and recurrent code constructs into macros, it becomes feasible to eliminate redundant code segments while preserving functional consistency. The encapsulation of routine operations within macro definitions allows for the automatic propagation of uniform interface properties across the codebase. Such abstraction facilitates a precise mapping from conceptual API specifications to concrete implementations. Furthermore, the compiler-enforced checks performed during macro expansion ensure that any deviation from the established templates is detected at compile time, thereby precluding the introduction of inconsistencies. In effect, macro-based code generation fosters an architecture in which uniformity is embedded in the very structure of the APIs, streamlining both development and maintenance processes while maintaining rigorous correctness guarantees.

Rust Code Snippet

```
//-----------------------------------------------------
// Procedural Macro Definitions
//-----------------------------------------------------
// Note: In a real-world project, the following procedural macro
// would be defined in a separate crate (e.g., "uniform_api_macros")
// with a "proc-macro" configuration. For demonstration purposes,
// the complete code is shown inline.

extern crate proc_macro;
extern crate syn;
#[macro_use]
extern crate quote;

use proc_macro::TokenStream;
use syn::{parse_macro_input, ItemFn};

#[proc_macro_attribute]
pub fn uniform_api(_attr: TokenStream, item: TokenStream) ->
↪  TokenStream {
    // Parse the input tokens into a syntax tree
    let input = parse_macro_input!(item as ItemFn);
    let fn_name   = &input.sig.ident;
    let fn_attrs  = &input.attrs;
    let fn_vis    = &input.vis;
    let fn_sig    = &input.sig;
    let fn_block  = &input.block;

    // Generate a transformed function that adds uniform logging
    let gen = quote! {
        #(#fn_attrs)*
        #fn_vis #fn_sig {
            println!("-- Entering uniform API: {} --",
            ↪  stringify!(#fn_name));
            let result = (|| #fn_block )();
            println!("-- Exiting uniform API: {} --",
            ↪  stringify!(#fn_name));
            result
        }
```

```
    };
    gen.into()
}


//------------------------------------------------------
// Declarative Macro for Uniform API Endpoint Generation
//------------------------------------------------------
macro_rules! generate_endpoint {
    ($func_name:ident, $http_method:expr, $route:expr,
    ↪    $return_type:ty) => {
        fn $func_name() -> Result<$return_type, &'static str> {
            println!(
                "Handling endpoint: {} [{}] on route: {}",
                stringify!($func_name),
                $http_method,
                $route
            );
            // Simulated processing logic: perform a simple
            ↪    arithmetic computation
            let value: $return_type = 42 as $return_type;
            Ok(value)
        }
    }
}


//------------------------------------------------------
// Application Code Utilizing the Macros
//------------------------------------------------------

// Note: In practice the procedural macro `uniform_api` is imported
↪    from its crate.
// For this complete example we assume it is defined in-situ.

// Apply the procedural macro to automatically wrap the API function
#[uniform_api]
fn get_user_info() -> Result<String, &'static str> {
    // Simulate retrieval logic for user information
    let user_info = String::from("User Info: id=1, name='Alice'");
    Ok(user_info)
}

// Generate another API endpoint using the declarative macro
generate_endpoint!(update_user_data, "POST", "/user/update", u32);

fn main() {
    // Call the function enhanced by the procedural macro
    match get_user_info() {
        Ok(info) => println!("Response: {}", info),
        Err(e)   => println!("Error: {}", e),
    }

    // Call the function generated via the declarative macro
    match update_user_data() {
```

407

```
        Ok(status) => println!("Status code: {}", status),
        Err(e)     => println!("Error: {}", e),
    }

    // Additional demonstration:
    // Compile-time expansion of an arithmetic algorithm
    ↪    representing the formula 3 * (4 + 5)
    let computed_value = 3 * (4 + 5); // Equation: 3 * (4 + 5)
    println!("Computed Value (3 * (4 + 5)) = {}", computed_value);
}
```

Chapter 65

Integrating Rust with C Libraries for Network Performance

Fundamentals of Foreign Function Interfaces in Rust

The incorporation of external C libraries into Rust applications is mediated through a foreign function interface (FFI) that serves as a bridge between the two languages. The technical mechanism underlying this integration is designed to permit the declaration and invocation of functions compiled in C while adhering to a strict application binary interface. This interface facilitates the direct communication between Rust and C, thereby enabling the utilization of mature, high-performance network libraries that have been optimized through decades of systems programming research. The process involves a careful replication of C function signatures, data structures, and memory layouts within the Rust type system, ensuring that every function and data type conforms to the conventions historically associated with the C language. In this manner, FFI bindings establish a robust foundation upon which seamless interoperability can be built.

Establishing FFI Bindings for High-Performance C Libraries

The establishment of FFI bindings is centered on the precise declaration of external function prototypes and the definition of corresponding data structures in Rust that accurately mirror their C counterparts. A critical aspect of this undertaking is the strict adherence to the C calling convention, which governs the method by which functions receive parameters and return values. Detailed examination of header files and C library documentation is required to identify the correct function signatures. Structural mapping is achieved by applying attributes that enforce a C-compatible memory layout, such as using the $repr(C)$ attribute in Rust. Furthermore, the translation of pointer types, arrays, and complex structures must be handled with due diligence, as these constructs often serve as conduits for transferring complex data across the language boundary. Through methodical binding construction, the performance characteristics inherent to the high-performance C libraries are preserved and made directly accessible within Rust's network code.

Memory Safety and Concurrency Considerations in FFI Integration

Rust's ownership model and its compile-time guarantees are among the language's most significant advancements in preventing memory-related errors. However, the introduction of external C components necessitates the careful demarcation of safe and unsafe operations. The integration requires that segments of code performing operations that could potentially violate Rust's safety guarantees be explicitly enclosed within designated $unsafe$ blocks. Such segmentation is essential when managing memory that has been allocated by C routines through mechanisms such as $malloc$ and subsequently deallocated by $free$. The discrepancies between Rust's automated resource management and C's manual memory oversight call for rigorous validation of interlanguage type mappings and a detailed scrutiny of lifetime semantics. In network service scenarios where concurrency and parallel data processing are prevalent, it becomes imperative to reconcile Rust's strict synchronization primitives with C's more relaxed concurrency models. This reconciliation ensures that shared resources remain protected without inducing performance bottlenecks or data races.

Performance Optimization in Mixed-Language Networking Environments

The integration of high-performance C libraries into Rust presents significant opportunities for enhancing network performance. By offloading computationally intensive tasks and time-critical operations to optimized C routines, developers can leverage established algorithmic efficiencies that are difficult to replicate solely within the Rust ecosystem. The design of such an integrated system is guided by the principle of minimizing the overhead incurred during the transition between the two language contexts. Detailed performance analysis typically involves quantifying the cost associated with FFI calls and identifying strategies to batch operations, thereby reducing call frequency and data copying overhead. Moreover, the zero-cost abstractions promoted by Rust can be effectively combined with the mature, low-level optimizations inherent in C libraries to achieve superior throughput and reduced latency. This synthesis of technologies necessitates a comprehensive understanding of both system-level performance metrics and language-specific optimization techniques, resulting in a network framework that capitalizes on the synergistic strengths of Rust and C.

Rust Code Snippet

```rust
use std::ptr;
use std::slice;
use std::mem;
use libc; // Ensure that the libc crate is added as a dependency in
↪    Cargo.toml

// External function declarations from the high-performance C
↪    library.
// These functions are assumed to be defined in a linked C library.
extern "C" {
    /// Computes a checksum over a given buffer.
    /// - buf: Pointer to the start of the data buffer.
    /// - len: Length of the buffer.
    /// Returns a 32-bit unsigned integer representing the checksum.
    pub fn compute_checksum(buf: *const u8, len: usize) -> u32;
```

411

```rust
    /// Processes a network packet represented by a C struct.
    /// - packet: Pointer to the packet structure.
    /// - size: Size of the packet structure.
    /// Returns 0 on success or a non-zero error code on failure.
    pub fn process_packet(packet: *mut Packet, size: usize) -> i32;
}

/// A C-compatible representation of a network packet.
/// The Packet structure directly mirrors the C struct layout using
↪   #[repr(C)].
#[repr(C)]
#[derive(Debug)]
pub struct Packet {
    header: u8,
    data: [u8; 256], // Fixed-size data buffer for consistency with
    ↪   C layout.
}

/// A safe Rust wrapper around the external compute_checksum
↪   function.
/// This function accepts a byte slice and returns the computed
↪   checksum.
pub fn safe_compute_checksum(buffer: &[u8]) -> u32 {
    unsafe {
        // Call the external C function using the pointer and length
        ↪   of the slice.
        compute_checksum(buffer.as_ptr(), buffer.len())
    }
}

/// A safe Rust wrapper around the external process_packet function.
/// It accepts a mutable reference to a Packet struct and returns a
↪   Result.
/// On success, it returns Ok(()), otherwise an Err with the error
↪   code.
pub fn safe_process_packet(packet: &mut Packet) -> Result<(), i32> {
    let ret = unsafe {
        process_packet(packet as *mut Packet,
        ↪   mem::size_of::<Packet>())
    };
    if ret == 0 {
        Ok(())
    } else {
        Err(ret)
    }
}

/// Allocates a memory buffer using C's malloc function for
↪   interoperability.
/// Returns a non-null pointer to a buffer of the specified size.
pub fn allocate_buffer(size: usize) -> *mut u8 {
    unsafe {
        let ptr = libc::malloc(size) as *mut u8;
```

412

```rust
        if ptr.is_null() {
            panic!("C malloc failed to allocate memory");
        }
        ptr
    }
}

/// Deallocates a memory buffer that was allocated using C's malloc.
/// It uses libc's free to release the memory.
pub fn deallocate_buffer(ptr: *mut u8) {
    unsafe {
        libc::free(ptr as *mut libc::c_void);
    }
}

fn main() {
    // Example 1: Using the compute_checksum function on a static
    ↪  byte slice.
    let data = b"Example network packet data for checksum.";
    let checksum = safe_compute_checksum(data);
    println!("Computed checksum: {}", checksum);

    // Example 2: Constructing and processing a Packet using the
    ↪  external C function.
    let mut packet = Packet {
        header: 0xAB,
        data: [0; 256],
    };
    // Populate the packet's data field with the example network
    ↪  data.
    for (i, &byte) in data.iter().enumerate() {
        packet.data[i] = byte;
    }
    // Process the packet via the FFI call.
    match safe_process_packet(&mut packet) {
        Ok(()) => println!("Packet processed successfully: {:?}",
        ↪  packet),
        Err(code) => eprintln!("Error processing packet. Error code:
        ↪  {}", code),
    }

    // Example 3: Demonstrating dynamic memory allocation via C's
    ↪  malloc.
    let buffer_size = 1024;
    let buffer = allocate_buffer(buffer_size);
    unsafe {
        // Initialize the allocated memory with zeros.
        ptr::write_bytes(buffer, 0, buffer_size);
    }
    // Convert the allocated memory to a Rust slice for processing.
    let dynamic_slice = unsafe { slice::from_raw_parts(buffer,
    ↪  buffer_size) };
    let dynamic_checksum = safe_compute_checksum(dynamic_slice);
```

413

```
    println!("Dynamic buffer computed checksum: {}",
    ↪  dynamic_checksum);
    // Clean up the allocated memory.
    deallocate_buffer(buffer);
}
```

Chapter 66

Composing Complex Service Pipelines

Routing Mechanisms and Their Semantic Implications

The design of routing mechanisms within a complex service pipeline is predicated upon the precise mapping of incoming requests to the appropriate processing endpoints. In this context, the routing subsystem is understood as the initial filter layer that disambiguates signals based on URI patterns, HTTP methods, and other metadata attributes. The underlying implementation often employs highly optimized data structures, such as prefix trees or hash-mapped indexing schemes, to ensure that the selection process incurs minimal latency while preserving predictable computational complexity. The mathematical rigor in the construction of these algorithms is underscored by the formal properties of finite automata, where the transition functions are analogous to state transitions in network protocol interpretations. The maintenance of semantic consistency across the routing layer is imperative, as any deviation from the prescribed mapping rules may compromise the integrity of downstream operations within the pipeline.

Middleware Abstractions for Multi-Layered Service Composition

Middleware components serve as the integrative fabric that binds disparate operational stages within the service pipeline. By encapsulating auxiliary functionalities—ranging from instrumentation and logging to error handling and request normalization—middleware provides a modular approach that decouples non-core concerns from primary business logic. Each middleware layer is conceptually analogous to a functional transformation or a monadic bind in the realm of functional programming, ensuring that modifications to the request and response objects are achieved without disrupting the inherent data flow. The composability of these middleware entities is achieved through adherence to a consistent set of interfaces and protocols, thereby enforcing a form of contractual design wherein each stage guarantees the preservation of context and state invariants. In environments where service-level agreements are critically evaluated, the middleware's role in enforcing quality-of-service parameters, such as throughput and response time bounds, cannot be overstated.

Authentication Strategies in Multi-Tiered Architectures

Authentication within complex service pipelines often necessitates the integration of robust security mechanisms that can operate seamlessly across multiple layers of abstraction. This integration is generally realized through the embedding of cryptographically secure identity validation protocols into a dedicated middleware tier. In such a configuration, authentication procedures may leverage token-based methods, certificate verification, or challenge–response schemes, each of which is undergirded by rigorous mathematical constructs from number theory and cryptography. The intricate balance between computational overhead and security guarantees is maintained through careful performance modeling, where the expected time complexity of authentication routines is analytically evaluated in relation to the overall service response latency. Furthermore, embedding authentication as an intrinsic component of the service pipeline necessitates a persistent and consistent mapping between transient network sessions and persistent user profiles, thus ensuring that each request is appropriately validated and authorized before subsequent processing stages engage with sensitive or critical operations.

Asynchronous Processing and Pipeline Coordination

The adoption of asynchronous processing paradigms is central to achieving the high-throughput and low-latency characteristics demanded by modern network services. Within the composite structure of a service pipeline, asynchronous processing facilitates the decoupling of interdependent tasks, thereby permitting simultaneous execution of routing, middleware evaluation, and authentication routines without incurring the traditional blocking constraints associated with synchronous processing models. The theoretical framework underpinning asynchronous operations can be characterized by non-deterministic finite state machines, wherein each state transition is activated by an external event or completion signal. This model is further refined by utilizing advanced scheduling techniques that exploit event-driven architectures to manage concurrent I/O operations. Coordination among asynchronous tasks is achieved through a combination of lightweight synchronization primitives and carefully orchestrated event loops, ensuring that the temporal ordering of operations is preserved even in the presence of concurrent modifications. The overall architecture of the pipeline is thereby transformed into a cohesive, multi-layered construct, wherein each individual component contributes to a harmonious balance between performance optimization and functional correctness.

Rust Code Snippet

```rust
use tokio::time::{sleep, Duration};
use std::sync::{Arc, Mutex};
use std::error::Error;

// Define the request and response structures.
#[derive(Debug, Clone)]
struct Request {
    method: String,
    path: String,
    token: String,
```

```rust
}

#[derive(Debug)]
struct Response {
    status: u16,
    body: String,
}

// Define the finite state machine states for routing.
#[derive(Debug)]
enum RouteState {
    Start,
    Home,
    About,
    NotFound,
}

// Simulate a finite automaton for routing requests based on the URI
↪    pattern.
async fn route_request(req: &Request) -> Result<RouteState, Box<dyn
↪    Error>> {
    // Start in the initial state.
    match req.path.as_str() {
        "/" | "/home" => Ok(RouteState::Home),
        "/about"     => Ok(RouteState::About),
        _            => Ok(RouteState::NotFound),
    }
}

// Middleware component: asynchronous logging of incoming requests.
async fn log_request(req: &Request) {
    println!("Logging: Received {} request for path {}", req.method,
    ↪    req.path);
    // Simulate an asynchronous delay representing logging I/O.
    sleep(Duration::from_millis(50)).await;
}

// Middleware component: token-based authentication.
async fn authenticate(req: &Request) -> Result<(), Box<dyn Error>> {
    // In a real-world scenario, this function could perform complex
    ↪    cryptographic checks.
    if req.token == "token123" {
        println!("Authentication successful for token: {}",
        ↪    req.token);
        Ok(())
    } else {
        println!("Authentication failed for token: {}", req.token);
        Err("Authentication Failed".into())
    }
}

// A simple implementation of a Token Bucket rate limiter to
↪    throttle request rates.
```

```rust
struct TokenBucket {
    capacity: usize,
    tokens: Mutex<usize>,
    refill_rate: usize, // tokens added per second
}

impl TokenBucket {
    // Create a new token bucket.
    fn new(capacity: usize, refill_rate: usize) -> Self {
        TokenBucket {
            capacity,
            tokens: Mutex::new(capacity),
            refill_rate,
        }
    }

    // Attempt to acquire a token. Returns true if successful.
    async fn try_acquire(&self) -> bool {
        let mut tokens = self.tokens.lock().unwrap();
        if *tokens > 0 {
            *tokens -= 1;
            true
        } else {
            false
        }
    }

    // Periodically refill tokens in the bucket.
    async fn refill(self: Arc<Self>) {
        loop {
            sleep(Duration::from_secs(1)).await;
            let mut tokens = self.tokens.lock().unwrap();
            *tokens = (*tokens +
            ↪    self.refill_rate).min(self.capacity);
            println!("Token Bucket Refilled: current tokens = {}",
            ↪    *tokens);
        }
    }
}

// The Pipeline struct composes routing, middleware processing,
↪    authentication,
// rate-limiting, and asynchronous task coordination into a single
↪    service pipeline.
struct Pipeline {
    rate_limiter: Arc<TokenBucket>,
}

impl Pipeline {
    fn new(rate_limiter: Arc<TokenBucket>) -> Self {
        Pipeline { rate_limiter }
    }
```

```rust
// Handle an incoming request by applying middleware, validating
↪    authentication,
// rate-limiting via the token bucket, routing based on finite
↪    automata, and asynchronous processing.
async fn handle(&self, req: Request) -> Result<Response, Box<dyn
↪    Error>> {
    // Step 1: Log the incoming request.
    log_request(&req).await;

    // Step 2: Authenticate the request.
    authenticate(&req).await?;

    // Step 3: Rate limiting using the token bucket algorithm.
    if !self.rate_limiter.try_acquire().await {
        return Ok(Response {
            status: 429,
            body: "Too Many Requests".to_string(),
        });
    }

    // Step 4: Route the request using a finite state machine.
    let route_state = route_request(&req).await?;
    let response = match route_state {
        RouteState::Home => Response {
            status: 200,
            body: "Welcome to the Home Page".to_string(),
        },
        RouteState::About => Response {
            status: 200,
            body: "About Us Page".to_string(),
        },
        RouteState::NotFound => Response {
            status: 404,
            body: "Page Not Found".to_string(),
        },
        // Fallback in case of an unexpected state.
        _ => Response {
            status: 500,
            body: "Internal Server Error".to_string(),
        },
    };

    // Step 5: Asynchronously update metrics or perform other
    ↪    non-critical tasks.
    let metrics_update = async {
        println!("Asynchronously updating service metrics.");
        sleep(Duration::from_millis(30)).await;
    };

    // Coordinate the asynchronous tasks. In this case, we only
    ↪    have metrics_update.
    tokio::join!(metrics_update);
```

420

```rust
        Ok(response)
    }
}

#[tokio::main]
async fn main() -> Result<(), Box<dyn Error>> {
    // Initialize the token bucket with a capacity of 5 tokens and a
    // ↪  refill rate of 2 tokens per second.
    let rate_limiter = Arc::new(TokenBucket::new(5, 2));
    // Spawn a background task that continuously refills the token
    // ↪  bucket.
    let rate_limiter_bg = Arc::clone(&rate_limiter);
    tokio::spawn(async move {
        rate_limiter_bg.refill().await;
    });

    let pipeline = Pipeline::new(rate_limiter);

    // Define a set of simulated incoming requests.
    let requests = vec![
        Request {
            method: "GET".to_string(),
            path: "/home".to_string(),
            token: "token123".to_string(),
        },
        Request {
            method: "GET".to_string(),
            path: "/about".to_string(),
            token: "token123".to_string(),
        },
        Request {
            method: "POST".to_string(),
            path: "/login".to_string(),
            token: "invalid".to_string(),
        },
        Request {
            method: "GET".to_string(),
            path: "/contact".to_string(),
            token: "token123".to_string(),
        },
    ];

    // Process each request sequentially for demonstration purposes.
    for req in requests {
        println!("\nProcessing new request: {:?}", req);
        match pipeline.handle(req).await {
            Ok(resp) => println!("Response: {:?}\n", resp),
            Err(e) => println!("Error encountered: {:?}\n", e),
        }
        // Simulate a delay between requests.
        sleep(Duration::from_millis(200)).await;
    }
```

```
    Ok(())
}
```

www.ingramcontent.com/pod-product-compliance
Lightning Source LLC
LaVergne TN
LVHW051420050326
832903LV00030BC/2920

9798312906639